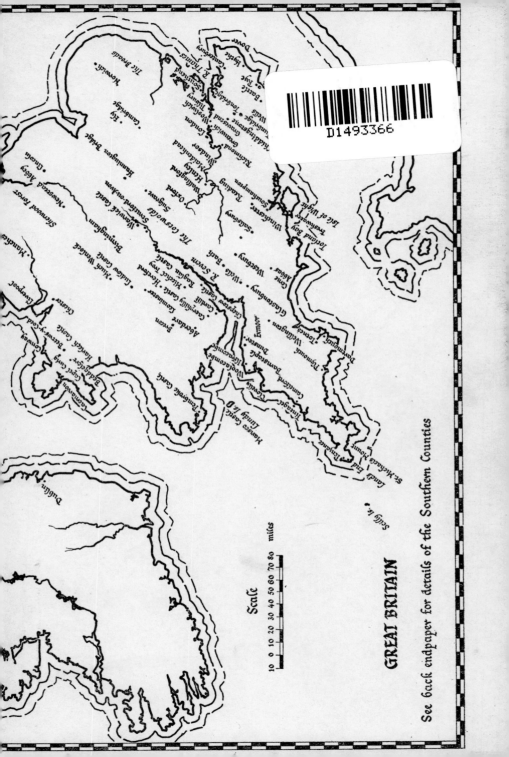

GREAT BRITAIN

See back endpaper for details of the Southern Counties

Scale

10 0 10 20 30 40 50 60 70 80 miles

Innocents in Britain

The Greyhound Hotel, Corfe

WILLARD PRICE

Innocents in Britain

HEINEMANN

LONDON MELBOURNE TORONTO

William Heinemann Ltd

LONDON   MELBOURNE   TORONTO

CAPE TOWN   AUCKLAND

THE HAGUE

First published 1958

© by WILLARD PRICE 1958

Printed in Great Britain
at The Windmill Press
Kingswood, Surrey

Contents

Illustrations

GRATEFULLY
TO
MARY VIRGINIA
PRICE

*Acknowledgment is due to
the National Geographic Society
for their substantial co-operation
in this project*

CHAPTER I

Over the Top of the World

Los Angeles Airport at midnight. Our plane is ready for its hop over the bald pate of the world. We ascend the steps and pass in through the door under the inscription, 'First over the Pole'.

This gives us a distinct thrill in spite of the fact that we know perfectly well that Peary got there first. And in spite of the fact that the inscription really does not refer to us at all, but to the airline, which was the first to inaugurate trans-polar passenger flights. And in spite of the fact that our route lies a few degrees away from the Pole, not precisely over it.

However, we shall be definitely within the polar regions, well inside the Arctic Circle, flying above the world's least-known ocean. And, since the airline began this route only eighteen months ago, we are among the first few hundred ever to make this fantastic journey.

Fantastic it would seem to Peary that, only forty-seven years after his nine-months trek by boat, sledge and dog train through the polar wastes, bored tourists winging across the same wastes should complain that it takes a whole day to get from Los Angeles to Europe.

"It's a tiresome trip," a travel agent had warned me, and I had nodded in sober agreement, neither of us reflecting that it had been rather more tiresome for Peary. How soft we are that we flinch at the prospect of sitting down for a day of champagne and fine food over a wilderness opened for us with such toil, danger and endurance.

We find our seats and look about us. The plane is not un-

I

usual. One might expect something like a space-ship for such a flight. This is an ordinary DC 6, four motors, accommodates fifty passengers, flies at three hundred miles an hour. It has a non-stop range of 4,200 miles. Its ten thousand horses give it as much power as that of the average Atlantic liner. It carries a crew of ten, says the steward. They sleep in the forward berths. Aft of that is the main cabin, the seats of which incline to form 'dormettes'. Then the galley, and then a section of Pullman berths quite like those on a train, minus the porter. So you may sleep tilted or flat as you please, the penalty for the extra indulgence being a matter of about fifty dollars.

We take off at 12.5 a.m. The captain's voice comes over the loudspeaker:

"Our flying time to Winnipeg is five hours and forty-five minutes. We pass over Las Vegas, Salt Lake City, Rapid City and Bismarck on the way to Winnipeg."

But instead of striking inland at once we circle out over the Pacific and fly south for a bit, the jewelled shore of California on our left. Then fog veils the view. When it clears we look down on the gleaming green serpent of Las Vegas, its brilliant main street glowing against the dark desert. A nightcap of sandwiches and champagne is served at 1 a.m. We sleep well despite a few bumps as we cross the Rockies. Morning brings sharp pains in the ears, a sure sign that we are coming down.

The Manitoba scene is amazing—flat country half submerged under frozen pools of water. We land at Winnipeg airport at 8.35 and walk out into chill air. All the airport staff have parkas attached to their overcoats. Winnipeg does not seem to be aware that this is late spring, April about to give over to May. The temperature is well below freezing and an icy wind is blowing. Hot coffee is served in the waiting-room. Taking photographs is not allowed.

"Why not?" Mary asks the chunky little customs officer.

"Oh, I don't know—military regulations of some kind."

He tells us about the floods. The Red River and the Assiniboine are out of control, much farmland has been inundated, hundreds of homes have had to be evacuated. "It happens every year."

After half an hour we are again in the air. We have an ample breakfast with real Danish pastry. At least we suppose it is real, since this is a Scandinavian airline with terminus at Copenhagen.

"No," says the stewardess when we ask her about it. "It's Danish pastry all right, but it's from the Brown Derby in Hollywood. Going the other way we stock up in Copenhagen. Frankly, I think the Hollywood Danish is an improvement on the original."

The captain: "Seven hours and thirty minutes' flying time from Winnipeg to Sondre Stromfjord, Greenland."

It is 5,600 air miles from Los Angeles to Copenhagen, according to the National Geographic map, 'The Top of the World', copies of which are placed in the hands of passengers. The route from Los Angeles to Copenhagen by way of New York would be a thousand miles longer.

We are flying over a sea so vast that we wonder at first if it can be Hudson Bay. But the map shows it to be Lake Winnipeg. Every school child knows of Lake Ontario, but here is a lake far larger that few people, juvenile or adult, have ever heard of. Nearly three hundred miles long and sixty wide, it lies in primeval splendour, with no human trespassers except at the southern end, where there are a few colonies of migrants from Iceland and some scattered posts of the Hudson's Bay Company. The surface is a solid floor of ice. What the temperature may be down there we don't know, but at our flight level it is 17° centigrade below zero.

The captain, strolling back to chat with his guests, tells us that this airline plans a trans-polar service from Copenhagen to Tokyo by way of Alaska. The flight will take about thirty-one hours against the present fifty-two or more around Asia.

Beside me sits a Dane who sleeps much of the time but rouses as if by instinct whenever the steward comes by with a new offering of potent spirits. I ask him if he has made the trip before. "Sixteen times." He explains that he is with the airline and gives me his card. He is Assistant Technical Manager for the Scandinavian Airlines System. His job involves keeping check on Douglas Aircraft's construction of DC 7s and DC 8s. The Eights will be ready in 1960. They will be twice as long as the Sixes, wide enough for six seats, and will provide twenty berths instead of the present twelve.

The Dane gives me his impressions of the United States. A short, stocky man whose accent places him somewhere in Central Europe joins in the conversation. He asks the Dane:

"What do you like best about America?"

"First," says the Dane, "the ice-cream. Second, the coffee. Third, the cigars."

The other man shakes his head.

"I would put liberty first," he says.

"Where are you from?"

"Czecho-Slovakia."

The Dane nods. "Then I understand why you would put liberty first."

The man of sixteen crossings says they are always like this— very smooth. The roughest spot is above the Rockies. But over these level land wastes and the Arctic Ocean the temperature is fairly even and the air currents without holes and humps. It is the world's smoothest air trip.

Now we really are over Hudson Bay. I look down upon it with a thrill of interest, remembering boyhood stories of the redskins and pathfinders, the deerslayers and pioneers, the explorers in search of a passage to India, the fabulous Hudson's Bay Company and the romance of the fur trade.

The plane, which usually maintains an altitude of eighteen thousand feet, now happens to be flying very low and every detail can be seen clearly. The western shore is flat and cut by

4

some of the thirty great rivers that pour into Hudson Bay. The surface of the Bay is a dazzling sheet of ice split here and there by black, winding cracks. Upon the edges of some of these cracks appear large bushy objects which upon closer view turn out to be bulky walruses basking in the comparative warmth of the sun of late spring. There is said to be good seal- and salmon-fishing in these waters but as yet there is no sign of the canoes and kayaks of fishermen.

The captain comes back to point out two herds of animals on the ice near the shore.

"Caribou and musk ox."

"The caribou look like reindeer."

"As a matter of fact they are reindeer. I looked it up. It seems that caribou is a French-Canadian name for the American forms of reindeer. There are great herds of them between Hudson Bay and Great Slave Lake. The Indians and Eskimoes would have a hard time without the caribou. The meat is good and the skins make warm clothing."

The musk oxen are as shaggy as Shetland ponies, as big-headed as bison, as humped as zebu cattle.

"The first time I've ever seen them outside of a zoo," my wife says.

"And could be the last time," says our flying encyclopædia. "They're disappearing fast. It's really time for them to go, because they belong in prehistoric days along with the dinosaur and mastodon. Their skeletons are found in deposits dating back to the Pleistocene. They used to be all over northern Asia and Europe, and this continent as far south as Kentucky. Now you can find them nowhere but here, in Arctic America. Fewer of them every year."

"Will we lose anything if they go extinct?"

"I think so. It seems to me we always lose when any of our animals die out. Balance of nature, you know. Musk ox meat is a bit tough and apt to be musky—but the Eskimoes don't mind that. The wool makes wonderful fabrics as soft as cash-

5

mere. Their hides are thick and warm. They can be tamed like cows and their milk is good."

I gazed with respect upon the vanishing musk ox.

The Dane looks for white whales but it is too early yet. They make Hudson Bay their summer resort. The ice breaks up into floes and bergs about the middle of June and the waters are open until the first of October. During his summer flights the Dane has seen as many as forty or fifty white whales at a time gambolling in the blue-green waters of the Bay.

"Are they really white?"

"White as polar bears. Not large—up to twenty feet long, weight about a ton. Steam whalers make a big business of whaling in these waters during July and August. The white whale—beluga is another name for it—gives the very finest oil and his skin makes good leather. It's an important part of the food supply of the Indians and Eskimoes. It's pretty exciting to watch them paddle out in their flimsy canoes right into the middle of a pod of whales and start peppering them with harpoons. The harpoons aren't too business-like—they are only poles eight feet long with a sharp bit of iron on the end. About a hundred feet of rope is attached to the harpoon and an empty oil-can tied to the other end of the rope as a float. After they harpoon a whale they follow it around until it tires, then either shoot it or net it, and tow it ashore.

"Sometimes it isn't as easy as that. A ton of lively whale can easily upset a fifty-pound boat and sometimes stave it in as well. These are toothed whales, not the baleen variety, and when they happen to be defending some young ones they can be really dangerous. Ordinarily they're as mild and playful as kittens. Not so many as there used to be. They may go the way of the musk ox unless more severe restrictions are put on the steam whalers."

The tremendous mineral wealth around Hudson Bay has hardly been tapped. The only important industry other than whaling is the fur trade, still carried on by the historic and romantic Hudson's Bay Company. The Company's sailing ships ply the waters of the Bay in summer, occasionally losing themselves because the compass fails to work. The proximity of the North Magnetic Pole, only seven hundred miles north of Hudson Bay, almost completely demoralises any compass. This is no ordinary bay where the shore is always in sight. It is some six hundred miles wide and nearly a thousand long; therefore a ship crossing it cannot depend upon landmarks, nor upon sun and stars since the sky is often overcast.

But some day these desolate waters may become a highway to Europe. Canada has sent many scientific expeditions to study the possibilities of inaugurating a through route by rail and steamer to carry the grain of the Canadian and American North-West to Europe. The distance from Edmonton to Liverpool by way of Hudson Bay would be nine hundred miles less than the usual route via Montreal. Ice is the great problem—but that is a problem that improved ice-breaking methods may solve.

The eastern shore of Hudson Bay leaps up in bold cliffs. Then we cross the tail of the province of Quebec, which we had not before realised extends farther north than Labrador. It is a bleak and treeless land, for we are three hundred miles north of the red dotted line by which the map designates the 'Northern Limit of Wooded Country'.

Across Hudson Strait, then over unbelievably huge Baffin Island, fifth largest island in the world. England, Scotland and Wales would not fill the half of it, and three Irelands would rattle around in the other half. Looking down on its cold white desolation I try to visualise the experiences recently recounted by the explorer Doug Wilkinson, who chose to spend a year in Baffin Island as the adopted son of an Eskimo family. He lived as an Eskimo, wore skins furnished by the seal and the caribou, lived in a sealskin tent in summer and an igloo of snow-blocks in winter, travelled more than a hundred miles a day by dog-sled when hunting and fished from a frail kayak, lived on a diet of meat alone, eating most of it raw, occasionally boiling it over

7

the seal-oil lamp. He came away with profound admiration for the resourcefulness of the people who make this savage yet beautiful wilderness their home.

Winging over an arm of the Arctic Ocean to Greenland, we look down upon icebergs as big as the *Queen Mary*. I refer only to the visible part, the part above the surface. Of course the submerged portion is six times as large. We are approaching the Arctic's chief iceberg factory. Greenland, the world's largest island, gives us a present-day example of what things were like in the Ice Age. Ninety per cent of Greenland is under ice. You would have to dig down through it a long way to find Greenland. The ice cap is a thousand to two thousand feet thick. It buries even the mountains and raises the level of interior Greenland to a maximum of about ten thousand feet.

There is nothing monotonous and static about the ice cap. It is full of action. Especially in summer under the melting effect of the never-setting sun, it becomes a chaos of impassable rivers, plunging cataracts, unfathomable abysses and large lakes.

Its chief action is more tremendous but less noticeable. This is its steady movement towards the sea. Like a half-congealed pudding it oozes gradually from the ten-thousand-foot heights down towards the coasts. It never finishes this trip, for it is constantly being replenished by new snows the weight of which maintain the pressure and continue the movement coastward. As it reaches the coast it is broken by the fjords and bays into more than a thousand glaciers which pour into the sea at a rate of from fifty to one hundred feet a day. Some of these glaciers are stupendous. Two of them have sea fronts more than fifty miles long.

As we come over the coast we see icebergs actually being born. The coast is abrupt and rocky, rising hundreds of feet out of the ocean. As the glaciers ooze over the edge of the cliffs and hang above the sea they naturally break into chunks, some of them only as large as a house, others as much as five, ten or twenty miles long and three hundred feet high. The cliffs of some of the fjords drop four thousand feet to the water and when a chunk of ice as big as a dozen Empire State Buildings makes this drop it must sound like the end of the world.

We see a piece go, but it is relatively small, perhaps only as large as Lincoln Cathedral. Yet the impact drowns the thunder of our four motors. This process is called the 'calving' of the bergs, and what mighty birth pangs it involves!

The only ice-free areas of Greenland are here and there along the coasts, and on one of these we land at the airport of Sondre Stromfjord. This is an American airbase maintained by permission and request of the Danes. Greenland is Denmark's only colony.

"She rules it well," says an officer of the base over coffee. "There's no exploitation of the Eskimo. The 23,000 Eskimoes of Greenland have the same rights as the thousand Danes."

After refuelling we fly on into the gathering darkness of the second night of our journey. It is more like early dawn than night because in another month Greenland will enter her long day. We are flying over the famous ice cap. It is by no means the level white field of our imagination, but a turbulent sea of congealed billows, breakers, whirlpools and chasms. Surface travel would be almost impossible and it is no wonder that much of Greenland still remains to be explored.

One hundred and fifty miles inland on an icy hill six thousand feet high stands a radio station maintained by the University of Michigan for the benefit of American weather bureaus.

We see what appears to be a bonfire on the ice. But this is plainly impossible, for there is no wood to make a fire. About the only way to make a blaze here would be to crash a plane. That sort of a fire would flicker, but this is a steady glow. It is roundish in shape and orange in colour and it takes us some time to realise that we are looking at the moon. It is the first time we have ever seen the moon rise below us. Yet this is the effect as from our perch four miles high we see the big fat orb push its way up over the edge of the ice cap.

The eastern coast is savage and precipitous, and here again is the noisy calving of bergs from the parent mass to send thousands upon thousands of the white monsters floating down towards the coasts of Labrador and Newfoundland.

Then sleep, as we pass on over the uninterrupted Arctic Ocean, warm and snug in the steel cocoon that protects us from the polar chill. During the night Iceland slides by underneath. We cross a bit of Norway early in the morning and come down at Copenhagen airport at nine.

The complete flying time from Los Angeles has been twenty-four hours.

At half-past ten we leave Copenhagen to fly over Denmark, Schleswig-Holstein, Heligoland and Amsterdam, to look down at last upon the fabulous green of rural England. We land at one o'clock, twenty-nine hours after leaving Los Angeles.

From London Airport the logical place to go to is London and our plane companions waste no time in doing so. But we shall see London later. We turn in the opposite direction towards England's slightly wild west.

CHAPTER 2

Down the Thames

Under a big ash tree was a stony well three feet deep. It seemed perfectly dry. I kneeled beside it, brushed away the pebbles at the bottom, and pressed my finger against the earth beneath.

There was a thin film of water on the tip of my finger.

"That," I said solemnly to my wife, "is the Thames."

We had found the source of Britain's chief river. On the trunk of the old ash someone long ago had cut the initials TH for Thames Head. At this point on the Government ordnance map appeared the words, 'Source of the River Thames'.

I wiped the Thames off on my slacks.

There is nothing in the upper reaches to suggest that this is one of the most important rivers in the world. It rises in a buttercup-spangled meadow in the dreaming Cotswold Hills. The place is not even as busy as it was nineteen centuries ago. Then the legionaries of a near-by Roman castle drilled in this meadow and brought their ewers to the well for water. The little well was not always dry. Old prints of Thames Head show a spouting fountain and a lake.

Even now in wet periods the well fills to the brim; in fact the entire meadow spurts thousands of tiny fountains whose streams join to form a crystal-clear brook starting on its 210-mile journey to the North Sea. On the way it is joined by other spring-fed streams so clear that the Upper Thames is called 'the sweetest of rivers' and is London's chief supply of drinking water.

Why were we to follow the Thames from source to mouth?

Primarily because we wanted to. Rivers have been a pleasant obsession of ours. We had shot Canadian rapids, cycled through the Rhine valley, paddled a dug-out on the Amazon, sailed the Nile from Nubia to Cairo in a 23-foot felucca, rafted a thousand miles down China's Grand Canal, canoed the Suwannee from its source in Okefenokee Swamp to the Gulf of Mexico, and voyaged via Japanese junk through the three thousand islands of the Inland Sea. In view of our love of waterways, particularly rivers, it was not surprising that we should want to go down the Thames. And when one desires anything very much, one has no difficulty in thinking up good reasons why one should have it.

So we rationalised our wishes with the excuse that there could be no better way to learn about England than to follow the great river that so completely epitomises the nation: its farms and villages, its towns and the greatest of its cities, its castles and universities and cathedrals, its industries and world commerce, all its romantic past and dramatic present.

Celebrating the beginning of our Thames journey, we had a gipsy breakfast under the great ash. Then we took off on our voyage down the Thames—afoot!

There was as yet no water and not even a channel, but the meadow sloped gently towards the centre. Following the low places, we came to a bridge, a culvert some four feet in diameter arched with stone under an ancient Roman road. What a contrast between this first Thames bridge and the last one, the mighty Tower Bridge at London, 142 feet high, affording passage for ocean liners.

From under the four-foot bridge we emerged into another quiet pasture. The path of the stream was now more or less clearly marked and we walked down the dry bed of it. High above, a skylark circled, spilling a cascade of melody. There was no other sound, and no one to be seen. The lovely hills stretched away to the horizon without a single house. Only a distant church tower rising from a clump of trees marked the position of the village of Kemble.

And yet all this region once hummed with activity. Only three miles to the north behind those woods was the second greatest city in Roman Britain, Corinium, now called Cirencester. It covered 240 acres to London's 330. It is interesting that Britain's two greatest cities were in the Thames Valley, one at each end.

But the Thames has always been the backbone of England. It was in the lush lands along the river that prehistoric man found the most favourable conditions: abundant water, fertile soil, plenty of game. And the Thames was the highway for invaders from Europe. It was a ready-made road to the heart of England.

England was considered a great prize. Roman emperors came in person at the head of their troops. Julius Cæsar was the first imperial visitor. Corinium was founded soon after the invasion of Britain by the Emperor Claudius in A.D. 43. An emperor-to-be, Vespasian, used it as a base for his personally conducted campaign to conquer the west country.

The city was heavily fortified behind a wall thirty feet high and a deep moat. It contained extensive barracks for troops, a colonnaded forum, a fine basilica used as town hall and court of justice, many temples to the Roman gods, and even a 'Regal Cinema'! This, however, was not a picture palace but a royal arena.

There was also a great amphitheatre where gladiators fought and bulls, bears and boars were killed. It is possible that followers of the new Nazarene cult were here thrown to the wild beasts, for Paul was teaching the heretical doctrine in Rome and some of the legionaries had adopted it.

There were noble homes in Corinium with fine sculptures, tessellated pavements and central heating (fires beneath that heated the floors). We even know what was eaten, the most unusual food being a fat snail cultivated for the purpose and leaving to this day many descendants. The implements of daily use together with lovely art objects may be found in the Corinium Museum, and not a few of them were dug up in the very fields we were now crossing.

The Romans stayed four hundred years. When they left, the countryside went to sleep. It did not wake until the Middle Ages, when it was discovered that the Cotswold Hills were ideal sheep pasture and the wool trade financed the building of lovely villages and beautiful churches.

The villages are still here, but the wool trade is gone and the Cotswold country has relapsed into a sort of perpetual Indian summer of charm and contentment, the loveliest sample of old England still to exist. It may have been the unique peace and beauty of the land that gave rise to the tradition that the county of Gloucestershire is more favoured by the divine presence than any other, an idea expressed in the proverb, 'As sure as God's in Gloucestershire'.

With such thoughts in mind we walked down the dry Thames through a meadow that showed signs of being a marsh in wet weather. There was still nothing to indicate that humans lived anywhere near or had ever lived here. Then we rounded a hillock and came suddenly upon a windmill.

Activated by a light breeze, it was lazily raising water from the underground Thames, supposedly for cattle. But there were no cattle about, and no farm-house near. Close to the windmill, which was modern, was a well, evidently very old. There was an air of mystery over all this and we resolved to ask about it if we should ever again meet a human being.

The Thames channel which served as our path was now a good ten feet wide and a lush garden from bank to bank. It wound under ash trees and elms and arching chestnut trees. The hawthorns dropped their white blossoms among the buttercups. Pigeons flew up with a heavy thrashing of foliage out of the willows—willows centuries old that had grown high, then given it up and drooped to the stream bed, only to come up again in vigorous new growth as if revived by the drink they got.

And now, the first surface water of the Thames. We came to two stagnant pools fringed with a green mat of algæ through which frogs poked their noses. We seemed to have come back into the world, for here were cattle and just beyond was a road bridge topped by a greater bridge for the railway.

We left the Thames for half an hour and walked down the road to the village of Kemble, which we had heard was the home of the man who owns Thames Head. He is S. J. Philips, proprietor of a great stretch of country around and including the source of the Thames, and a number of villages such as Kemble, where he lives in a mansion called Kemble House.

He was not at home but his attractive sister received us cordially, told us we were just in time for morning coffee, and welcomed us into the cool, restful beauty of the great house. We told her of our interest in Thames Head.

"You did well to find it," she said. "I'm afraid we don't make it too accessible. People have suggested that we turn it into a tourist attraction, put up signs, build a road in to the spring, charge admission and all that. But we feel it would spoil the place. Don't you agree?"

We did agree. We asked about the windmill.

"Yes," she said, "there's more to that than meets the eye. It does bring up water for the cattle but it has another purpose. You noticed that the well is deep and full of water. There is always plenty of water, no matter how dry the season. The underground Thames never dries up. When the surface channel goes dry it's a hardship to farmers along the river, so it became the custom, during periods of drought, to pump water from that well up into the bed of the river to keep it flowing. So when Thames Head is dry the real source of the river is the windmill well. The Thames is the only river in the world, so far as I know, that is started with a pump. However, it isn't necessary now—you'll find plenty of water in the stream below this point. Would you like to see the house?"

We were indeed interested to see the home of a typical country squire of old England. The great house was a beautiful old structure, much of it dating from the sixteenth century. But we soon found that, like many others of the stately homes of old England, it had suffered a great change, yet without humiliation. It still had vast dignity, in spite of the fact that all the stables and the barn had been converted by the squire into houses and the main building had been remodelled to make two apartments upstairs and a home for the Philips family below. But on both floors the windows were still magnificent bow windows of leaded glass looking out on a frontage a mile wide—a lovely park with flower gardens, lawns and great trees.

These splendid surroundings now give pleasure to some twenty families instead of one as in the old times. Who shall say that this is not better?

Of course there is much more sharing possible. A frontage a mile wide is hardly needed even by twenty families. But such a frontage is modest in comparison with many English estates. The Earl of Bathurst's private estate at Cirencester is crossed by a straight private road five miles long. We have heard much of the breaking up of the old estates and this process is going on, but there are still hundreds of gigantic holdings in England. One can scarcely go fifty miles in any part of the country without coming upon a wall that skirts the road for mile upon mile to enclose the property of a single family.

Refreshed and informed, we returned to the river. Beyond the double bridge there were more pools, lying always closer together until presently we were walking along beside a continuous ribbon of standing water. A duck flew up, leaving her ducklings to struggle ashore as best they could. Three horses came to taste the water, disapproved of it, tossed their heads and went off to find something fresher in a watering trough.

People emerged from a thatch-roofed farm-house and looked at us curiously as we waded through the high grass beside the water. If this was their property, they raised no objection to our crossing it. That is a delightful characteristic of English country folk. So long as visitors behave themselves they are welcome and property owners may even provide paths and stiles for the use of the public.

Here, however, there was no path, for what stranger in his senses would want to walk beside a strip of swamp? At the fences there were no stiles and we had to crawl scratchily through barbed wire.

Another bridge, and another. Then an exclamation from Mary:

"Look! It's moving!"

The grasses in the stream bed were bending towards London. The stripling Thames was actually on its way.

After the stream took to flowing the water seemed to wash its face and become bright and sparkling, minnows appeared in it, then three fish, then many fish, a mole swam across to his apartment in the bank, a snake slid out of the grass, chaffinches, crows and swallows obeyed the lure of running water.

Going was easier now. With shoes removed, we simply waded down the shallow stream.

The banks were a botanist's delight. The teasel lifted its bristling head: this wiry tuft was once used to raise a nap on woollen cloth. The purple loosestrife and purple fritillary showed how different two purples can be. There was water-loving comfrey, gathered by country folk to make cough mixture and used to congeal wounds. There was water betony with purplish flowers like small helmets: the juice crushed from the leaves is good to cleanse ulcers and relieve sunburn. Having encountered some nettles, we rubbed the irritated skin with leaves of the tall, coarse water dock, a popular antidote. It did seem to relieve the itch. The Thames shore is a natural pharmacy, as well as a source of many wild foods; and of dyes of superior quality for those who have the patience to extract them. The yellow iris yields a blue, the teasel a yellow, the water-lily a brown, the meadowsweet a black, the devil's-bit scabious a blue, centaury and agrimony a yellow, and from the roots of the lady's-bedstraw one may get a brilliant Turkey red.

We had to leave the river briefly to see the village of Somerford Keynes—for there are no villages directly on the river. While searching for the church we stumbled into the grounds of the manor house. The door opened and a lady with an inquiring and slightly alarmed expression on her face came out. After our battle with brush, weeds and river, we looked like two tramps.

"Oh-oh," said Mary. "I think we're going to be thrown out."

Explanations followed. Half an hour later we were sitting at lunch with Mrs. Foyle Fawcett, lady of the manor and widow, who told us that her husband's ancestors had bought this place in 1556 together with much of the Thames country through which we were walking.

She asked if we had noticed some ponds or small lakes along the way. We had.

"They are gravel pits filled with water."

"Rain water?"

"No. Water from beneath. Throughout all this region there is water only two or three feet below the surface. When gravel is taken up for use on the roads, that top layer is removed. The result, a lake. And there are now dozens of these small lakes occupying abandoned gravel pits. In wet weather the lakes overflow and even the apparently dry land bubbles up in thousands of springs. That's what makes the Thames."

She took us out to see her topiary. It is practically an unknown art in America but widely practised in England, this trimming of trees into fanciful shapes. Most amenable to such treatment are the box and the yew. Here some yew shrubbery had been artfully trimmed to represent two grey-hounds chasing a hare.

Walking through the village, I trained my camera on a house so old that some of the rafters had fallen in and flowers, weeds and a tree of considerable size were actually growing out of the thatch roof. A woman came out of the next house.

"Why don't you photograph *my* house?" she said. "It's a hundred years old and it was 'lapidated just like that one, but we fixed it up."

I congratulated her, then photographed the ' 'lapidated' house. The woman was disappointed and not satisfied until I took a picture of her house also.

We peered through a hedge into a lovely garden. A lady in her Sunday best, wearing a hat and carrying an umbrella, evidently on her way home from church, stopped beside us.

"Would you like to see the garden?"

She took us in and, after seeing the flowers, we were invited into the house for a glass of Madeira.

A favourite American misconception is that the British are cold, aloof, do not readily receive strangers. One wonders if those who pass such judgments have ever been in England.

Only after the Madeira did anyone trouble with introductions. Upon hearing our name, Mrs. Macmillan recalled that she had read a book by an author of that name and had a pleasant word to say about my British publisher, Heinemann: "Any book of theirs is good." Copies of *National Geographic* lay on her reading table. Warmed by these evidences of fellow-feeling, of which one is so much more sensible in England than in non-English-speaking countries, we returned to the Thames and took off our shoes.

Fish were so numerous that they bumped against our feet as we waded. But a farmer told us, "Not many fish here now. Men came with nets and scooped them up and took them away to fish ponds. Afraid the river would dry up. When we get some wet weather and the river fills again, they'll bring them back."

The seventh bridge over the Thames led only into a barnyard. Here the farmer showed us his old mill, run by Thames water. It used to serve all the countryside but now it only grinds 'corn grain' for the family.

"It was here when I was a boy," said the farmer. "Must be well over a hundred years old."

I looked about for some sign of the corn but could see only some wheat straw. Then it occurred to me that the English use the word corn in the biblical sense, not the American. Corn means any cereal crop such as wheat, barley, rye or oats. What Americans think of as corn the English call maize or Indian corn, and they know little about it, for it grows poorly in England.

The farmer had a big place, 350 acres, two-thirds of it in pasture, the rest in 'corn grain'. He had 200 head of cattle. His two boys, both in their twenties, run the place now.

"They're full of modern ideas," he said. "Look in this shed."

The shed was full of complicated farm machinery. We were to find the same sort of thing throughout England. The farms of England are among the most highly mechanised in the world.

One of the boys came rumbling up on a motor-cycle.

"Where are you going?" asked his father.

"To get the cows."

I remembered my own cow-getting days. I didn't go on a motor-cycle. I went afoot, and barefoot at that. I stared unbelievingly at the motor-cycle cowboy.

"I've been wondering," I said, "how you keep the cows from getting out of the pasture. We used to have rail fences and they would sometimes even break through those. But you have only hedges. Any determined cow could wriggle her way through a hedge."

The young farmer smiled. "Come down and I'll show you."

We followed him down the Thames-side path to the eighth

bridge, which was the simplest yet, only a single plank with a guide rail. Beside it was a shallow ford leading to a pasture gate. He rode through the ford while we walked the plank, then opened the gate and showed us an electrically charged wire half-concealed in the hedge.

"It runs around the whole pasture," he said. "The cattle soon learn to keep away from it."

It was an immense pasture, with the cattle at the far end of it, and it would have been a slow job for a barefoot boy to get them out. But in an amazingly short time the motorised cowhand had them splashing through the ford while he rolled through after them.

"Do you milk them yourself?" I asked as he chugged by.

"Automatic," he called back. "No more of that hand stuff."

The Thames plunged into a picturesque forest that arched over the river, admitting only long arrows of sunlight. The stream was two or three inches deep and the bottom was a level spread of small pebbles. The water was as transparent as air and looked like a coat of clear varnish over a tessellated pavement.

But the tessellated pavement did not feel as romantic as it looked, therefore we dried and shod our weary feet and walked along the right bank.

The pebbles gave way to weeds which threatened to choke the stream. Presently we came upon a gang of Thames Conservancy men who were clearing them out.

"If we don't," said the foreman, "we'll have all these farms flooded the next time the river rises. It looks harmless enough now but during the spring rains it can be a real menace. Back in 1947 we had it pretty bad. The river below Chertsey was three miles wide. People all down this valley love their river, but they're afraid of it too."

So that was evidently why villages were seldom built close to the river.

We left the stream to walk through the pleasant and peaceful village of Ashton Keynes. The decapitated cross in the main street was evidence that the place had not always been peaceful. Cromwell's Protestant army systematically knocked off the heads of village crosses, which they regarded as Papist symbols.

We were pretty tired and ready to quit for the day, but there was no inn to be found at Ashton Keynes. We returned to the river, a little disturbed about heavy cumulus clouds that were rolling up from the east.

A stream with the realistic name of Swill Brook joined the Thames. Swill Brook, as if trying to prove itself worthy of a better name, ran crystal-clear.

CHAPTER 3

Seven Sprites of Seven Springs

A peal of thunder ripped the sky just above us. Where the sky had been torn apart, a lake fell out. Travelling light, we had not encumbered ourselves with umbrellas or raincoats. In two minutes we were soaked.

That would not have been so bad if a cold wind had not whipped up. We tried to keep warm by putting on speed, but it was no use.

We deserted the Thames and took shelter under a hay shed near a farm-house. It was warm there, and dry. We stretched out comfortably on the hay and had about resigned ourselves to the idea of spending the night here when a gruff "Good evening" roused us. A farmer stood by us with a murderous-looking pitchfork in his hand. I made haste to explain matters before he might be tempted to use it.

"Of course," he said. "We saw you come in. But you are wet. Come along to the house."

The house was made of the famous honey-coloured Cotswold stone. It was covered with climbing roses and roofed with rough-hewn stone shingles colourfully mellowed by moss and lichens.

The interior dated from Queen Victoria, but Queen Elizabeth II evidently felt quite at home here, for she smiled at us pleasantly from above the fireplace.

The farmer's wife was most solicitous. "First you must get those things off. Come into the bedroom. I think we can find something for you to put on. May not fit very well, but . . ."

We protested that we would just sit by the fire for a while and warm up, then walk on to Cricklade.

"Indeed, you won't do anything of the sort. This is a real storm. It won't let up. You had best stay the night here. Now, this is the bathroom, and there are towels, and there's plenty of hot water. I'll get some clothes for you and when you're ready we'll have some tea."

There was no resisting such hearty hospitality. We stayed the night.

The farmer, typical of the well-to-do and well-informed English countryman, knew his Thames. He was an amateur naturalist and something of an archæologist as well.

"We've dug up many interesting things hereabouts. I like to think of the Thames as it was long ago. Of course you know that England wasn't always an island. Winston Churchill reminded us of that recently but the scientists knew it long before. England was part of the Continent. The North Sea was not a sea but a great plain. The Thames ran out into this plain and joined the Rhine—hard to imagine, isn't it?—and together they flowed into the Arctic Ocean. I have a book here somewhere that tells about it."

He fished out an old copy of *Scenery of England* by Lord Avebury, opened it and handed it to me. I read:

"We must therefore picture to ourselves a state of things when England formed part of the continent of Europe . . . when the North Sea was a great plain and the Thames, after joining the Rhine and subsequently the Humber, ran northwards into the Arctic Ocean. It was along the banks of this great river, and over the surrounding plains, that the bears and lions, bisons and elks, rhinoceroses, hippopotamuses and elephants lived whose remains are so abundant on the bed of the North Sea as well as in many of our river valleys."

"They've found remains of the giant mammoth," said the farmer, "and the musk ox, and the grizzly bear—the huge one —and the hyena, and the great elk, and the lion. Look at this."

He turned up a page in his copy of *Treasure in the Thames* by archæologist Ivor Noel Hume.

"The reader who believes that the only lions that ever sat in Trafalgar Square were put there by Sir Edwin Landseer would be wrong. Bones of the lion have been found in terrace gravel both there and in Fleet Street, while a rhinoceros lay down and died in Pall Mall. Bones of another were found under the Old Bailey, and remains of a hippopotamus were uncovered in Waterloo Place."

The thunder growled and roared and it was easy to believe that prehistoric beasts were besieging the farm-house.

But the morning was clear and bright and we met nothing more fearsome than a weasel as we walked on to Cricklade.

Cricklade is an ancient market town with memories of King Alfred and Canute. The name probably comes from the Saxon word *creccagelad* which means 'the stone ford'.

Of course there have always been innumerable places where the baby Thames could be forded by oxen and men. But the bottom is soft and would not tolerate an army on the march with many horses, chariots, carts and equipment. Such a crossing required not only a solid bottom but solid approaches on both banks and there were only two places in all of the Upper Thames where such conditions existed, Oxford and Cricklade. Of the two, Cricklade was for centuries the more important, since it carried a great Roman road direct to the mighty Roman city of Corinium.

Cricklade was well known to Celtic chiefs, Danish generals, Saxon kings and Roman emperors—and Christian saints. We stood in St. Samson's Church and admired the fine stained-glass window depicting the arrival of St. Samson, who, according to tradition, brought Christianity to the Upper Thames Valley from Brittany in the fifth century and became a teacher in Cricklade.

.   .   .   .   .   .

Just outside of Cricklade the Thames is joined by the Churn, a river that has churned up no end of controversy. It is a more lusty stream than the Thames itself and reaches many miles farther back into the hills. Therefore many persons contend, and with some reason, that it should be called the Thames, and what is called the Thames should be considered a tributary. These persons scorn the official acceptance of Thames Head as the source of the Thames. The true source, they say, is Seven Springs, which gives birth to the Churn.

After a night in Cricklade we journeyed in a hired car up the road of generals, kings and emperors, to spend a few days in the Cotswolds. Our first objective was Seven Springs. I drove in silence, for I had a problem. It would be good to have a picture of the rival source of the Thames. But it's hard to make an interesting picture of a dribble of water. How could we inject some human interest into such a subject?

"I've got it," I said at last. "We'll have seven beautiful maidens grace the seven springs and drink a toast of pure spring water to the infant Thames."

"Very nice," said Mary, "but where would we dig up seven beautiful maidens?"

That required more silent thought. "We'll apply to the mayor of the nearest town. That would be Cheltenham. He could find seven pretty girls."

"He'd call a meeting of the town council. They could never decide which débutantes could be chosen without offending the families of others. We'd probably wind up with seven society matrons with hats. More likely, only six would turn up and the whole idea would be spoiled."

This was all too true and I abandoned the notion.

But, for once, fate befriended the photographer. While searching for the spring, we drove in at the gate of what appeared to be a large estate. I knocked at the door of the lodge just inside the entrance. The woman who came to the door gave me the necessary directions. Then I asked about the estate.

"Oh, it *was* an estate," she said. "Now it's a school."

"A beautiful place," I said, looking up the flower-planted slope to the stately building on the hill-top.

"My husband is the gardener," she said.

A school! Seven beautiful maidens! It might work.

"I suppose it's a school for boys," I said, prepared for disappointment.

"No. Girls only. Why don't you go and see the principal, Miss Brown? She would love to show you around."

"We'll see the spring first—then go up to the school."

We backed out and drove a few hundred feet down the road to a bit of park that dropped down to a rocky hollow—and there were the seven springs bubbling bravely out of the rocks and flowing in a clear-as-glass stream two feet wide to a culvert which took the newborn river under the road to form a little lake on the other side where ducks swam and cows drank. Emerging rather reluctantly from the lake, as if it knew what it was in for when it got into the oily, sooty grip of London and the world's greatest port, the river started on its long journey to the sea.

The local authorities had been so firmly persuaded of the justice of their claims that they had engraved a stone above the spring with the words, '*Hic Tuus, O Tamesine Pater, Septem-geminus Fons*' (Here, O Father Thames, is Thy Sevenfold Source).

While we were looking over the ground, dreaming how seven beautiful maidens could be staged to make a picture, the gardener's wife appeared.

"I've just seen the principal and she wants you to come right up. I know you will be interested in the school."

Keeping our plot to ourselves, we followed the gardener's wife through a small gate up through lovely gardens to a fine old house. A lady as young and fresh and cool as a June morning in England came out to meet us.

"This is Miss Brown," said the lodge-keeper, and to her:

"These are the Americans who would like to see the school."

"And most welcome," said Miss Brown. "Do come in and have some coffee."

A stranger in England comes to regard this as a threat rather than an invitation. But this time the coffee was good, the lady was delightful, the school was excellent and our roving eye saw lovely maidens by the score. And when our plan at last was broached, it wasn't twenty minutes before seven charming young things had donned colourful dance costumes, equipped themselves with drinking glasses, and were tripping along beside us to the springs. There we took two dozen pictures, in colour and black-and-white, in rapid succession as the seven sprites of Seven Springs raised their glasses of spring water in a toast to Father Thames. The affair ended in a near riot, as the girls, quite evidently intoxicated by their drink, whipped off shoes and stockings and danced in the cool stream while their teacher pleaded with them to get back to their classes.

When they had gone, I straddled the infant river, one foot on one side and the other on the opposite shore, and thought what a Gargantua it would take to span it in the lower reaches where it spreads to a width of six miles and bears the burdens of the Seven Seas.

We circled through the Cotswold villages of the Thames watershed, as quaint and unusual as their names: Chipping Camden, Chipping Norton, Moreton-in-the-Marsh, Bourton-on-the-Hill, Bourton-on-the-Water, Stow-on-the-Wold, Upper Slaughter, Lower Slaughter. Bibury has been called "the loveliest village in England", but so has Broadway, and we could not decide between them.

Winchcombe also claims a superlative. The townspeople say: "We have the most beautiful and kindest ghost in all England." Any night, they told us, she may be seen walking through the garden of Sudeley Castle, wrapped in a long mantle of dark blue, a white veil over her coif, her eyes on a small book in her hands.

CHAPTER 4

Canoe and Solitude

Some days later found us back in Cricklade to pick up a canoe that had been delivered by lorry from a boat-house down-river. We slipped the canoe into the two-inch-deep Thames. When we got aboard, it sat placidly on the bottom. This seemed to amuse an ancient Crickladian, who chortled:

"You'll have to carry that dem thing more than it'll carry you."

We proved him wrong. We didn't carry the canoe more than a third of the time.

Actually we didn't carry it at all, but frequently had to go overboard to walk it through shallows, haul it through weeds, or let it down gently through stony riffles. There was just enough exercise to relieve canoe-cramp. Fast water only finger-deep alternated with quiet stretches several feet deep. The sun was bright, the air warm, the countryside a paradise of perfume and song.

The river-banks were a continuous delight. Wild roses climbed up into the willow trees to escape the competition on the ground where Queen Anne's lace, blue forget-me-nots, yellow charlock, elderberry, wild iris, buttercups, blackthorn and poppies fought for space. Yellow water-lilies floated on the quiet pools. Over them hovered blue-black dragonflies.

The silence of the gliding canoe allowed us to hear the wind in the grass, the 'peek, peek' of the moorhen, the dart of a startled fish, the paddling of a stoat in pursuit of a water rat. We found ourselves speaking in whispers.

The incredibly green and pleasant land stretched away without a house to a wooded skyline. It was good to think that here was something unchanged in a changing world. "In such a landscape," John Buchan has written, "you can cheat the centuries, for all that is presented to your ear and eye is what medieval England heard and saw."

We pulled out on the shore to have lunch—vegetable soup heated on a Tommy Cooker (the British counterpart of Sterno), cheese, biscuits, apples, oranges and milk chocolate—mixed with warm sunshine, solitude and comfort.

According to the map we passed two villages but they were too far from the river to be seen. Then came the tiny settlement of Castle Eaton, with no sign of human life, and, a mile farther, a small group of houses known as Kempsford. Here are the remains of a castle and if you listen with imagination you can hear the twang of bowstrings as English bowmen practise archery in preparation for their fight at Harold's side against the invading William at Hastings in 1066. There are a few thatch-roofed houses, a square-towered church built in the fourteenth century, and a cemetery whose peace seems to have pervaded the village.

At Hannington Bridge we saw our first human since Cricklade. He had come up from Swindon for a day's fishing.

"Any luck?"

"Must have close on fifty."

"What do you get?"

"Chub and trout."

I asked about fishing rights in the Thames.

"It's a complicated business," the fisherman said. "The rights belong to the farmer who owns the land. He takes a fee from anybody who wants to do some fishing. Some landowners charge a little, some a lot, some nothing. Some charge by the day and let anybody come in, some lease the rights to a club and make everybody else stay out. In this particular stretch there's no day fishing—that is, you can't buy a ticket for a shilling or so for a day's fishing. The farmer has leased his rights to a fishing club in Swindon at a yearly rental."

We shot some brisk rapids, then paddled down a long, lovely and solitary stretch to one of the most interesting spots on the Thames. A round tower like a castle keep marked the point where the Thames, the Coln, and the Thames-Severn Canal join. Near the tower was a house. And in the garden by the shore a 'Van Dyked' gentleman was taking his ease in a long chair.

He turned out to be Eric Edmunds, proprietor of one thousand two hundred acres of Thames and Coln country. The roundhouse and house adjoining are his home and he has transformed this confluence of three waterways into a charming estate with connecting bridges. On a point of land between the two rivers he has his studio—for in his spare time after managing large family interests, including the farming of one thousand two hundred acres and running a chain of draper's shops, he paints. And the little studio is ingeniously contrived to turn on its base as the position of the sun changes.

He took us through the house and the quaint two-storey roundhouse, his daughter served tea, and we heard the story of the famous and ill-starred Thames-Severn Canal.

It was opened in 1789, the year of the inauguration of Washington as first American President, the year of the storming of the Bastille. As implied by its name, its purpose was to connect the Thames and Severn rivers, thus providing a navigable waterway clear across England from sea to sea. There were many locks on the canal, the last one located at this point, and the lock-keeper lived in the round stone tower.

Barges to the number of 150 a day, each barge of from thirty to seventy tons burden, passed through the canal carrying grain, cheese, groceries and metals to London; merchandise, timber, hides and gunpowder to Bristol, Worcester and Liverpool.

Then came the railways to provide swifter and more efficient transportation and the canal fell into disuse. Now it is a dry moat overgrown with hawthorn bushes and wild flowers.

From this point the Thames is deeper and wider as befits a thoroughfare for barges. But the barges are gone. With the closing of the canal, they disappeared. While the world grows steadily busier, the Upper Thames has relapsed into medieval peace. Once a highway for trade, it is now a river of pleasure and history. Not until well down towards London does the Thames begin to think of buying and selling.

Ahead of us was Lechlade with its centuries-old church spire celebrated by Shelley:

> Thou too, aerial pile, whose pinnacles
> Point from one shrine like pyramids of fire,

and its 600-year-old hotel which bears the contradictory name of New Inn. Here we turned in our canoe and, the next day, hired a punt.

It is only in recent centuries that this fantastic craft has become the favourite on the upper river. The ancient Britons used a still more extraordinary vessel, the coracle. We were later to ride a Welsh river in coracles and admire the genius of the ancients who invented them. It is possibly the lightest craft man has ever used on the water. A full-blown coracle weighs twenty-five pounds, half the weight of a small canoe. It is nothing more nor less than a roundish basket covered with tarred canvas. It floats on the water as lightly as a leaf and can easily be picked up and carried on the back from one lake to another or around rapids.

But the coracle is anti-social, since it will accommodate only one person. On the Thames it gave way to the punt, which will take the whole family and the dog. They can flop about in it without peril, eat in it, sleep in it, play games in it. It is dangerous only to the person who poles it.

CHAPTER 5

Perils of the Punt

We had sailed the world's waters in almost every sort of craft but this was our first experience with an English punt. Before starting out, we asked the boat-house attendant for a few points on punts. Most important—the pole: how should it be used?

"If you've never used a pole," he said grimly, "my advice to you is to leave it severely alone."

"But there always has to be a first time."

"Yes, but aren't you beginning rather late?"

I ducked that one and examined the pole. It was as long as four men placed end to end and seemed about as heavy. It terminated in a metal prong.

"You stand in the stern," the man said. "If you try to work it from the bow, the after part of the boat will wag back and forth like the tail of a dog—or go around in circles."

"Do you operate it over the middle of the stern, or at the side?"

"At the side."

"Changing sides when necessary?"

"If you swing the pole across the boat from one side to the other you are quite likely to knock your passenger's head off. You keep it on one side and press in or out on it to steer the boat."

That was reassuring, for it was just what you did with a paddle. This was probably even easier than paddling. I comforted myself with the reflection that poling was a primitive art practised by untaught savages for thousands of years before the use of the paddle was learned.

33

"Let's get along," I said, and we got along, but used only the paddle until we were through the bridge and out of sight of the boat-house man. Then I laid down that light, lithe and beloved implement and took up the twenty-foot pole.

The upper end of it promptly snagged a willow tree and the punt all but passed on without us before it was extricated. By this time the punt had turned about and was headed back through the bridge.

"This tub has no keel," I complained. "It spins like a top."

"Quick, do something," my wife advised me. "He'll see you with that pole."

Since this was something that obviously must not happen, I pronged a pier of the bridge and swung the boat back under the willow.

Then I tried to reach bottom with the pole. The bottom was only some ten feet down and the pole was twenty feet long, so this should have been easy. However, when the pole was thrust into the water at an angle its wooden buoyancy promptly lifted it to the surface and no amount of pressure could get it to the bottom. It was necessary to thrust it straight down.

This I did with a mighty thrust—with the result that it went deep into the muddy bottom and stuck there. I heaved and strained to get it out. In the meantime the punt was going on. There was a grave decision to be made. Should I stay with the punt or with the pole? The stretch between them was getting dangerously long. I decided on the boat and let the pole go, then paddled the boat back to retrieve it.

"Better stick to the paddle," my wife suggested. But my blood was up now. The pole and I were going to fight this out if it took all summer.

For a while it was simple. The wind was accommodating and pushed us along rapidly in the right direction. I had only to go through the motions of manipulating the pole, which actually never touched bottom. It was very easy and perhaps even graceful. A girl walking along the towpath with her man stopped and gripped his arm.

"You see, Henry," she said, "that's the way it's done."

Fortunately some of the Frisian cattle that graze on Thames banks came between the couple and us before a bend of the river brought us into the wind and I was forced to give up the pole for the paddle. But at least I still had the glow of having thrilled a feminine heart and inspired deep envy and even resentment in a male one.

With either pole or paddle, the keellessness of the boat was trying. It would turn readily, but never knew when to stop turning. And it was peculiarly sensitive to the wind—a good point while sailing with the wind, but it slid backwards or sideways as easily as forwards. Sudden gusts of wind did different things to the bow and stern—the boat was so long that the two ends were in different weather zones. Both ends were blunt and wide and stood clear out of the water. The craft really had two back ends, so it could hardly be blamed for not knowing which way to go.

Now paddling, now poling, now walking the towpath and dragging the boat into the teeth of the wind while Mary fended it offshore with the paddle, we were grateful that Lechlade is not built directly on the river-bank. A broad field and screening willows separated us from the village. We passed the 600-year-old New Inn, passed Shelley's church, passed the blockhouse erected in World War II to protect the village and bridge from enemy air attack, passed the entering Ray River, so small that one could jump over it, and approached St. John's Lock, where a green flag labelled *Wreck* floated over a sunken motor-boat. Since we were only a lone punt, the lock-keeper made us wait quite a time before he filled the lock and opened one of the upper gates.

Entering a lock when winds and currents are contrary can be like threading a needle in a cyclone. Under the critical scrutiny of the lock-keeper, his wife and his daughter, I took up the pole. Noticing that everyone including my wife wore a strained expression, I tried to set them at ease with an air of complete nonchalance. This was shaken slightly when we collided with the flagpole of the wreck. At that moment my guardian angel gripped the pole with me, and together we propelled the craft into the lock with a flourish so highly professional as to bring a smile to every face.

Dismissing my angel, and quite ready to take all the credit to myself, I tied the painter to a ring-bolt and settled down in the boat with my copy of Jerome's *Three Men in a Boat*, for the scene of that tale was this very Thames. I turned to see what Jerome had to say about locks.

"I am fond of locks. They pleasantly break the monotony of the pull. I like sitting in the boat and slowly rising out of the cool depths up into new reaches and fresh views; or sinking down, as it were, out of the world, and then waiting, while the gloomy gates creak, and the narrow strip of daylight between them widens till the fair smiling river lies full before you, and you push your little boat out from its brief prison on to the welcoming waters once again. They are picturesque little spots, these locks. The stout old lock-keeper, or his cheerful-looking wife, or bright-eyed daughter, are pleasant folk to have a passing chat with. You meet other boats there and river gossip is exchanged. The Thames would not be the fairyland it is without its flower-decked locks."

I was aroused by a scream from Mary. She was clutching the gunwales to keep herself from tobogganing down the punt into the swirling waters of the lock. The bow was high in the air and the punt was tilted like the roof of a house. At every moment the tilt grew worse.

I saw the reason. The painter snubbed tight to the ring-bolt held the bow of the punt up while the stern went down as the water level in the lock fell.

"The rope!" I shouted. "Untie it."

But my wife had all she could do to hang on. If I tried to climb the boat from my place in the stern the result would certainly be an upset. The inside wall of the lock was wet and slippery and there was no way to climb it. The lock-keeper and his wife and daughter had all disappeared.

Then the rope parted under the strain and the punt slapped down upon the water. The lock-keeper came running from his house with a scone in his hand. He had evidently been enjoying tea with his family while the lock emptied. He looked down into the dark abyss where we lay and said:

"Anything wrong? I thought I heard you call."

I looked up from my book. "No," I said mildly. "Nothing wrong." My wife spoiled it by telling all.

The lower gates opened and we slid out into the sunshine. This was the first of the forty-five locks of the Thames. We were to witness many misadventures in the locks, but the memory of our own in the first one gave us the proper attitude of sympathy and understanding.

Thames locks are all more or less alike. At each there is an island. If no natural island exists, one is made. On one side of the island, between it and the mainland, is the lock. On the other side is the weir or dam. These three obstructions, lock, island and weir, impound the water in the stretch of river above so that it is deep enough for navigation. Thus the Thames, which was once a ramp of fast-flowing water so shallow that nothing but a coracle could float on it, is now a staircase of forty-five level steps of fairly deep water.

This is the work of many centuries. The early Britons could not control the Thames. The Romans could but would not, since they had little need for it; their commerce moved on Roman roads. When they departed and their roads deteriorated, traffic began to move up and down the river, but under the greatest difficulties. Wherever there was a sharp drop in the stream the local landowner would put up a mill, then build a weir across the river to get a sufficient head of water to turn the mill wheel. This of course completely blocked navigation and boats must be dragged around the obstruction. Of course bargemen complained lustily. This led to a cure almost as bad as the disease.

The mill owner, seeing his chance to turn a shrewd shilling, made a gap ten or twenty feet wide in his weir and blocked it temporarily with boards. When a boat required passage he would collect a substantial toll, then remove the boards and let the boat go through.

This was simple enough if the boat was going down-stream; it would plunge through as if shooting rapids. If bound up-stream it would have to wait until the water level was about the same above and below the weir, then it could be hauled up through the gap by men or horses.

The plan worked very badly. If the mill was busy the miller quite naturally did not want to lose his head of water and might make boats wait for days before letting them through. He was inclined to charge heavy tolls, because after the basin had been drained his mill might have to stand idle for days until the river rose to the necessary level.

The boatmen would face a similar problem; the stretch above, having been drained of its water, might take days or in dry seasons even weeks to fill deep enough for navigation. It was a common saying that it was quicker to cross the ocean than go up the Thames.

The weir with a closable gap was called a 'flash lock' because of the flash or flush of water that poured through when the gap was opened. This sudden cataract could be very dangerous and many lives were lost in the flash locks, especially when the river was in flood.

For centuries the struggle went on between mill owners and barge owners. And all the time the solution was in plain sight. The pound lock—by which water impounded or dammed could be let into a kind of cistern to raise or lower boats from one level to another—had been invented by Leonardo da Vinci. It was already in use in the year 1488 on the Mortesana Canal built to supply Milan with water. But it was almost a century before it came to England, there to be installed in 1563 in the Exeter Canal. And the Thames had to wait another century for its first pound lock.

The Thames was now a great commercial highway despite the difficulties of navigation, and the quarrel over water rights finally stirred Parliament to action. A commission was created to control Thames navigation and the first pound locks were built during the middle of the seventeenth century, the rest during the eighteenth and nineteenth.

Ironically enough, thirty years after the entire lock system had been completed the Thames ceased to be important to commerce. The steam engine had been invented. The river was supplanted by the railway.

And so the pleasure boats of today have the grimy barges of centuries past to thank for easy passage up and down one of the most delightful rivers in the world.

True, you need plenty of time for a Thames trip. Locks have changed but little in a hundred years; they are old and slow and their tranquillity seems to have affected the lock-keepers, who cannot imagine why anyone on the Thames should be in a hurry. "People in a hurry go by road," one said to us when we showed slight impatience. Of course he was right—yet the half-hour we sometimes had to wait before the lock-keeper appeared seemed a bit too much. When after such a wait at one lock we landed and routed the keeper out of his house he fixed us with a sad eye and said reprovingly: "A man must have his tea, you know."

After all, a man does need his tea for the hard labour of working the heavy, cumbersome gates. Every lock on the river is still operated by hand. Meanwhile the lock-keeper in Europe sits in a control tower and presses buttons. This might seem to mply that the Continent is more up-to-date than the island.

But it may just as well be taken to mean that the Continent still relies upon the snail-slow transportation afforded by rivers and canals long since abandoned in England in favour of swift delivery by railway and road.

Leaving St. John's Lock, we brought the punt around the island and up into the foaming waters below the weir. To the thunderous music of falling water we lunched in the punt. Then, in order to practise the use of the pole under the most exacting conditions, I spent much of the afternoon making perilous near-misses in the conflicting currents produced as the Thames overflowed the weir and dropped its thousands of tons to the lower level.

Weary of this, we landed to visit a quaint pub named The Trout Inn. We entered an ancient taproom with a beamed ceiling that all but grazed our heads. The chubby proprietor was talking.

"Born within sound of Bow Bells, I was. Brought up for the stage, I was. For years on end I made the rounds of the halls—the music halls. Never thought in those days I'd wind up in a convent. That's what this was, you know—a nunnery built round about the year 1200. Then it became the Priory of St. John Baptist. Lay brothers and lay sisters—whether they lay together I don't know." He laughed heartily and expected us to join in, which we did. He was still the music-hall trouper.

The taproom had age-old plaster and wattle walls, a stone floor, a black cat called Sooty, an orange-coloured fire on the hearth, a huge pike in a glass case on the wall. He saw us admiring the pike.

"Pretty good fish, yes? Wore me down to the bone, that one did."

"You caught it yourself?"

"Of course. He gave me a time of it, he did."

I caught a twinkle in his eye.

"Have you ever read *Three Men in a Boat*?" I asked.

"Can't say I have."

I went out to the punt and got the book. While the old trouper settled down behind his counter among the beer mugs I read aloud the story of the big trout on a taproom wall much like this one—how Jim Biggs claimed he had caught it, how when he had left the room Joe Muggles came in and attributed the catch to himself, how in turn Mr. Jones claimed the honour and then old Billy Maunders. And how the proprietor of the inn laughed when he was told of these extravagant claims, and explained that he had caught the fish himself, years ago, when he was quite a lad, with a bent pin on the end of a string:

"He was called out of the room at this point, and George and I again turned our gaze upon the fish. It really was a most astonishing trout. The more we looked at it, the more we marvelled at it. It excited George so much that he climbed up on the back of a chair to get a better view of it. And then the chair slipped, and down it came with a crash, George and the chair on top of it. 'You haven't injured the fish, have you?' I cried in alarm, rushing up. 'I hope not,' said George, rising cautiously and looking about. But he had. That trout lay shattered into a thousand fragments—I say a thousand but they may have only been nine hundred. I did not count them. We thought it strange and unaccountable that a stuffed trout should break up into little pieces like that. And so it would have been strange and unaccountable, if it had been a stuffed trout, but it was not. That trout was plaster of Paris."

We looked again at the big pike. The old trouper laughed, and waved his hand.

"Well, perhaps I didn't catch it, but I can tell you one thing, that fish is not plaster of Paris, no, sir. I'll take off the case so you can smell it. There—am I right?"

He was right.

We slept under twelfth-century rafters in a gigantic canopied four-poster once used doubtless by the lay brothers and/or lay sisters.

CHAPTER 6

Five-Room Flat Afloat

The river now being deep enough for motor-boats, we had
arranged with a boat-house down-river for delivery of such a
vessel at this point.

The next morning, there it was—a sleek, trim cabin cruiser
some thirty feet long, crisply painted blue and yellow and carrying the British flag at her stern.

The tip of the flag divided her name, leaving 'Gosh' on one
side and 'awk' on the other. The first part suggested profanity
and the second part sea-sickness. It seemed an unfortunate
name for a boat.

Then the wind blew aside the flag and we realised that the
name was not Gosh-awk but Gos-hawk, an excellent name for
a boat, for the goshawk (originally goose-hawk) was that
famous bird much used in falconry to bring down geese, hares,
rabbits, pheasants, partridges, and celebrated for its power,
speed and courage.

Just as puzzling as the name had at first been was the black
mop that now projected itself from the wheel-house. Coils of
black hair shot off in all directions, some standing up like
cobras, others drooping over the face and all but obscuring
the eyes, but stopping just short of an ear-to-ear grin. The
owner of that magnificent tousle of serpents must have had
Harpo Marx as his father and Medusa as his mother. From
under this ferocious snake nest came a remarkably gentle
voice.

"You are Mr. and Mrs. Price? I'm Herbert."

42

Herbert, eighteen-year-old-about-to-turn-nineteen boat builder's apprentice, had brought the boat up-river and would accompany us down. In ten minutes we were aboard and examining our floating home.

It was actually a five-room flat with sun-deck and back porch. Reading from the front: the head, crew's cabin with two berths, the wheel-house, main cabin with two berths, galley, cockpit. And all within thirty-one and a half feet fore-and-aft and nine feet of beam.

The limitations of space were most noticeable in the head (lavatory to landlubbers). It was practically form-fitting. Once inside with the door closed, you were in a suit of armour. There was one good thing about it: if the boat should roll you would not and could not fall. If you should drop anything on the floor and wish to pick it up it would be necessary to open the door to get room enough to bend. It was a chemical toilet and the chemicals were evidently effective, for it was odourless. It would not require bits of perfume hung up in the room in the Japanese fashion.

Needless to say, it was an enormous convenience, much better than the fields of tall wheat which had served on our felucca trip down the Nile.

The forward cabin was a bit short on headroom but Herbert, who occupied it, was well protected from the beams by his thick thatch. The after cabin had plenty of headroom, six windows for light and ventilation, space between the berths for a table. The galley was just large enough for a sink on one side and a stove on the other. The cockpit in the stern and the decks overall afforded plenty of space for sun-bathing if the temperamental English sun should decide to favour us. The boat was equipped with electric light and bottled gas for cooking, also a fresh water tank that would hold twenty-six gallons.

Two propellers made easier the constant turning required on the winding Thames. The boat was a quarter-century old and the engines of very modest power, but speed is definitely not desirable on the Thames, since a violent wash would upset canoes, skiffs and punts.

We had not finished the first day's run before we realised what a prize we had in Herbert. He could take the wheel when there were photographs to be taken or notes to be written—and that was much of the time. Every bend in the river revealed something picturable and memorable. He did most of the hopping about that was necessary to get the boat safely through the locks. He pumped the water from the bilges, swept the floors, swabbed the decks, filled the gas and water tanks, emptied the pails, dug holes to bury the garbage. No waste could be thrown into the river, for the Upper Thames is London's chief water supply.

He was hard to roust up in the morning. That, however, was not an individual peculiarity but a national one. The Englishman is not aware that there is any daylight before 10 a.m. We were usually awake at six or seven and fretting to be off, since the sun, the photographer's best friend, generally shone during the early hours, then hid itself behind banks of clouds for the rest of the day. However, Herbert's schedule was really the more sensible, because the lock-keepers were Englishmen too. There was no point in starting early only to wait at the first lock.

Once up and with the dew of sleep brushed from his eyes, Herbert was willing and cheerful. His manner was as mild as his hair-do was aggressive. He spoke so softly that it was usually necessary to ask him to repeat. Even then it was hard to understand him because of his pronunciation. 'Pound' was 'pahnd' and 'railway' was 'rilewy'.

Shyness muted his voice. Conscious of his own difficulties, he was taking a correspondence course in conversation and showed us the manuals. We tried to convey to him that his conversation problem would be ninety per cent solved by a little more volume. What he said was always sound enough when one could hear it. He had a good mind, good manners and a good heart.

The river meandered through lush meadows to Buscot Lock. This has no keeper of its own, but the keeper of St. John's Lock occasionally rides over on his bicycle to Buscot to see if anyone wishes to go through!

In due season we were in and out again and sailing sweetly through the Vale of the White Horse, so called after the 374-foot figure of a horse cut into the flank of a hill at Uffington and believed to be either the work of the early Britons or a memorial of the victory of King Alfred over the Danes in 871. How deep in history is this lovely land! Dreaming back over the centuries one suddenly feels a thousand years old, and it's a good feeling.

We disembarked to walk through Kelmscott Manor, a fine old gabled house once the home of William Morris, the amazing man whose versatility almost equalled that of Leonardo da Vinci. He painted pictures, wrote poetry, printed and published beautiful books, executed stained-glass windows, drew patterns for textiles, designed tapestries, built furniture, revived handicrafts, translated from the Latin and the Icelandic, stimulated social reform.

His chief rôle, perhaps, was that of an inspired interior decorator. He is credited with having revolutionised the homes of the English middle class. As one historian says: "His mission was to teach the mass of his fellow-countrymen that ugliness, artificiality, meaningless complication in their houses, in their furniture, in their general surroundings, were not merely a mistake but an evil." He fled from London to this rich Thames country with its abundant grass, stately elms, meadowsweet, loosestrife, multitudinous willows, and he wrote of it:

> See, we have left our hopes and fears behind
> To give our very hearts up unto thee;
> What better place than this then could we find

By this sweet stream that knows not of the sea,
That guesses not the city's misery,
This little stream whose hamlets scarce have names,
This far-off, lonely mother of the Thames?

All day the river was scarcely wider than our boat was long. Cattle grazed near the shore. All land along the river was pasture, the cultivated land being half a mile back and on higher ground so that crops would not suffer in case of flood.

Swallows dipped and twirled above us. Two big herons rose, trailing long legs. Ducks chattered past.

The most distinguished birds were the swans, stately white caravels sailing without the least apparent effort. As the ibis is the bird of the Nile, so is the swan the bird of the Thames. From the point where the stream is so shallow that the birds' paddles scrape the bottom, all the way down to the Port of London, it is hard to go a mile without encountering some of these conspicuous beauties.

We came upon one sitting on her nest among the rushes at the water's edge. She had the air of a queen on her throne. She turned a haughty eye upon us as we nosed the boat close in and stopped within five feet of her so that I could get a picture.

"Go easy," Herbert advised. "When they get angry, they're bad."

I went easy, but the click of the camera made her hiss and glare, and her mate came steaming over from the other side of the river to defend his home. Mary bribed him with a crust of bread and he, craven soul, left his spouse to take care of herself.

The queen in the meantime had decided to ignore us. She ruffled her feathers, stretched herself, and rose, revealing seven eggs the size of giant hen-eggs.

Then we saw a remarkable sight, and it was the only time we were to see it on our entire journey. Mother Swan placed her beak under an egg and deftly turned it upside down. She went on to do the same with all the other eggs. Then, with a disdainful look at us, she settled down to fry them on the other side.

When the bread was gone the male suddenly bethought himself of his paternal duties, picked up a stick, and brought it to his wife. She took it and tucked it into the great pile of sticks and twigs that constituted the nest. When we tried to lure her from her nest with an offer of food she complained softly and turned her head away. But when the morsel was passed to her on the blade of a paddle she did not refuse it. Then she hissed something that might have been, "Get along now. Don't you see you're bothering me?" and we left her in peace.

As common as the swan but less conspicuous is the moorhen. Her nest is a scraggly affair designed to look exactly like the bush in which it is built. She has reduced concealment to a fine art. In a dead bush we found a nest of dead twigs, in a live bush a green nest. The eggs are brownish and spotted to blend with their surroundings. When the bird leaves the nest she covers it with rushes in the manner of the pheasant and the partridge.

"What are those holes in the shore?" I asked Herbert. The perpendicular bank was pierced with openings like miniature cave dwellings.

"The wet ones, low down, are made by the water rats. The dry ones are used by the kingfishers. They make their nests out of the bones of the fish they catch."

After a five-lock day we tied up for the night in the shadow of New Bridge. Like New Inn at Lechlade and New College at Oxford, New Bridge is of great antiquity. It is quite possibly the oldest bridge on the entire river, its only rival being Radcot Bridge.

New Bridge was already more than two centuries old when Columbus discovered America. It is hard for an American mind to stretch back to the year 1250, when this beautiful stone bridge of five pointed and groined arches and projecting piers was built.

Let those who are aged and yet without achievement take heart, for this bridge was four hundred years old before it rose to fame. Then it played a part in one of the greatest social revolutions of all history, the extinction of the theory of the Divine Right of Kings and the birth of democracy. It was here that Cromwell fought King Charles I and sent him packing northwards to final defeat.

At this point the Windrush, beautifully named, enters the Thames after a journey through charming Cotswold villages past medieval castles.

The wind that has defied the wheel all day has died down. As darkness comes on, the river looks like a sheet of black glass reflecting the illuminated windows of an inn on the farther shore. The inn also is beautifully named. It was once The Old Rose, but after it burned down and was rebuilt it was appropriately renamed The Rose Revived.

Mary has an argument with the gas stove, which grudgingly agrees to co-operate, the table is set up between the bunks, and Herbert joins us at dinner. The chill May air makes everything taste wonderful.

And the chill May air together with a dense river fog followed by heavy frost makes for a very uncomfortable night. The temperature drops to four degrees below freezing. The next morning we telephone a requisition for more blankets.

CHAPTER 7

Ghosts

At Northmoor Lock we left the boat with Herbert in charge and walked a mile over the fields to Appleton village in search of the home of Sir Basil Blackwell.

All Englishmen and tens of thousands of readers the world over know the four-storey, block-deep bookshop in Oxford, one of the two or three greatest bookshops on earth. If any author wishes assurance that the public still reads books he has only to witness the surging crowd of book-hungry people who lose themselves in the labyrinthine mazes of Blackwell's. The house fills a dual rôle, not only selling books but publishing scholarly volumes by university dons. No less distinguished a pen than John Masefield's has honoured this institution:

> There, in the Broad, within whose booky house
> Half England's scholars nibble books or browse,
> Where'er they wander blessed fortune theirs:
> Books to the ceiling, other books upstairs;
> Books, doubtless, in the cellar, and behind
> Romantic bays, where iron ladders wind.

In his letter inviting us to stop off from our river journey for Sunday dinner at his country home, Sir Basil had given us typically English directions:

"My house, Osse Field, lies behind a tallish hedge three hundred yards from the village cross along the road to Netherton."

By ways as labyrinthine as the bookshop's we came at last upon a great house in large grounds radiant with daffodils and tulips. We were admitted to the library, a spacious and wonderful room richly walled with books from floor to ceiling and, through big leaded windows, overlooking acres of private parkland.

Sir Basil and Lady Blackwell had been joined for the day by their two married daughters and three teen-age grandchildren. Throughout the cigarette-and-Dubonnet period in the library and the lunch of roast mutton with currant jelly, fruit topped with custard sauce and whipped cream, cider, coffee, the conversation, by some chance, centred upon one fascinating subject: ghosts.

A daughter recounted how an American gentleman had actually laughed when told of English ghosts, and she had had a hard time convincing him that they actually exist.

I said: "Perhaps American houses are too new to be haunted. At any rate, we almost never hear of such a thing."

This caused much astonishment, and stories were told about the very active and numerous ghosts of England.

Sir Basil knew a man who had visited Tintern Abbey in the dusk and had seen a monk in long white robes walking two feet above the ground. It seems that the floor in the time of the monks had been two feet above the present ground level. The visitor was a clergyman. He challenged the monk with:

"I adjure you by the living God to leave me."

The ghost vanished. Sir Basil felt that this was no way to treat a fellow religionist. Why didn't the visitor grasp his opportunity and ask the ghost to stay and tell him of the ancient days of the abbey?

But, someone asked, do ghosts ever talk? Yes indeed. Instances were cited of remarks and even speeches made by spirits. Which led the handsome daughter who was taking a course at the London School of Economics, but is more imaginative than that fact would suggest, to speculate as to whether things, once said, imprinted sound waves upon the air so that they may at some time long after be recalled and heard again.

Speaking of mysterious voices, Sir Basil told of a verger who saw in the dim church a stranger tampering with the poor-box. He cried: "What the hell are you doing with that bloody box?" The man fled in the greatest terror. "You know," the verger said when he told of what had happened, "I believe he thought it was the voice of God himself."

Sir Basil began a story but his wife stopped him. She wouldn't have that story told, it was too terrifying, and might distress us, sleeping alone on the Thames.

Later when she had left the room Sir Basil said mischievously: "Shall I tell that story now?" Everyone voted for the story, and here it is.

Four men were talking about the malicious ghost of a man buried in the near-by cemetery. One of them said he was not afraid of ghosts. In a fine spirit of bravado, he took down a dagger from the wall and declared he would go to the cemetery and plunge it into the grave.

The next day he was not to be seen. The other three, becoming anxious, went to the cemetery and found him stretched out upon the grave, face-down and dead.

Turning him over, they discovered what had happened. The man who had boasted that he had no fear of ghosts had died of fright when, after he had plunged his dagger into the ground and tried to get up, he felt himself held by an invisible hand.

His dagger had pinned down the corner of his overcoat.

Lady Blackwell came back just in time to hear the end of the story. She shivered. "It could have been an accident," she said. "But—who knows?"

To American ears it was nothing short of amazing that highly intelligent people in this twentieth century should profess to believe in ghosts. And yet what could be more natural in this land of ancient mansions and castles, creaking floors, echoing

51

corridors, unused rooms, gloomy dungeons, secret passages, all steeped in a long, romantic and bloody history? The American is like a cut flower, no roots. The Englishman has roots and sometimes longs fiercely to get away from them but cannot, and is a more interesting person because he cannot.

We started back to our boat, quite prepared to meet ghosts in the fields or find them under our bunks. We said something to this effect. Sir Basil smiled. "It's not their natural habitat," he said. "But during the war it might not have been safe to walk across those fields after dark—not because of ghosts, but thieves. For a while England became a nation of thieves. That reminds me . . ."

And he told us one more story. A man parked his bicycle outside a church. He went to a friend's house and stayed until late, forgot the bike, and his friend drove him home. The next day he remembered. He assumed that the bicycle had been taken. But, passing that way, he was surprised to see it exactly where he had left it. So he went into the church to offer a prayer of thanks. When he came out the bicycle was gone.

"I suppose there's a moral there somewhere," said Sir Basil.

We met neither ghosts nor thieves as we made our way back across the starlit moor to the sleeping river.

We stopped in the morning to see the old-time ferry which is still, as in Matthew Arnold's day, "crossing the stripling Thames at Bablock Hythe". It was already ancient when Arnold saw it. A manuscript of 1692 states that "Bablock Hythe has a great boat to carry over Carts and Coaches". In a document of 1279 there is reference to "the ferry of Babbelak".

Of course this is not the same vessel but is of the same type and worked in the same way, by sheer arm-power. The ferryman stands amidships and grips a cable that runs from shore to shore. He simply pulls the boat back and forth across the stream, but this is some feat, since the craft may be loaded with two or three automobiles and many passengers.

And yet a girl once operated the ferry, and thereby hangs a tale. She was Betty Rudge, the ferryman's daughter. The Rudges were of very humble and unpretentious stock and it was a great thrill to Betty when a viscount took an interest in her. He was young William Flower, second Viscount Ashbrook, a student at Christ Church College in Oxford, and he had come for a day's fishing. He forgot about his fishing when he saw Betty. It was love at first sight. He found her utterly enchanting, until she opened her mouth. Her speech was not precisely Oxonian. He realised what a gulf lay between them. However, further meetings intensified his longing for her. He must have her, but not without an Oxford accent.

He solved the problem by placing her in a family of gentlefolk whose fortunes had declined but whose accent and manners remained intact. It is not recorded how long the tutoring continued, but finally Galatea passed all tests with honours and the two were married in Northmoor Church in 1766. Nor is it just a pretty story, for we found their names on the old register.

Contrary to the gloomy prophecies of friends, the marriage was a very happy one. In fact Betty reaped a double dividend, for that chance meeting at the ferry gave her two happy marriages. After giving the viscount eighteen years of wedded bliss together with two boys and four girls, she was married again, following ten years of widowhood, this time to a distinguished scholar of Jesus College, Oxford. Doubtless this completed her conquest of the famous accent and when she died in 1808 she was referred to in the public press as "a courtly old grandame". Her children and grandchildren carried the humble blood of the Thames ferryman into the veins of the aristocracy of England. One of her granddaughters married the sixth Duke of the house of Marlborough, that famous clan ancestored by the seventeenth-century Sir Winston Churchill and climaxed by the Sir Winston of the twentieth.

Another Oxford student who frequented Bablock Hythe was

Shelley and it is said that a lark rising from its nest in the near-by meadow inspired the lines:

> Hail to thee blithe Spirit!
> Bird thou never wert,
> That from heaven, or near it,
> Pourest thy full heart
> In profuse strains of unpremeditated art.

We spent many days exploring the near-by villages, most interesting of which was Cumnor, a mile from the river across the meadow where Shelley's skylarks still rise like rockets of song.

Above: what a contrast between this first Thames bridge and the last one, the mighty Tower Bridge at London, 142 feet high, affording passage for ocean liners

Below: the seven sprites of Seven Springs drink a toast to the infant Thames. A tablet in the wall bears the inscription, "Here, O Father Thames, is thy sevenfold source"

CHAPTER 8

Mystery of Amy Robsart

Cumnor is the scene of a murder mystery never quite solved. The chief figure in the mystery was the man who fell in love with Queen Elizabeth I; or, at least, fell in love with the power she wielded and longed to share it.

The handsome Robert Dudley, Earl of Leicester, was much favoured by the young Queen; but he was already married to Amy Robsart. This awkward fact was all that stood in the way of a royal wedding.

Then Amy was found at the foot of a staircase with her neck broken. Her husband maintained that it was an accident. He himself had a perfect alibi. He was away from home when the 'accident' occurred. The Queen herself could testify to this, for he was with her.

But so widespread was the suspicion that he had contrived the death of his wife that the Queen's marriage to him would have been a public scandal. Elizabeth's trusted adviser, Lord Burleigh, counselled her to abandon her plans for the marriage because Leicester was "infamed by the murder of his wife".

As the years passed, details leaked out. And although the guilt of Dudley was never conclusively proved, the evidence as finally assembled by the English antiquarian, Elias Ashmole, in his *Antiquities of Berkshire*, was overwhelming.

According to this account, the men Dudley engaged to act for him were his friends Sir Anthony Forster and Sir Richard Varney. They, finding the neglected wife very unhappy, tried to persuade her that she was suffering from melancholia and should take a potion which they would provide. She refused, suspecting the worst. Then they appealed to a reputable physician, Dr. Walter Baily, to prescribe a potion. The doctor was also suspicious, fearing they would add poison to the medicine before it was administered, and declined to have anything to do with the matter.

The killers then resorted to death by violence. On a morning when the servants had gone to market they seized upon Amy, strangled her, flung her down a flight of stairs and broke her neck, leaving her in such position that it might appear either accident or suicide.

The murderers were evidently men of some conscience. Forster, writes the antiquarian, "being a man formerly addicted to hospitality, company, mirth and music, was afterwards observed to forsake all this, and being affected with much melancholy (some say madness) pined and drooped away". Varney on his death-bed cried miserably and lamented that all the devils in Hell were tearing him to pieces. Another death-bed confession, that of the wife of a kinsman to the Earl, gave damning evidence.

Then there was the suspicious fact that Dudley had hastily buried his wife before the coroner could hold an inquest. Amy's father insisted that her corpse be taken up and an inquest held. It was held, but with no effect, it being believed that Dudley bribed the coroner to silence.

To quiet the talk that was going around and to prove his great love for his wife, Dudley caused her body to be reburied in St. Mary's Church in Oxford with great pomp and solemnity. The chaplain rather spoiled the effect of this magnificent gesture. In his funeral sermon his tongue slipped and he referred to the *'murder'* of the late Amy when he meant to say 'death'.

One man who was convinced of Dudley's guilt was Sir Walter Scott, and millions of readers of *Kenilworth* have wept over the fate of Amy Robsart.

Both of the women in Robert Dudley's life are memorialised in Cumnor Church. A statue of Queen Elizabeth bears the inscription: "This statue was supposed to have been sculptured by order of Robert Dudley, Earl of Leicester, and placed as an ornament in Cumnor Place Gardens in compliment to his Royal Mistress." And on the wall near-by are preserved some melancholy letters written by Amy Robsart shortly before her death.

Crossing on the hand-pulled ferry, we walked a mile from the other shore to the village of Stanton Harcourt, where Pope's Tower rises above the thatched roofs. Here the irascible and erratic Alexander Pope, with only a guessing knowledge of Greek, translated the *Iliad*. Self-taught, his knowledge of languages was meagre, and he relied largely upon translations already made by others. Whether or not he deserves criticism on this score, his version was recognised as a noble poem in its own right and won him immediate fame. Still preserved is a bit of red glass from one of the tower windows on which he scratched: "In the year 1718 Alexander Pope finished here the fifth volume of Homer."

We came to a lovely bridge with an unlovely name, Swinford, from Swine-ford, in loving memory of the pigs that used to ford the river here when there was no bridge.

The bridge is private property. It was built by the Earl of Abingdon in 1777 and in fifteen years the tolls had paid for it. But the tolls continue to the present day, a penny a wheel, thus twopence for a bicycle, fourpence for a car, an inexhaustible gold mine for the fortunate owners.

Beyond the bridge rises Beacon Hill, where signal fires burned to warn England of the approach of the Spanish Armada, and where, more than a millennium before that, the Britons fortified themselves against Roman invaders.

We are brought suddenly back to today's world by a red flag

waving in the middle of the river. Herbert, at the wheel, steers to port of it. At the eleventh moment a dredger by the shore blows its whistle and a workman calls to us to go to the right of the flag.

But it is too late to turn. To pass on the other side it will be necessary to back water first. Herbert throws the engines into reverse.

Nothing ever happens promptly when this is done, and doesn't happen at all now because the current is pulling us forward more powerfully than the engines can take us backward.

Again the call from the shore: "Go back." We don't go back. Thinking that the helmsman may not have heard, I call down from my camera perch above: "Go back if you can."

"I can't," Herbert answers. "One of the engines has gone off."

He tries a bit longer. But the current is too strong. We continue to slide forward.

"I'll have to try going ahead."

We strike with a jolt that dumps me from the wheel-house roof on to the forward deck and sends all the pans tumbling in the galley.

The stern of the boat begins to swing round in the current. In a moment we are broadside in a most precarious position, listing far over and threatening to capsize under the powerful push of the current. Men from the dredger come running along the shore shouting unhelpfully.

Herbert stops the engine to save the propellers from grinding themselves to bits against the shoal. We all throw our weight on the up-stream side to restore the boat's balance, but it does no good.

Then there is a grinding sound beneath. The stern of the boat passes over the obstruction and we are now pointed upstream. We deposit all our slight weight in the stern, the bow lifts, the current pushes us off, and we are free, floating down-stream backwards. Herbert starts the engines and turns the boat about.

Our pulse-beats slow down—but only for a moment. A big cruiser comes ploughing up-stream. Noting the side on which we have passed the flag, they assume that they should do like-wise. Our shouts and those of the dancing men on the bank fail to register until they are stuck high on the shoal. The skipper calls: "Why didn't you warn us?"

He tries reverse but his boat does not budge. We throw him a line and, after an hour's manœuving, get him off.

"What's the use of putting out a red flag," grumbles the dredge foreman, "if you fellows pay no attention to it?"

But Herbert will not argue.

"Got a line?" he says. Obtaining one, he ties one end on shore and the other to the flagpole. We wait to see how it works. The skipper of the next boat sees the line blocking the dangerous passage and steers his boat to the other side of the flag.

But we make no convert of the foreman. When we leave, he is still grumbling about people who can't see a red flag.

The pages of romance opened again as we looked at the tumbled walls of Godstow Nunnery where Fair Rosamond lived and sinned and now lies buried.

Sin was not a stranger in the nunneries, else why the pro-verbs, "Nuns wear their virginity easily" and "Clerks should not haunt nunneries neither early nor late"? However, there was still another proverb, "A king can do no wrong", and perhaps that was the excuse of Henry II when he seduced fifteen-year-old Rosamond in Godstow Nunnery, then carried her off to his palace at Woodstock.

He did not instal her in the palace since that was already occupied by his Queen, Eleanor of Aquitaine. In a far-away corner of the vast estate he hid Rosamond in a secret bower which, according to a mixture of history and legend, was a maze of arches and winding walls with 150 doors. To find their way back and forth through this labyrinth Rosamond and her royal lover used a silken thread. For several years the secret was evidently well guarded and two sons were born to Rosamond, one of whom became Earl of Sarum and the other Archbishop of York.

But the day came when the retreat was discovered and the Queen faced Rosamond. The historian Holinshed says: "The Queene found hir out by a silken thridde, which the Kinge had drawne after him out of hir chamber with his foote, and dealt with hir in such sharpe and cruell wise that she lived not long after."

The many ballads that have been written about the fair Rosamond give various accounts of her death. The most commonly accepted seems to be that the Queen offered her death by torture or by poison, and she chose poison.

> She gave this comelye dame to drinke,
> Who took it in her hand,
> And from her bended knee arose,
> And on her feet did stand,
>
> And casting up her eyes to Heaven,
> She did for mercye calle,
> And drinking up the poyson stronge,
> Her life she lost withalle.

She was taken back to the nunnery for burial and her King saw to it that she was provided with a magnificent tomb set about with lighted candles and curtains of silk. Possibly some of the more pious nuns did not approve of the burial of such a woman in a nunnery chapel. They may have been responsible for the rather dubious epitaph placed on her tomb:

> Here lies beneath the earth without hope of coming
> up again, Rose of the World, not a pure Rose,
> Not smelling as a decent corpse should, but sweet as
> usual with cosmetics and perfume.

There she lay until two years after Henry's death. In 1191 the Bishop of Lincoln, discovering the fine tomb and being told it was Rosamond's grave, cried: "Take this harlot from hence and bury her without the church."

It was done. But after the Bishop had gone "the chaste sisters gathered her bones, and put them in a perfumed bag, enclosing them so in a lead and layde them againe in the church under a fayre large grave stone". And seven centuries later Peacock, on a river excursion to Godstow with his friend Shelley, wrote:

> The windflower waves, in lonely bloom,
> On Godstow's desolated wall:
> There thin shades flit through twilight gloom,
> And murmured accents feebly fall.
> The aged hazel nurtures there
> Its hollow fruit, so seeming fair,
> And lightly throws its humble shade
> Where Rosamonda's form is laid.

At Godstow Lock I took a ducking. Stepping on the gunwale with the intention of leaving the boat, I left it, but not as planned. A rope on the gunwale rolled under my foot and I found myself with one leg hip-deep in the lock. My other foot was still on the boat and my hands on shore, and the gap between was widening. In my hand was a Leica camera.

After having lost a Contax in the Nile, a Leica in Nassau, and a Retina in the Inland Sea, I have acquired the habit of thinking of my camera before myself. When Herbert came running along the lock side to help me I said: "Take the camera." He took the camera and I dropped into the water.

A lock is not a good place to go bathing. The water rushing out from under the lower gates creates a dangerous undertow. The boat's deck was too high to reach and the lock wall was higher. I swam through the churning waters to the upper gates where the undertow was least and was ignominiously hauled up at the end of a rope. But the wetting seemed unimportant when Herbert handed back the camera, dry and safe.

We all cringed as we went under Osney Bridge, fully expecting that we would scrape our top. This is the lowest bridge on the entire river, and affords only from seven to eight feet of headroom. We skimmed through with an inch to spare.

We must have interrupted the lunch or siesta of the keeper at Osney Lock, for he emerged, pulling on his coat, only after a quarter-hour wait and a dozen horn blasts. He went about grumbling, as if he had something better to do than open locks. He reminded us that it was against the law to toot. But just how he would be aware of our presence if we did not use the horn, he failed to explain.

Perhaps he had been saddened by his surroundings, for the river was now, for the first time, smothered between grimy warehouses and factories. For thirty miles there had not been a town or village on the river. We had been passing through a green paradise that, except for the locks, had changed but little in long centuries.

Here, white swans were the only beautiful things. They refused to be daunted by the black cliffs, belching steam, growling machinery. Even the crowning horror, the gas works, did not lessen their majesty and pride.

CHAPTER 9

Dreaming Spires of Oxford

So this was Oxford, called by some the most beautiful city in England. Where were the 'dreaming spires'? All we could see was factory chimneys. When would Oxford follow the example of so many other cities and turn its waterfront into a riverside park?

Our first glimpse of another Oxford came when a majestic stone tower shouldered its way up out of the warehouses. This was the last remaining tower of Oxford Castle, built in 1071 by William the Conqueror as one of the three strongholds with which he intended to control the valley of the Thames. The other two were Windsor Castle and Wallingford Castle.

We could see in imagination the figure of a woman being let down at the end of a rope from the dizzy battlements to the ground, for it was here that Matilda was lowered one dark winter night and fled over the snows to escape the wrath of King Stephen.

And now one of the chief streets of Oxford crossed the Thames before us by way of Folly Bridge. Curious buildings are often called follies, and the tower on the bridge is not only curious but has a curious history.

It is built upon the site of Friar Roger Bacon's study, in which he performed mysterious experiments that gave him a reputation as a magician and wizard. Bacon has been called the founder of modern scientific inquiry. He was a scientist born long before his time. He did pioneer work in mathematics, physics and philosophy. Many inventions are credited to him.

He invented spectacles and devised a telescope. He discovered errors in the calendar and prepared a new one. Charges of witchcraft were made against him. Accused of black magic, he was exiled to Paris, where he was confined for ten years without writing materials, books or instruments.

The man of learning also had a sense of humour. During his residence on the Thames bridge, some Cambridge scholars came to challenge the Oxford dons to a contest in Latin verse. Hearing of this, Bacon dressed as a workman and put himself in the way of the visiting scholars as they crossed the bridge. When they spoke roughly to him he answered them in Latin verse and challenged them to a contest.

Amazed that even the common workmen of Oxford should be skilled in Latin, the Cambridge men despaired of their chances in a contest with Oxford scholars and returned to their own university in humiliation and alarm.

Passing under Folly Bridge, we moored the boat just below it and enjoyed the change in view. Here there were no more tawdry buildings, but green lawns and gardens sweeping up to the colleges. Moored along the opposite shore were the famous college barges which serve as floating boat-houses for student racing crews. The ornate, colourful, fantastic barges make a brilliant scene during the races of Eights Week. "The oddest little street, this row of motley Noah's Arks," D. T. MacColl has said of them. "And when the high poles shake out their amazing flags and the men come down in fearless college colours and a vast and diverse millinery decks every foot of standing room the roof can give, there would seem to be some touch of an Arabian Night about a very English day, were it not that the vigorous people wear many more colours than Arabia would allow."

The Eights, so-called because of the number of oars to each boat, are also known as the bumping races. The boats are placed one behind the other, a boat's length apart. Each crew does its best to overtake the next boat and bump it. Then in the next race the boat that bumped and the boat that got bumped exchange places and in this way a winning shell may gradually work its way to 'the head of the river', that is, the head of the line and victory.

This beautiful tree-shaded stretch has also more placid memories. Here a young Oxford professor used to take two little girls out rowing. As he rowed them along he improvised a story to while the time away. The children liked it, and he wrote it down. It was *Alice in Wonderland*.

As we climbed to Folly Bridge and walked up St. Aldate's the glory of Oxford unfolded before us, all the more amazing because of our first bad impression. Matthew Arnold was right after all about "that sweet city with her dreaming spires". They rose like a forest of fine architecture, each one different, but all lovely.

Beside us loomed Tom Tower, housing the seven-ton bell called Great Tom which strikes the nightly curfew at five minutes after nine. All students are supposed to be inside before the last of the 101 strokes has sounded. Then the college gates are closed.

But it isn't quite as grim as it sounds. A side door is left open. Late-comers must pay a fine of from one penny to sixpence according to the lateness of the hour up to midnight. But that really is the zero hour. He who wanders in thereafter must appear before the authorities the next morning and is quite likely to be 'gated', confined for a number of days to the college precincts.

In the cathedral at Christ Church we stood in awe at the wonder of the ceiling, where intricate designs had been worked out in solid stone as smoothly as if it were modelling-clay. Some of the superb stained-glass windows had been designed by William Morris, the same whose home we had visited far up the Thames.

In the dining-hall a student showed us a picture of William

65

Penn. "We're proud of him now," he said, "but when he was a student here we expelled him."

We turned into High Street and soon found why it is called "the noblest old street in England". The colleges of Oxford are marvels in stone. One would be quite enough for a city. But Oxford University consists of twenty-eight colleges. That does not mean twenty-eight buildings. Each college comprises many fine buildings, and the visitor's astonishment grows when he realises that this vast concourse of noble institutions is provided for the education of only a few students. In America such a plant might accommodate fifty thousand. Oxford University with its twenty-eight colleges has eight thousand under-graduates. For the objective of Oxford is not the education of the masses but the training of leaders.

A young man goes to Oxford from his public school at about the age of eighteen and spends four years reading for an honours degree. What he studies is not so important as what soaks into him without study. Oxford is a mental and moral climate. Its traditions and standards and codes have a conditioning effect quite independent of the subjects taught. There is little compulsion to study. No one worries very much if you choose not to attend classes.

There are many distractions—but these distractions are of an intellectual nature. There are lectures by the dozen on every conceivable subject, concerts, operas, plays, club meetings, debates, and, above all, conversation with intelligent and stimulating friends. The result is a liberal education that may have little to do with text-books.

It is gradually being recognised that even women may be trained to be leaders. Women are now admitted to Oxford but their number is limited by statute to one-fourth of that of the men. Of the twenty-eight colleges, four are for women.

Students come from many lands to Oxford, and particularly from Canada and the United States, thanks to the Rhodes

Scholarships, the gift of the empire-builder of South Africa, by which a promising student may be awarded a grant that will give him three years at Oxford.

Every college has its chapel, most of them with dramas in stained glass that tell Bible stories more vividly and colourfully than they could be told by any other means. How grateful we should be that the old-time artists, refusing to be bound by the fact that the Hebrews wore white, clothed them in garments of every hue. And what enduring colours! Windows that the sun has beat upon for half a millennium still glow with rich reds, deep blues, royal purples, golden yellows, strong and true, while the gaily coloured prints our women buy fade to a dish-water neutrality in a decade.

The emphasis on the chapel in every college grows out of the fact that Oxford was Church-born and is still largely under Church influence, Cambridge being more independent. And yet even Oxford may be more liberal than most American universities, for it would be hard to imagine one of them dedicating a memorial to an atheist. In University College, Shelley, who was 'sent down', expelled from the college because he refused to repudiate his paper, 'The Necessity of Atheism', now lies in white marble in a room of his own.

This is a peculiarly English trait, the ability to look on both sides of a question. In fact it may be said that some Englishmen become so adept in this art that they can see both sides of a question that has only one.

It was not always so. We stood in Broad Street and looked at the cross in the pavement which marks the spot where Latimer and Ridley, accused of "sundry erroneous opinions", were burned at the stake.

Oxford's beauty is enhanced by its waters, the noble Thames, and the sparkling Cherwell up whose embowered stream we lazed in a punt. Of course Oxford couldn't call it the Cherwell, because that is its name. Here it is 'The Char'. And the lovely college of Magdalen which borders the stream is of course

'Maudlin'. And High Street which crosses it is 'The High'. And the Thames which it runs into under a little wooden bridge arched like an affectionate cat's back is not the Thames but 'The Isis'.

These little intellectual affectations may be forgiven in view of the fact that Oxford really is genuine and the Cherwell is a very honest river winding through untouched wildwoods just as it did in pre-man days when the mammoth and rhinoceros waded in its cool shallows.

It's a pleasant change from the formal beauty of the extensive college gardens designed by Capability Brown and others. No criticism of the gardens is intended—they themselves are a blessed relief from the roaring and gaseous 'High'. Oxford is a city of amazing contrasts—motor traffic like Time Square's or Piccadilly's thundering past fourteenth-century façades that shut in quiet quadrangles and acres of green lawn, woodland and flower gardens where students may quietly walk and think.

Father of the contrast is William Morris—not the versatile genius of the Upper Thames, but a man who was more single-minded and therefore made more money. This William Morris stuck to one thing, the making of wheeled vehicles. His admirable enterprise may yet destroy Oxford, unless a solution is found.

He began with a bicycle shop. In 1902 he made and sold his first motor-cycle. In 1910 he produced his first motor-car. Today William Morris, become Viscount Nuffield, is a multi-millionaire and king of the gigantic Nuffield automobile empire which employs over 25,000 people, and has converted the quiet streets of the old university town into one of the noisiest, smelliest, and riskiest traffic bottlenecks in all England.

Daily the situation grows worse. True, the colleges are sealed off from this bedlam by high walls. But they cannot remain permanently unaffected. If industry completes the conquest of

Oxford the university may wither and die. Able men, including Viscount Nuffield, who want to save it, are deep in plans for by-pass roads and industrial zoning.

To see Winston Churchill's birthplace we journey north a few miles to Blenheim Palace. It proves to be as colossal as the man, as large as a dozen great hotels rolled into one. It is sur-rounded by a vast park with a lake a mile or more long, a river as broad as the Upper Thames, acres of formal pools, fountains and waterfalls, glorious flower gardens, wild woodlands and pasture, bronze and marble statues springing up at the most improbable places.

The building itself is imposing in a rather brutal way, bold as a bludgeon and as unbeautiful. Constructed in Italian style by an English architect it is about as successful as *pizza* from a Cockney cook.

The interior is a different story. It too is non-English, but in this case the designers were French and Italian and the furnish-ings were made on the Continent by Continentals. In decora-tion and design, the English habitually trust Europe more than they trust themselves. One is constantly reminded of this fact in Blenheim as the guide calls attention to Savonnerie carpet, Venetian cradle, Sèvres china, Gobelin tapestries, Spanish lace, Genoese damask, Renaissance ceilings, fine furniture in the styles of Louis the Thirteenth, Fourteenth, Fifteenth and Six-teenth.

It is a truly magnificent home, vying with Windsor Castle itself. The estate was a royal gift to John Churchill, Duke of Marlborough, as a reward for his victories over the French in the early years of the eighteenth century.

The room in which Winston Churchill was born is plain and modest in comparison with the others and we are happy to find it so.

The present Duke of Marlborough (second cousin to Winston Churchill) still occupies a wing of the palace, which is so vast that he and his family can hardly be disturbed by the daily thousands of sightseers who pay three shillings each for the privilege of parking a car at the gate and wandering for miles through rooms and gardens that might have come out of a dream.

One room, the library, is 183 feet long and glows with the beauty of ten thousand volumes in rich morocco. The room is so high that the full-sized pipe organ standing at one end of it seems incidental. The great pipes gleam like silver but are actually tin, which, more expensive than silver, will not tarnish. The treasures in the house, particularly the splendid tapestries, are of incomparable beauty and value.

Outside, the English landscape architect, Capability Brown, has done an English job and done it well. In Winston Churchill's own words: "Natural simplicity and even confusion are the characteristic of the park and gardens. Instead of that arrangement of gravel paths, of geometrical flower-beds, and of yews disciplined with grotesque exactness which the character of the house would seem to suggest, there spreads a rich and varied landscape."

Long before Blenheim, the adjacent village of Woodstock was famous as the home of kings, Saxon, Norman and Plantagenet, and it was here that Fair Rosamond was hidden in a secret bower and discovered by the jealous Queen.

We stay the night in a village inn where the rooms are as innocent of running water as a thousand years ago, and, the next morning, see an industry that has persisted since the eleventh century, the manufacture of gloves. In the old days commoners were not allowed to wear them—only the nobles and the clergy. The latter were deaf to the protests of disrespectful people who wanted to know: "Why should the clergy wear gloves? Did Jesus?"

Even within the clergy there were class distinctions; only the higher orders were allowed to wear gloves made of deerskin; the monks were limited to sheepskin. Gloves are still made by hand and methods have changed but little in nine hundred years.

Returning a few days later to Oxford, we bought in one of its delectable shops a huge white cake with red rosebuds and pink angels and nineteen candles and bore it to our waiting boat below Folly Bridge. Herbert could hardly believe his eyes when it was borne blazing into the cabin at dinner-time to a chant of Happy Birthday. Our sympathy for him because he could not spend his birthday with his family was perhaps misplaced. He had been having the time of his life in Oxford indulging his great passion, going to 'the pictures'. He bore out the statistics which indicate that England *per capita* is far ahead of America in cinema attendance. The birthday dinner had to be curtailed a bit because he must not be late for the seven o'clock show. He set off with a piece of birthday cake and an angel in his hand.

CHAPTER 10

Hazards of a Holiday

The lasher at Sandford Lock is a good place to drown yourself. A lasher, well named, is the pool of thrashing, foaming water just after it has tumbled over a weir. The drop at Sandford is the greatest on the entire river, eight and a half feet. The tumbling tons of water create whirlpools and strong undercurrents. A monument stands on the bank as a reminder of the drowning of two Oxford students. The plinth of the monument is used as a diving board by young men who want to see if the pool really *is* dangerous.

Above the weir a large sign warns of danger. But that did not help the boating party whose engine had failed just at the critical moment. As we came up we saw their boat being sucked past the danger sign towards the weir.

The occupants of the boat seemed to be in a state of complete paralysis. The man and two women were staring at the white edge of river where it disappeared over the weir.

I happened to be at the wheel of the *Goshawk*; Herbert was having a cup of tea. Herbert set down his cup long enough to call a bit of advice to the bewildered trio: "Get a rope over the sign."

The three turned to look at us, their mouths drooping open. Perhaps this was the first time they had ever been in a boat. Thames boat-houses hire out their craft to anyone without inquiring as to experience. The boat had doubtless been delivered to them with the engine running and they had not been told what to do if it stopped.

Herbert repeated his suggestion and this time managed to make it loud enough to top the roar of the weir. The man picked up a rope and flung it at the sign. Since he had not troubled to make a noose, the rope slipped off and fell into the water.

In the meantime I had been bringing the *Goshawk* around, her stern towards the other boat. Herbert ran aft and flung a line to the drifting cruiser. The line landed neatly between the man and one of the women but they made no move to grab it. It slipped off into the river.

Herbert gathered it in and threw it again. "Hang on to it!" everyone on the *Goshawk* called in chorus. The man did nothing, but one of the women seized the rope and tried to hold it. It did not occur to her to fasten it. The boat was drifting more rapidly now with only a few yards more to go before the plunge. As the distance between the boats lengthened the rope was being dragged away.

"Put it over a cleat," Herbert called.

"What?"

"A cleat."

The word meant nothing to them. Mary seized a rope and put it over a cleat on the *Goshawk*. "Like this."

Just in time they made the line fast and I revved up the *Goshawk's* engine—not engines, for one of the two had gone silent that morning. Both engines had been acting rather temperamentally for days.

The rope tightened and at the first heavy pull my engine went dead. I pressed the starter button and got only a whirr. Now both boats were drifting, stern on, to destruction. The engine grumbled and spat but would not take hold.

"The anchor!" I shouted. If the anchor rope had been lying in a tangled mass as we had seen it on most cruisers we would have been in for real trouble. Herbert always kept it coiled neatly and it spun away clean when Mary dropped the anchor overboard. Would it take hold, or would it drag?

What a relief when it took hold! At the first touch of the button the engine started, like a naughty boy who suddenly becomes very good when he's caught.

We towed the little cruiser safely out of the current. Only then did it occur to the man to try his own engine. It started immediately.

"How far are you going?" we called.

"We're going," said the man, "straight back to the boat-house. We've had enough."

Pale-faced Londoners pour out by the thousands to the Thames of a week-end and trust themselves to craft of every sort without previous experience. The Thames is fairly safe for such experimentation, yet every year it takes its toll of lives.

As distressing as the engine that won't start is the engine that won't stop. We came upon a motor-boat wildly racing round and round, dodging other craft only by inches.

"The throttle's jammed," yelled the driver. "I can't stop her."

Everyone screamed advice, but no one advised him to stop his boat by crashing into a stone wall, which is what he did. The boat sank in a dozen feet of water.

Then there is the irresponsible skipper who sets his course down a wide, empty stretch of the river and calmly leaves the wheel, to step into the cabin for his packet of cigarettes or a box of matches. His wife detains him for a moment and in the meantime other boats have appeared or the river has curved and the driverless boat is headed straight for a cement pier and a salvage job.

Most English holiday-makers have a high regard for the rights of others, but there is the occasional Teddy Boy, or hoodlum, who is looking for trouble. One such came charging down the river standing atop the wheel-house and calling down to the boy at the wheel to go faster. He howled with delight as the wash of his cruiser nearly capsized punts and skiffs and he hurled back ribald taunts at anyone who dared to remonstrate. But the whole river had the satisfaction of seeing justice done when the cruiser's wash dashed against the hull of a steamer and recoiled upon the boat that had made it, and the wallow sent the man on the wheel-house roof toppling into the Thames. He came up feet first, to the delight of all observers.

We step back a dozen centuries at Abingdon as we enter the abbey founded in 675 by a Saxon king. There the Benedictines, the true missionaries of agriculture in England, made the country rich and productive, incidentally enriching themselves. The abbey became so powerful and arrogant that the people of the region rose in revolt, sacked the abbey and burned a great part of it. Henry VIII completed its extinction when he destroyed or confiscated most of the too-powerful abbeys of England in 1538.

Abingdon remained a "famous city goodly to behold, full of riches, encompassed about with very fruitful fields". Apparently its citizens were as fruitful as its fields if we are to judge by the memorial in St. Helen's Church to Lee, five times mayor of Abingdon, but more noteworthy because he "had in his lifetime issue from his loins two hundred lacking but three". The accolade accorded to him for this achievement would hardly be repeated today in overcrowded England. The too-large family may still be noteworthy, but hardly praiseworthy.

The loveliest book ever written on the Thames is *Sweet Thames, Run Softly* by Robert Gibbings. We found him in a six-hundred-year-old cottage at Long Wittenham, a picturesque village with thatched roofs close to the stream.

Opening the door to us was a great paunchy man with Jovian white curly hair in a great burst over equally luxuriant whiskers. In fact he looked as if he might be Father Thames himself.

He lost no time in serving us tea and cakes, later a glass of sherry, and entertained us with stories of his intellectual adventures—for he is an antiquarian, naturalist, writer, artist, printer, ethnologist and carpenter, and as full of curiosity as of years.

He told us of the electro-numbing of fish recently carried out in a Thames tributary. Because the Windrush was a trout stream, pike were not wanted in it, but they were wanted in the Thames. So an electric wire was stretched through the pike pools with just enough charge to bring the fish to the surface in a stunned condition, whereupon they were scooped up and shipped to the Thames.

Beyond his colourful garden was his studio, well skylighted, and here he had not only drawings in progress, but all sorts of subjects for future drawings, from Cook Island spears to the yard-long forks that were once used to turn loaves of bread in the deep ovens.

A small robin followed him everywhere, perching on his hand whenever the hand stayed still long enough. He fed it seeds, which it never swallowed, but stuffed down the throat of its young one following behind.

Now he is writing another book on the Thames, a sort of sequel, therefore he intends its title to be *So Ends My Song*, reminiscent of Spenser's line, "Sweete Themmes! runne softly, till I end my Song".

Only a half-mile from the village of Father Thames and close to a peaceful red bridge spanning the river is the village of Clifton Hampden, a fairyland of Christmas-card cottages with thatched roofs, latticed windows and beamed walls, blue smoke rising languidly from the chimneys. There is hardly a house in the village less than a half millennium old.

We deserted the *Goshawk* to spend a night in The Barley Mow, one of the most ancient and oddest inns on the Thames. Here Jerome K. Jerome is said to have written a good part of *Three Men in a Boat*. He says of The Barley Mow:

"It is, without exception, I should say, the quaintest, most old-world inn of the river. Its low-pitched gables and thatched roof and latticed windows give it quite a story-book appearance, while inside it is even still more once-upon-a-timeyfied. It would not be a good place for the heroine of a modern novel to stay at. The heroine of a modern novel is always 'divinely tall', and she is ever 'drawing herself up to her full height'. At The Barley Mow she would bump her head against the ceiling each time she did this."

The kindliness and old-time courtesy of the village is expressed in a sign at the entrance to a riverside meadow. Instead of a brusque 'Keep Out', the sign gently reminds you that this is private property but invites you pleasantly to enter and enjoy it, and have a picnic if you wish, it being understood between friends that you will leave no litter.

All over England we were to find the same polite consideration in the signs. If anything was forbidden the reason why it had to be forbidden was stated. There was none of the fierce *Défense* or *Verboten* of the Continent. There was almost a note of apology in some signs. They seemed to say: "We know we are no better than you are and don't wish to give you orders but merely supply you with a little necessary information." This sort of thing took more words than a crisp 'No Admittance!', but it left a much better taste in the mouth.

But there is no rule without an exception. The exception in this case was the sign posted by the Thames Conservancy Board at all of the forty-five Thames locks under its control. The sign read as follows:

NOTICE

All persons using the River Thames and the locks, works and towing paths thereof must take them as they find them and do so at their own risk.

BY ORDER

It is the phrase 'take them as they find them' that particularly offends users of the locks. It is only another way of saying: "If you have any complaints, shut up. These are our locks, not yours, and it is pretty generous of us to allow you to pay handsomely to get through them." This is quite a contrast to the polite 'Suggestions will be Welcome' that one sees so often elsewhere. It is to be doubted that a pay-up-and-shut-up rudeness protects the locks from misuse as well as this could be accomplished by a more co-operative attitude. One would think that in a country where the public is sovereign, officials daring to post so arrogant a notice would soon find themselves replaced.

But this sort of thing is conspicuous only because so rare in Britain. In no country is more respect shown to the people by their public servants. Nowhere—to take a single example—will you find the police officer less officious and more helpful.

CHAPTER 11

Home of the Poet Laureate

"Doesn't John Masefield live near-by?" I asked the proprietor of The Barley Mow.

"Yes indeed. At Burcot village. He dined here recently and signed the visitors' book." And with great pride he showed us the large, rough signature of the Poet Laureate of Great Britain.

I was seized with the desire to meet the man who was not merely Britain's most honoured poet but author of adventure books that had given me much delight, *Victorious Troy*, and *Bird of Dawning* in particular.

Burcot is so small a village that we were through it before we realised that we had been in it. Turning about, we stopped where some men were plastering a house and asked one who appeared to be the foreman:

"Where does Mr. Masefield live?"

He looked puzzled. "Maze—what's the name?"

"Masefield—John Masefield——" And as he still showed no spark of recognition, I added: "You know—the Poet Laureate of Great Britain."

It was plain he didn't know. "Oh, not 'ere, sir, we don't go in for that sort of thing 'ere, sir, no, not 'ere!"

We rolled on a few hundred feet to the door of a pub. Publicans know everyone, including those worth knowing.

"Of course," said the man, "just down at the corner—the place with the big gates—you can't miss it."

We found the place with the big gates and, just inside, a large and comfortable gatehouse. Since we were coming uninvited and unannounced it seemed wise to seek permission here before invading the grounds. I knocked repeatedly but got no response.

What should we do? It would be brashly American to walk in without a by-your-leave. And yet it would be stupid to let such an opportunity pass. After all, it was not our fault if there was no one on duty at the gatehouse. Leaving the grim gates behind, we ventured up the drive.

Through a quarter-mile of great trees the road wound, to come out at last before a large grey-stucco mansion of indeterminate age redeemed by a pleasant though shaggily natural setting of flowers and forest. There were no formal gardens, no yew trees trimmed to look like animals or ships, no lawns with a crew cut and a knife edge. This was quite evidently not a show place to impress visitors with the importance of the owner, but had been chosen for its seclusion and quiet.

Pomposity I could have taken, but this shyness disarmed me, and feeling very much the interloper I knocked at a side door. A pleasant-faced housekeeper opened the door and invited us in.

No, she was very sorry, Mr. Masefield was not at home—could we come again?

Unfortunately our itinerary would not bring us again to Burcot—and at any rate, I said, Mr. Masefield had doubtless established himself here to be free of visitors and enjoy his retirement in peace. The housekeeper laughed.

"Not retirement," she said. "He didn't come here to rest, but to get on with his work. He says he has so much still to do and so little time to do it in. He is never unoccupied; he works far beyond his strength."

The interior of the house bore out her words. It was not the over-decorated home of a soft, rich, eighty-year-old man content to relax among the accumulated treasures of a lifetime. It had the severity of a school or a business office. Furniture and furnishings were at a minimum. There were no Greek gods or

Ming vases or Japanese screens or Gobelin tapestries—and I mentally contrasted the house with the gorgeously crowded museum-like rooms of other mansions we had seen. Here there was a vista of large rooms almost empty, as if the occupant had moved in last week—or perhaps a quarter-century ago—but had preferred putting the treasures of far seas and lands into novels and poems rather than shelves and corners. It was the house of a working man.

Some days later I received a note of regret from Mr. Masefield in his own hand with his prized signature, which, upon my return home, I would cut out and paste into my copy of *Victorious Troy*.

John Masefield has always been a lover of the Thames and of the great waters into which it flows. As a boy he explored England's rivers, then the far seas as a sailor before the mast. His experience covered many lands and many jobs, including that of farm labourer, and bartender in a New York saloon. Of his formidable list of a hundred and more works a good proportion have to do with the story and romance of the world's waters. And now he prefers to spend his twilight years far away from the acclaim of London in a quiet village by the Thames.

From Day's Lock we look up to one of the strangest pair of hills in England. Side by side, they slope up bare and smooth, and each is crowned with a thatch of beeches. They look for all the world like the breasts of a giantess. But the country people prefer to think of the giantess as lying face-down. For some reason they call her Mother Bunch and the hills are known as Mother Bunch's Buttocks. But the English flair for salty names does not stop at this and the twin hills are also called the Berkshire Bubs and the Wittenham Clumps, while on maps they are more formally labelled the Sinodun Hills.

We climb to the twin peaks to see the remains of ancient fortifications. They are complete with vallum, fosse, scarp and counterscarp, all this suggesting that they may have been built by the Romans. But archæologists probing beneath them believe that the earliest stronghold far antedates Roman times and may have been constructed by primitive man as a refuge against wolves and later strengthened to withstand the attacks of Celts, Romans, Saxons and Danes.

If the country notion that nettles grow where blood has been spilt is true, there has been plenty of blood-letting here, for the nettles rise hip-high. Where the soil has been loosened by the plough we poke about with a stick and in an hour's time turn up a spearhead, an arrowhead and half a dozen pieces of pottery.

We look out over pleasant England and try to imagine ourselves two thousand years back in time. It is not so difficult, for the view cannot have changed much since those days. Even then the Thames wound like a silver snake through the valley, the grass was incredibly green all the year round, the hills were soft and gentle, the same trees grew in the woods and the same unpredictable weather brought patches of honey-coloured sunlight and muddy shadow. We have to ignore Day's Lock and one or two houses, but otherwise the scene is probably little changed. There is something to be said for an urban nation, one that concentrates its population in cities, leaving great stretches of countryside unspoiled by 'modern improvements'.

We moored for the night beside the ruins of Wallingford Castle and entertained eleven swans at dinner. The great birds had an insatiable appetite for bread, and indeed would accept almost anything that looked like food. One gulped down a lighted cigarette, drank a little water to quench the flame, and came back for another. However, they drew the line at fresh fruit.

A bus crossing picturesque Wallingford Bridge startled the birds and they took off with a tremendous splashing as they beat the water until they gained altitude and flew with long necks stretched out goose-fashion.

Wallingford reeks with history. Its streets still lie as the Romans laid them out and bits of the city wall may still be seen. William the Conqueror built the castle on the site of another of unknown antiquity. It is a question whether the town has declined in piety—in William's time there were fourteen churches, now there are three.

It is an orderly and progressive town, but takes pride in the whiskers of age. One carefully preserved old relic is the George Hotel. Persons about to enter the taproom are faced with the sign 'Beware of overhang'. However, this does not mean hangover. The warning is intended for lorries and buses, which must look out for the overhang of the second storey.

The innkeeper took me up to the room said to have been occupied by Dick Turpin. In the floor of the room is a trapdoor provided for the bandit's convenience. In case of danger he would drop through the trapdoor upon his horse and gallop away.

In another room the wall is covered with oversize tear-drops. It seems that when William II was regent, Princess Amelia ran away with a commoner from the Court. They were traced to this inn, and her lover was killed in the courtyard, while she was confined in this room. For every day she was kept here she moistened soot from the chimney with her tears and drew a tear-drop on the wall. There they are now, fat tears, an inch or more across, all in neat rows and too many to count.

Some of the islands on which the lock-keepers have their homes are very charming, but a bit isolated.

"It's a nice place to live," Mary said to the lock-keeper at Cleeve.

"It is that, in summer," he agreed. "But it's not everybody's cup o' tea in winter. You can't reach it except by boat. And the river gets so high and the current so strong that it is very dangerous to try to cross."

And at Benson Lock the keeper's wife had told us of the big

trees that come floating down in winter and how the water floods the weir path so that it is impossible to go on foot to the mainland. The only way to get supplies is to row a dinghy across, and that isn't safe. When the current becomes too strong they are marooned for days.

The river can be savage. The village of Goring still remembers the day when a boat was swept over the weir and sixty persons were drowned in the pool below.

Everyone on the Thames knows perfectly well that he should climb the hill at Streatley for the view. But the lazy life on a boat puts one into a sort of torpor, and the hill looks very high and steep. So one rebellious traveller wrote:

> The air is clear, the day is fine,
> The prospect is, I know, divine,
> But most distinctly I decline
> To climb the hill at Streatley.

With some difficulty we fought off the inclination to agree with him, and climbed the hill, to be rewarded with a magnificent view over the Chiltern Hills.

The scenery became really dramatic as we sailed down through the Goring Gap, walled with steep hills upholstered in purple marjoram and yellow bedstraw and mignonette and bell-flower and agrimony and St. John's wort, and drifting flowers in the form of black-and-orange butterflies rising among the flowering chestnuts.

Paradise with Peacocks

Then we came upon an astonishing sight, a paradise complete
with peacocks. The glorious birds wandered about a sort of
palace under construction on the right bank. Around it was
some sensational statuary and, beyond, a lovely lily-covered
lake.

We landed and looked. The statuary proved to be a noble
fountain with beautiful figures representing Nereids in full
abandon, sporting in the waters. Standing about in the field
were other naked nymphs and fauns, gods and goddesses,
patiently waiting to be placed where they might adequately
display their charms. Some were still in crates.

We went to the palace-like building and inquired. It was to
be a summer pavilion, a workman told us, and was being constructed by Gilbert Beale, of Carter's Seeds, who had more money
than he knew what to do with. So he was sinking a fortune in
this boggy Thames-side pasture to transform it into an exotic
pleasure garden complete with lagoons, lakes, bridges, waterfalls, fountains—and peacocks. The lordly birds picked their
way around among the statues. Already there were 190 of
them in this, the largest peacock colony in England.

We went down the lane to Church Farm, where we found
spry eighty-seven-year-old Gilbert Beale in a mansion running
over with art treasures. The overflow of exquisite art objects
was in the barn, the cow-barn, and the hay-loft. Some of them
had been imported direct from Italy; many of them he had
picked up at auction sales, the effects of country estates whose

owners had found living like a lord too costly in this busy century. So the old order changes. Men who serve the public with seeds or machinery or what not supplant those who live on the achievements of their forefathers. Inherited wealth disappears, earned wealth takes its place.

Whether a rich man's money should go into palaces and peacocks rather than into research for the cure of cancer or something of the sort is a question. But, after all, we have many health foundations but no provision for palaces and peacocks. Mr. Beale plans to open his fabulous pavilion and lagoon gardens to the public and they are bound to be put to good use by the thousands of wayfarers on the river and the near-by trunk road from London. The peacock paradise on the Thames will become famous as an example of how a rich man can bring pleasure to many.

It may seem odd to train sea captains on a river, but that is just what is done at the Nautical College near Pangbourne. We were taken through the extensive buildings where masters lean over relief maps of the seven seas and give instruction in all the details of seamanship. The college has a frontage on the Thames with two boat-houses and shipwright's workshop. Practical instruction is given in manœuvring under power, sail and oars. The river is alive with dinghies, whalers, gigs and skiffs of practising cadets. They learn not only the vagaries of wind and stream, but gain resourcefulness and self-reliance. Deep-sea experience is acquired by assignment to training vessels or merchant ships on trips to all parts of the world.

Poking about in a riverside church we came upon an inscription which made us happy that the good old days are gone— the days when murder by poison was too common to make news and a king must employ someone to test every food before he dare eat it. A brass commemorates Sir Thomas Walysch, food-taster to the fourth, fifth and sixth Kings named Henry. It was a post requiring a high order of courage as well as gastronomic

Above: deep enough now for a canoe, the stripling Thames affords pleasant picnic spots along its flowering shores

Below: the Upper Thames flows through a land of lonely beauty and deep content. This is the view from quaintly-named Tadpole Bridge

fortitude and we were glad to see that Sir Thomas had been rewarded with a manor at Whitchurch.

A ghost haunts Mapledurham. Henry Blount, lord of the manor, killed a manservant. That was in the time of Alexander Pope, friend of the Blounts, but the manservant may still be seen, they say, prowling about in search of his murderer. As for Blount, he was punished in a way best calculated to hurt a pedigree-proud gentleman. He was deprived of his coat-of-arms and ordered to adopt instead as his device a weeping eye. The eye still weeps over the gates of the old manor house.

Then Reading, the first important town of the Thames since Oxford. The clattering city hardly suggests poetry, yet it was here that the imprisoned Oscar Wilde wrote:

> I never saw a man who looked
> With such a wistful eye
> Upon that little tent of blue
> Which prisoners call the sky
> And at every drifting cloud that went
> With sails of silver by.

Well, it is about as hard to see the sky today through the smoke of Reading's factories that turn out everything from agricultural implements to biscuits, beer and marzipan.

The greatest disaster in Reading for three hundred years struck the city in 1947 when the Thames overflowed, driving hundreds of people from their homes. Reading did not suffer alone. Water stood six feet deep in the streets of Maidenhead. Eton College had to be closed and its eleven hundred boys went home. Many villages were turned into isolated islands. The flooded river swelled to a width of three miles.

Another sensation put Reading in the news during the spring of 1956. A monster was seen swimming up the Thames. An American looking for thistles on the bank saw a great black fin projecting from the water four or five feet high and moving up-stream at a speed of about one and a half knots. He took a picture of the Thing and, upon reaching London, went to see the editor of the *Daily Telegraph*.

The editor was not unduly sceptical. If Loch Ness could have its monster, why not the Thames? At any rate it was an interesting story, and it was printed along with the photograph. The *Telegraph* followed up by sending its own reporter up the Thames. He saw the 'creature' and photographed it again. A scientist said it looked very much like the dorsal fin of a dimetrodon, a reptile known to have existed two hundred million years ago.

So long as it stayed in the river, that was one thing, but when it came ashore in an inhabited place there was real alarm. The *Telegraph* reported:

"Twenty-five mysterious and muddy 'footprints' which appeared overnight on Riverside, Henley-on-Thames, have given inhabitants an alternative topic to the two horror films showing at a local cinema. A steady stream of people has been to see the 'footprints', five-toed, two feet long and eighteen inches in breadth with ten feet between strides."

A rival newspaper, the *Daily Sketch*, could not believe that part about the man looking for thistles. An American might look for a good investment or even buried treasure but certainly not for thistles. They went to see him and found it was true. He was a student botanist and crazy about thistles. If one could believe this, it was not so hard to believe in the dimetrodon. And so the legend grew. And it could not be denied that more people every day were seeing the monster and taking pictures of it.

It always appeared in quiet stretches of the river where there were very few people and these few were confined to one bank, the other bank being wooded or otherwise inaccessible. But one day a reporter managed to scramble through the underbrush and see the Thing's other side. Concealed behind the fin and attached to it was a small rubber boat propelled by a young man with a paddle.

And so the story came out. The fake fin had been fabricated by two students at Reading University and they too had been responsible for the footprints on the Henley shore.

Fire is one of the ever-present hazards on a motor-cruiser. For several days we had been distressed by gas fumes. We telephoned the firm that had rented us the boat and, although it meant a round trip of more than a hundred miles, they promptly sent two men to repair the leak. They were always most accommodating in such emergencies. The men worked for two hours on the gas stove and the pipes connecting it with the tank and departed well satisfied that they had found the trouble and corrected it.

Probably they had, and it may have been the vibration that reopened the connection. At any rate, we had more trouble, and this time it could have meant a burned boat and a face scarred for life.

Mary was getting dinner. She opened the oven door and introduced a burning match. Gas that had accumulated in the bottom of the oven exploded in her face, scorching her eyebrows and hair and setting fire to near-by papers. She called for help and the fire was promptly beaten out. Soap bubbles applied to the pipe revealed the leak and the joint was tightened. With abbreviated eyebrows, Mary wore a slightly startled look for several days.

Sonning is a fairy-like little place, more like a stage village than a real one, and smothered in roses. Its White Hart Inn near the bridge is no more or less lovely than a dozen other riverside inns scattered all the way from Oxford to Richmond.

The river was no longer wild and lonely, but no less beautiful for the well-kept lawns that came down to its edge, the attractive homes near the shore and the well-ordered park-like appearance of the hills, dales and woodlands. We had long since decided that, while it was not the most dramatic, the Thames was the loveliest river we had ever travelled.

And so down the exquisite stretch past Shiplake and Wargrave to Henley. This is a delightful small city with hospitable inns well deserving the words that someone wrote a century ago on a window of The Red Lion:

> Whoe'er has travelled life's dull round,
> Where'er his stages may have been,
> May sigh to think he still has found
> The warmest welcome at an inn.

I would amend this in only one particular. A little better than an inn is a boat, a home afloat.

We had timed our arrival to coincide with the beginning of the famous Henley Royal Regatta and for four days we watched shells from all over England and abroad race from Temple Island up the straight course of a little over a mile to the finish line near Henley Bridge. Besides many English colleges, the contenders included the Royal Air Force, the French Army, Princeton University, rowing clubs from Sweden, Poland and Canada. The three chief trophies went overseas, the Diamond Sculls to Poland, the Thames Cup to Princeton and the Grand Challenge Cup to the French Army. The thousands of spectators, most of them of course British, were as warm in their applause of these winners as if they had been British too.

CHAPTER 13

Windsor Castle and an Island

We had seen Windsor Castle before but were never so thrilled by it as when, rounding a turn in the river, we saw its fabulous walls and towers mirrored in the still surface of the Thames. Set on a hill with the Thames forming a natural moat on the north and east, the castle sends up rank on rank its "towers and battlements bosomed high in tufted trees". No wonder it is considered the most regal building in the world. The Kings and Queens of England from William the Conqueror down have made it their residence and it is still the home, or one of the homes, of the reigning monarch.

Most conspicuous is the immense Round Tower. Once it was called the Rose Tower because that was its colour. How gay the grim castle must have been when the Crusaders brought back from Byzantium the custom of decorating buildings in bright colours.

The history of the place runs back into legend, which has it that King Arthur himself sat in council on this hill. William the Conqueror built a wooden castle to control England's chief highway, the Thames. Henry III in 1272 built the first stone tower and there has not been a century since without additions and elaborations. It is far from being an architectural unit, but is the more bewildering and thrilling because it is not.

We spent a day and could have spent many days wandering like two moonstruck children in Disneyland through the State Apartments, seeing the Queen's Doll House, King's Drawing-room, Queen's Ballroom, St. George's Chapel, Albert Memorial

Chapel, up the two-hundred-and-some steps to the top of the Round Tower, along the battlements, through the endless gardens with their flowers and fountains, lakes and waterfalls.

Across the river from Windsor is Eton, the largest, most expensive and most exclusive of all English public schools. Of course it is to be understood that 'public' is English for 'private'. A young man may as easily get into Eton as a camel may pass through the eye of a needle. However, a camel having undergone this experience would be a changed camel, and Eton does change boys. Perhaps one reason for its effect is that there is one master for approximately every ten students, so there is always close contact between teacher and taught. Chiefly responsible are the monastic notions of discipline which rule the stern old school.

An arm of the Thames embraces Eton and we found the 'wet bobs' rowing their racing shells. If a boy goes in for rowing he is a 'wet bob', if he prefers land sports he is a 'dry bob'. The surroundings of river and woodland are enchanting. The view of Eton is particularly fine from the north terrace of Windsor Castle. It was from there that Thomas Gray, Eton student, looked down upon the dreaming valley where "wanders the hoary Thames along his silver winding way" and wrote the 'Ode on a Distant Prospect of Eton College'.

We are the guests of the Queen of England for lunch. We moor alongside Home Park, one of the private parks of Windsor Castle, failing to see the conservatively small sign: 'Crown Land —No Mooring.' One half-hour later a caretaker appears and courteously informs us of our error.

"But I see you are just about to have lunch," he says. "Stay until you have finished."

Royal courtesy, that.

If one were asked to single out the most important document in the history of human freedom one would probably name the Magna Charta. It might be supposed that the spot where it was signed by King John, 15th June, 1215, would be the Mecca of pilgrims from all over the world; for there is not one person on earth who has not been affected directly or indirectly by what was done on Magna Charta Island seven centuries ago. The bold conception that the people are the real sovereigns and must be obeyed by their rulers was not only the seed from which today's democracies have grown but remains the thorn in the flesh of the tyrannies that still exist.

Yet this little island in the Thames where King John made his mark (he couldn't sign his name) is practically unknown. It has not been made a national shrine. It is not included in any tour. It is private property and anyone who has the temerity to land upon it is greeted by a pack of growling dogs. Yet the castle-like, abbey-like stone house that stands upon it contains a relic of great interest to the human race—the stone on which King John is said to have signed the charter of freedom.

As we approached the island, dark clouds rumbled over it, adding to its air of mystery. Shaggy trees thick with under-brush covered it. The old stone house had a sternly forbidding look. No life was evident, human or animal.

But as we slid our boat up against the high bank (there was no dock), animal life appeared in the form of a number of Alsatian wolf-hounds, one of the breeds commonly used in America as police dogs. It was quite evident that they were prepared to police this island. They rushed at the boat as if about to chew it to bits.

We held a council of war. Perhaps it would be just as well to by-pass King John's stone. After all, it was only a stone.

And yet it meant more to all of us than any other stone we could think of, even the Rosetta Stone or the Stone of Scone. We wouldn't risk a life to see it, but it might be worth a nip or two. Dogs were barking furiously and someone, sometime, somewhere had said that barking dogs don't bite.

Gingerly, I tested the theory. With soothing words and slow movements I stepped ashore and approached the house, the dogs whirling around me in a dervish dance.

It was a surprise to find an electric bell button beside the ancient door. I pressed it. Even if it didn't work the inmates must know from the canine din that they had a caller. There was a confused sound within but no one came.

I looked around. It was a place for plots and murders. The aged trees cast a heavy shade over the stained-glass windows, the cold stone walls, and the great bell that I now noticed for the first time above the door. I pulled the chain that hung from it. The resulting boom drowned even the thunder and the dogs. The sound started tremendous barking inside the house. I heard voices. But still no one came.

This was becoming a mystery that must be solved. It was plain that someone was at home. I went around to the back door. A sign was pinned to the door: "Do not leave letters. The dogs will destroy them."

There was another large bell here and a pull rope, which I pulled and repulled. More din of dogs within, and the outside dogs went mad with excitement.

Around to another door, which I rapped, without effect. Back to the first door, where I rang the big bell again, then used the knocker. Movements inside. The door opened. If a fire-breathing dragon or the ghost of King John had stepped out of it I should not have been surprised.

An elderly lady in green sweater and red slacks greeted me pleasantly. "You're American, aren't you?" she had evidently been studying me through the leaded panes. "I am too. I was born in Boston, Massachusetts. You would like to see the charter room?"

I called Mary and Herbert and we entered the strange place, half expecting that we would be dropped into a dungeon. The ceilings were heavily beamed and the walls as thick as battlements. It was an ancient manor house, Mrs. Bigelow told us,

Above: the ornate 'college barges' moored along the left bank below Folly Bridge serve as clubrooms for Oxford boat crews

Below: beside the Thames a flower-seed magnate has turned a swamp into a 'paradise with peacocks' adorned with fine imported works of art

built upon the spot where King John signed the Magna Charta. There was no house here at the time of the signing.

"And this is the charter room."

We stooped to enter a small, dark room lighted only by two stained-glass windows. One depicted King John, the other his brother Richard. In the middle of the room was a great round stone, flat on top and several feet in diameter. On it we read the inscription:

"Be it remembered that on this Island in June, 1215, King John of England signed the Magna Charta; and in the year 1834 this building was erected in commemoration of that great event by George Simon Harcourt, Esq., Lord of the Manor, and then High Sheriff of the County."

We tried to visualise the scene. The barons had risen in force against King John and he could not choose but bend to their will. He would not trust himself in their camp, nor they in his. So he called for a conference on neutral ground, a sort of no-man's-land, this bit of an island in the Thames.

The King and his followers camped on one bank of the river, the barons and their great armies covered the large meadow of Runnymede on the other. Their delegates met on the island between them. Using the broad flat stone as a council table, they spread out the great parchment upon it and there signed it. And we have in Holinshed a quaint account of how John felt about it:

"Having acted so far contrary to his mind, the king was right sorrowful in heart, cursed his mother that bare him and the hour in which he was born; wishing that he had received death by violence of sword or knife instead of natural nourishment. He whetted his teeth and did bite now on one staff, now on another as he walked and oft brake the same in pieces when he had done."

In one corner of the room was some fresh stonework. "It was the entrance to a secret tunnel leading beneath the river to the shore," Mrs. Bigelow said. "There were two other secret passages besides this one. No one knows why they were made. I was nervous about them, so I had them walled up."

"It would be interesting," I said, "to know all the strange things that have gone on in this house."

Mrs. Bigelow laughed. "I think I'd rather not know," she said. It was an isolated spot for a woman living alone. "But I keep busy. I raise dogs—Alsatians and poodles." And she brought out one of the poodles, a very lively, friendly dog being groomed as a prize-winner.

She had thirty-six grown dogs and eighteen puppies—no wonder there had been a dog din to greet me. The police had advised her to keep dogs, she said, because there were so many Teddy Boys about—teen-age gangsters who wear sideburns, long coats and tight trousers, carry knives and brass knuckle-dusters and raise hell generally. She has had visits from a few of them and had to call the police.

I asked if there was any fee for our admission to the charter room. No indeed. And wouldn't we stay to dinner? Well, if we must hurry on, how about coming back later to stay over-night?

All quite amazing cordiality after the chilly and sinister beginning.

Shopping for food on a Thames boat trip is not too easy. The supermarket is not known in England, except in a few of the great cities. The chain store has not yet monotonised English towns. And even the chain grocery that does exist is by no means a supermarket. Its range of foods is strictly limited, and this is even more true of the small individual shops that have been kept as family enterprises down the years. The butcher whose father was a butcher and whose grandfather was a butcher would not think of branching out and selling milk as well as meat. The average butcher will not even sell chickens— that is the business of the poulterer. To buy milk, meat, fish, paper napkins, cold cream, groceries, fruits and baked goods it is necessary to go to eight different stores rather than one. You will find milk only at the dairy, meat at the butcher's, napkins at the paper store, cold cream at the chemist's, fish at the fishmonger's, canned goods at the grocery, fruits at the fruiterer's or greengrocer's, and bread at the bakery. And in many a store it will be necessary to stand in line to be waited on. We developed great respect for the patience and endurance of the English housewife.

It being one of Britain's breathing spells between crises, the shops were free of restrictions and there was an abundance of food. The bakeries especially were amazing in the variety and excellence of their products. Surprisingly enough, there was plenty of fresh fruit, though England is decidedly not a fruit country. Apples are home grown, but the beautiful pears, grapefruit, oranges, luscious grapes, are imported. There is no Californian variety of fresh vegetables and the carrots are runty, but there are canned vegetables aplenty and even frozen foods may be had. The many butchers' shops are well stocked. The eggs and milk and cheeses are very good.

Little provision is made for carrying packages. Foods are wrapped in flimsy paper without string or tape to hold the package closed. Sometimes there is no wrapping whatever. We bought four cartons of milk and they were set out on the counter for us. Our request that they be put in something so that we could carry them was met with an astonished "Oh!" A thin bag was found, and when supplemented by two more thin bags at other stores the milk was carried with reasonable safety.

But the English housewife carries a shopping bag and all her purchases go into that, so it does not matter if they are not separately wrapped. This method, of course, means a great saving in wrapping-paper.

The salesmen and saleswomen we found always pleasant, accommodating and honest, and of course the prices are fixed, not vacillating as in Latin or Asiatic lands.

CHAPTER 14

The Secret of the Maze

With quickened pulse we approached the largest and finest palace in England. We tied up to the right bank just short of the bridge beyond which rose the mellow red-brick walls of Hampton Court Palace.

It was Sunday and a warm day and people had come in swarms to the river. They lay on the green grass, they waded or swam, they navigated in punts, canoes, skiffs, sailing boats, kayaks, and motor-boats—but we had not seen one scrap of paper floating on the water all day, not one orange peel or eggshell. I am not saying that all trippers behave this way on land, but they don't defile the water London drinks.

Walking across the bridge and through the palace gate, we visited a few of the thousand rooms of this residence of twelve of the Kings and Queens of England. It was built for a man who thought himself, in some ways, more important than kings and queens. Cardinal Wolsey, son of a very humble home, had attained to high position and enormous wealth and was famous, or notorious, for his lavish extravagance. He built the palace and there lived in incredible luxury. His servants and retainers numbered five hundred persons. Two hundred and eighty beds were not enough for his guests, who sometimes numbered five or six hundred. Art treasures from all over the world were poured into the public rooms.

One of the guests was King Henry VIII. He pleased Wolsey by saying that he liked his palace very much. Wolsey was not so pleased later when the King told him that he liked his palace so *very* much that he would accept it as a present. Wolsey moved out and Henry moved in.

If Wolsey thought that he could so satisfy the envy that his wealth had inspired in the heart of the Sovereign he was sadly mistaken. Four years later he was stripped of his honours, driven from the Court, and brought to trial on a charge of high treason. He died on his way to prison.

Henry spent much of his time in Hampton Court Palace and you may still see on a gateway a love knot containing the initials H. A. for Henry and Anne. In turn he brought Anne Boleyn, Jane Seymour, Anne of Cleves, Catherine Howard and Catherine Parr to the palace as Queen.

You are painfully conscious of their ghosts as you walk through the great dark rooms and corridors. Visitors may chatter elsewhere but never in the Haunted Gallery, where they listen for the scream of Catherine Howard and strain their eyes to catch a glimpse of her frantic figure rushing towards the chapel.

Hearing that Catherine had been unfaithful to him, Henry locked her in her room and went to the chapel to pray for divine guidance. She escaped and ran down the gallery, hoping to reach him in the chapel and plead for mercy. She was intercepted just at the entrance to the royal pew and dragged back by the guards, shrieking, to her room. Henry, unmoved by her screams, went on praying.

A few weeks later Catherine Howard was beheaded at the Tower of London on the very spot where Anne Boleyn had died.

Ghosts are evidently erratic. One would think that Anne would haunt the palace. She does not, but observers declare that Catherine may still be seen rushing along the Haunted Gallery towards the chapel. Then something seems to stop her short. Her body is contorted as if in a desperate struggle and her agonised screams echo through the palace. "A most unquiet, upsetting ghost," Pepys said after he claimed to have seen this manifestation.

Jane Seymour is a more placid ghost. Gowned in white and carrying a lighted taper, she comes from the Queen's room, passes through the Silver Stick Gallery and down the stairs. She is not seen as often as Catherine. The reason appears to be that she has another job elsewhere. She spends a good part of her time haunting the vicinity of her old home in Hampshire, reliving perhaps those happy days when she was courted there by the King while her predecessor, Anne Boleyn, awaited execution.

Sibell Penn, nurse of the King's son, Edward, having no more children to care for, spends her time at the spinning-wheel. It is said that many people have heard the sound of the wheel but could see nothing. There was no record of there ever having been a spinning-wheel in or about the Haunted Gallery. But one day during renovations of the Haunted Gallery by the Office of Works a secret doorway was discovered leading to a small room and in the middle of the room stood a spinning-wheel. Evidently it had been much used, for the treadle had worn a groove in the floor.

We walked through the magnificent gardens to the Maze. Now I had a particular reason for wanting to take Mary through the Maze. I knew the code and she didn't know that I knew it. Before we had left America I had come upon it in the *Encyclopædia Britannica* and had memorised it. She would certainly be impressed when I would lead her through the labyrinth without a moment of hesitation and she would say I was wonderful, and I would say it was nothing, just a sixth sense.

We paid our threepence apiece and entered the narrow passage between high hedges. We came to a passage leading both left and right and I confidently turned right. That was what the code had said, always turn right. Or was it left? Anyhow we went on, my wife's amazement growing as we swept around every corner without a moment's pause for thought.

Other people stood about debating, arguing, complaining, but we forged ahead at full speed.

The Maze is not large and with luck you should not have to go more than a hundred yards or so to reach the centre, a round place with benches where you may rest, then the same distance to get out. After we had gone about half a mile my wife showed signs of flagging. I was beginning to have a few doubts myself.

"I'm tired," Mary said. "Suppose we give it up?"

"Just a little farther and we'll come to the centre. You can sit down there and rest."

A half-mile more. Then we dragged to a halt and looked at each other.

"Let's go back," Mary suggested. "Do you know the way out?"

"Well, I think so."

If you kept to the right on the way in you would keep to the left going out. We kept to the left and in five minutes walked into the centre. This surprised my wife, but I pointed out that it was just what I had been trying to do all the time.

We rested while I pondered. The code must have said left, not right. Then going out you would keep to the right, not left.

We took to the trail again, keeping always to the right. In five minutes we were back in the centre. It was getting dark now. We were hungry. The other visitors had gone, or had died of exhaustion somewhere in the labyrinth. A cold rain was beginning to fall.

I shouted. No answer. Had the gatekeeper gone home? We both shouted, but without effect. I picked up a pebble and threw it. If it happened to crack the pate of a gatekeeper I didn't much care. But it brought no curse, no sound at all. More stones, and more shouts.

Then a beautiful sight. A guard appeared on a high platform just outside the Maze.

"All out," he called. "Closing time."

"Which way?" I inquired.

"I'll come in and get you."

He led us out. To save our face he said kindly: "Of course I know you could get out by yourselves, but that might take longer and it's time to close."

I let it go at that.

Later I saw the code, this time not in the *Encyclopædia Britannica* but in the tourist magazine, *Coming Events*. Here it is, but don't try to carry it in your memory. Paste it in your hat.

Og tfel no gniretne dna neht no eht tsrif owt snoisacco erehw ereht si na noitpo og thgir. Retfa taht peek ot eht tfel.

CHAPTER 15

The Swan Upping

It was time to up the swans. The annual 'swan upping' is one of the few historic pageants still to be seen on the Thames and we did not want to miss it. We went to see the Worshipful Company of Vintners' Swanmaster, Richard Turk.

He was co-operative. "The B.B.C. has chartered a launch to follow the swan uppers and take photographs. I believe they would be quite willing to take you along."

He told us the story of the Thames swans. Of course the swan is not native to England. Legend has it that the first pair of swans was brought to Britain by King Richard Coeur-de-Lion. The story goes that on his way home from the Holy Land he was shipwrecked on Cyprus. The Queen of Cyprus fell in love with him. When he finally left the island she gave him a parting gift of a pair of white swans as a token of her affection.

"Ever since," said the Swanmaster, "the swan has been a royal bird and, like the stag, is protected by royal decrees and laws. All swans belonged to the King unless he chose to give them to his friends. Edward III was always in need of funds to carry on his wars and some of the people who helped him were given the right of owning swans. Most of these rights have now lapsed, but the Vintners' Guild and the Dyers' Guild still share with the monarch the ownership of the swans on the Thames."

"And just what is the swan upping?"

"The swan upping is the rounding up and marking of the young swans to indicate who owns them, the Queen, the Vintners or the Dyers. Every year we must dress in the colourful liveries prescribed by custom and row up the Thames in six boats, banners flying. When we sight the first pair of swans with cygnets there comes the operation of surrounding or 'upping' the birds and eventually catching them, ascertaining to whom the parents belong, and marking the young."

"Do the birds put up much resistance?"

"The adult birds have to be held while the cygnets are being marked or they would attack us viciously. It's quite an art to catch and hold them. It's not the beak that is dangerous but the wings. They can hit harder than I can punch. Give them a chance, and they can break an arm or a leg. Ordinarily, of course, swans are not dangerous; it's only when they are defending their young.

"The swan is a great family bird. Swans mate for life and really seem devoted to each other as well as to their young. They build a nest every year, usually in about the same place. They prefer a backwater or an island hidden from view.

"The nest is made of twigs and rushes and both birds help in the building. They show remarkable common sense. During flood times I have known swans to keep raising their nests to prevent them from being flooded and washed away.

"The male bird is called a cob and the female a pen and some people believe that this was the origin of the name of the writing pen, which was formerly made from the quills of swans.

"The pen lays an average of six eggs, covers them loosely with moss or down, and sits for from thirty-two to thirty-eight days. Sometimes the cob takes a turn at sitting on the eggs but this is unusual. The cygnets are grey when born and remain so until almost a year old, when they begin to turn snow-white like their parents. During that period the cob and pen guard their reach of the river jealously and fight for it against all comers. And it's while they are in this mood that we have to mark the cygnets."

During the intervals when he is not acting as keeper of the swans for the Worshipful Vintners, Richard Turk runs a pair of boatyards. It was because he was an expert licensed water-man that he was appointed to his post as Swanmaster. The same qualifications made his brother, Frederick Turk, Her Majesty's Swanmaster, and L. J. Robinson Swanmaster for the Dyers.

We watched all three of them set out one morning with their crews from the dock of Hampton Court Palace. They had already done the lower reaches of the river on previous days. Today they would do the stretch from Hampton Court to Staines. Each Master sat in majesty in the stern of his boat, directing his oarsmen. The Queen's Swanmaster wore a royal scarlet blazer, scarlet jersey and white slacks; the Vintners' Master, green and silver; the Dyers', blue and gold. Royal crests were embroidered on their coats. The crews too were brightly uniformed. Each Master commanded two boats, making six in all, and with colours flying, cameras snapping, spectators cheering, they presented a brave appearance as they struck off up the river.

We followed by courtesy of the British Broadcasting Corporation in a launch that provided plenty of elbow-room for two acrobatic television men and their camera, a reporter from a news agency, and ourselves.

Not far above the bridge one of the watermen called, "All up!" the signal that a brood had been sighted. Two stately white swans and seven smaller grey ones hovered near the bank.

The boats were ordered to quarters, that is, in line, one boat's bow touching the stern of the next. Slowly they were rowed up until the swans were between them and the shore. Then the last two boats turned their bows to the shore, keeping their sterns together, thus forming a V in which the birds were trapped. The other boats were beached and the men leaped out to prevent the swans from climbing ashore and escaping.

They were just a shade late and the big cob was already on the bank. He hissed angrily, struck one of the men a blow strong enough to leave a blue bruise for many days, and then took off at a run, beating his great wings to increase his speed. The men promptly gave up, for a swan using both leg power and wing power can outrun any man.

The cob did not go far. He stopped and looked back anxiously to see what was happening to his family. Then he came charging back, furiously flapping and hissing. The men scattered like chaff out of his way. But one brave fellow dropped on the bird as it passed him and hung on.

The man and bird were about the same length, some five and a half feet, but one would think that the one hundred and fifty pounds of man would completely crush the thirty pounds of bird. Not so. The bird kept right on going as if he were merely carrying a few extra feathers. Other men raced in to add their weight but could not get there in time. Over the bank went swan and man and dropped five feet to the water. The splash soaked the proud uniform of the Queen's Swanmaster. The man who had taken the plunge had somehow slipped about so that he was now under the bird and under water.

So far this had been good comedy, but it could end unhappily. The struggling man was beaten down whenever he tried to get his head above the surface. Several men leaped in and fought to get the bird under control, being rewarded by smart blows on the head and shoulders from the flailing wings.

One seized the swan's neck and it promptly went limp. Apparently the neck of the swan is its Achilles' heel. The swan was dragged dripping into a boat and the submerged man came up with mud in his hair and a grin on his face. It was all part of the job.

The wet swan's legs were crossed over its tail. For some reason that only an anatomist could explain, this makes the bird helpless. Then the markings were examined to see whether the swan belonged to the Queen, the Vintners or the Dyers. It has been the custom to mark the Vintners' birds by two nicks on the bill, those of the Dyers by one nick. It is not thought

necessary to mark the Queen's swans. All swans found unmarked are presumed to belong to her. In this case the cob
was unmarked, therefore the Queen's. The pen bore the mark
of the Vintners.

The cygnets were hauled into the two flanking boats by
means of a stick with a hook on the end like a shepherd's crook.
If the parents had belonged to the same owner the cygnets
would all have been marked in the same way. Since there were
two different owners, three would be assigned to each owner
and the odd bird to the owner of the cob. So, in this case, the
Vintners acquired three birds and the Queen four.

The entire family, when released, rushed away like speed-
boats, but soon stopped and began preening their feathers,
apparently not too much disturbed by their experience.

A smart rain began to fall. We were protected in the launch,
but the skiffs were open to the weather and the uniforms soon
became a little dull and the banners drooped. But the men
sturdily rowed on up the river and the Masters sat erect under
the downpour without recourse to mackintoshes or umbrellas.
The honour of the realm was at stake and would be maintained
at the risk of pneumonia. Other broods were captured and
marked. The rain continued. It was unpleasantly gusty and
wet even under the roof of the launch. The B.B.C. decided it
had all the pictures it could use. At Walton we turned about,
while the swan fleet went stubbornly on to Staines.

This sort of exposure for days on end must be trying, and
two of the Swanmasters were elderly men. Yet they would
probably prefer to die on duty than give up their royal pre-
rogatives.

Their work is not confined to the annual swan upping. They
are responsible for Thames swans throughout the year. There
are more than two thousand swans on the river. They are
usually well treated but occasionally a bird will be injured by a
heedless or malicious Teddy Boy. Then the Swanmaster is
called and the culprit goes to court. Because of the bird's royal

status, the offender may be severely punished. In the old days the penalty was death. Injured birds are taken to the swan hospital in London. Dirty birds also go to the hospital for a cleaning up. In the lower reaches of the Thames their plumage gets covered with oil. The same thing happens of course to smaller birds such as gulls and terns, whose wings become so heavily loaded with oil that they cannot fly. To attempt to rescue them all would be impracticable. Hundreds of dead birds are scooped from harbour waters every year. But nothing like this is allowed to happen to the royal swans, who are cared for as tenderly and expertly as any human patient.

CHAPTER 16

London's Widest Street

At Kingston we saw our first tugs, all boats above this point having been pleasure craft. This was our first warning that we were about to enter another Thames, a quite different Thames, a river not of green splendour and picture-card villages, but of grinding industry and great ships.

"Where are you going?" the lock-keeper at Teddington challenges us.

"To Southend."

"But Bushnell never allows his boats to go down-river. Too dangerous. Too much traffic."

I explained that we were covering the river from end to end and produced the owner's letter authorising us to sail the boat below Teddington provided we took on a pilot. Shaking his head, the lock-keeper let us through.

Now we were in the tidal Thames. Teddington is the last full lock on the river. Above this point the water is fresh. Below, it is brackish. Above, the level remains more or less the same except in flood. Below, the river restlessly rises and falls twice a day as the ocean tides make themselves felt sixty miles up-stream. Just below the lock is a stone that marks the division between the Upper Thames, controlled by the Thames Conservancy Board, and the Lower Thames, supervised by the Port of London Authority.

It is required by custom if not by law that an experienced pilot be aboard every boat in the crowded lower reaches. This had been arranged for and Denis Hoolahan, licensed waterman, was waiting for us at the boat-house by the weir. He came on at once and we sped down-river. Denis was a very pleasant and competent Irishman. He began by asking for a cup of tea. This was the first of some ten thousand cups of tea he consumed on the way to the mouth of the Thames. Just as the engines ran on petrol, Denis ran on tea.

While Teddington is the last full lock, there is a half lock at Richmond. This is an ingenious contrivance by which, when the water level below the weir rises to the same height as above the weir, gates in the weir are opened and boats may pass freely, thus avoiding the delay and expense of going through the locks. As the tide begins to drop, making a difference in level below and above, the weir gates are closed and boats are locked through in the ordinary way. We arrived just before the moment of closing and shot through the weir on a swiftly flowing ebb.

We visited the gorgeous gardens of Kew, then just below Kew Bridge called at the branch office of the Port of London Authority. One of the functions of the Authority is to patrol the Thames and I was curious to see how it was done.

The Thames is London's widest street and one of the busiest. It used to be even more busy than now. Three centuries ago it was the city's main thoroughfare. The streets were bogs and it was easier to go from Westminster to the Tower by water than by mud. The river is still used for loads too big for any lorry. Tugs tow immense barges filled with goods from ships in the port up-stream to power plants and factories. Excursion boats filled with tourists or schoolchildren ply up and down daily, mainly to Richmond or Oxford in the one direction and Greenwich in the other.

Someone has to see to it that the street behaves itself—for it is not a settled thing like a city street. It is temperamental and moody, rises and falls eighteen feet or more with the tides, is broad enough to lash itself into a fury under a strong wind, tears away timbers from the docks and tosses them in the way of

Above: a rarely seen and seldom photographed event in the life of
Mother Swan. She turns her eggs to warm them on the other side

Below: The Barley Mow, Clifton Hampden, one of the oldest and
oddest inns on the Thames. Here Jerome K. Jerome wrote a good
part of *Three Men in a Boat*

steamers, swells under heavy rain until it rushes through bridge arches like a mill race to the dire peril of small craft and often undermining the great stone piers of the bridges.

There has to be someone to patrol the river, as a 'bobby' does his beat on city streets. Patrol launches, about a dozen of them, do the job.

In the Authority office I was fortunate to meet Captain L. J. Lovell, Harbourmaster for the Port of London Authority for the stretch from Kew to Tower Bridge. Handsome in his blue uniform and the gold bars of his rank, he was a heavy-set man of a hearty hand-on-your-arm type and promptly agreed to take me on a run in a patrol launch, just about to leave. He would go with me to explain things.

The launch *Ranelagh* looked like a tugboat that has come up in the world. Its woodwork was as rich as mahogany and its brass dazzled the sun. The boat ploughed down-stream without incident until a floating bale of sparta grass was sighted.

"That wouldn't be so good in a ship's propellers," said Captain Lovell.

We pulled up alongside. One of the men dangled overboard and broke up the bale with an axe.

"Bales, boxes, timbers, all sorts of floating obstructions, we get thousands of them."

"How do they get down through the locks?"

"They don't come down—they float up from the port on the tide."

A motor-cruiser lay on the beach, quite evidently disabled. We drew up by it. Three men were making repairs. Captain Lovell called to them:

"I'll take that gear now."

Some heavy tackle and equipment was passed on board our boat. As we went on, the captain explained.

"Salvage gear," he said. "We used it yesterday to get the boat up."

"How did it happen to sink?"

"Just one of those stupid things. They had the boat on the beach, working on it, and when they knocked off at night they forgot that they had left the sea cocks open. During the night high tide floated the boat out into deep water and it filled and sank. Of course it's up to us to keep the river clear of obstructions, so we hoisted it and deposited it on the foreshore. From there on, the owners must look after it."

We passed under the fairly new Wandsworth Bridge.

"See the streamlined piers? We insisted upon having them built that way. Otherwise the impingement of the tide is such that it splays out, interfering with navigation underneath."

Up the river came a tug towing six heavily loaded barges, any one of them three times as big as the tug. Captain Lovell called to the skipper:

"Short-haul your line."

The men on the tug lost no time in obeying.

"Very dangerous," Captain Lovell explained, "to have a long line between the tug and the first barge. Tremendous momentum there. If the tug suddenly had to stop, the barges would run over it. Short-hauled, that can't happen."

One man was noting down the name and home port of every outgoing ship. "That's for Lloyd's," said the captain. "No ship can move secretly on the Thames. Its position and direction go down on the record."

By the time we had gone to Tower Bridge and back to Kew I had developed high respect for the men who keep order on London's great water boulevard.

Our own boat passed through London at night and it was one of the great experiences of a lifetime. Floodlighting has greatly enhanced the beauty of London and nowhere are the floodlit buildings seen to greater advantage than in the black mirror of the Thames. Every illumination is doubled and at the same time given a wavering, ethereal unreality. It is a sight that not many tourists see, for few excursion boats ply the

Thames after dark. To be sure, you may see it in detached snatches from the bridges and banks, but London at night pours into Piccadilly and Leicester Square and Soho and is quite unaware of the night glory of the Thames. My various sojourns in London had totalled about two years but I had never seen anything like this.

Even the Battersea Power Station was a thing of terrific beauty, its four immense chimneys reaching up like giant arms, and the enormous smudges of smoke, transformed into golden draperies against the night sky.

The gleaming white stone and bold statues of the Tate Gallery show no sign that the famous building was severely damaged by air-raids in 1941.

The Parliament tower rises darkly, unilluminated because it is under repair, but the great clock dial glows like an enormous moon and a white light at the top of the tower signifies that the House of Commons is in night session.

Most gorgeous is the façade of the stately London County Hall, illuminated in four colours. Festoons of light complete the picture, which gains contrast from the blackness underneath the bridges as we pass through.

Cleopatra's Needle is silhouetted in black against the two-colour floodlit front of the skyscraping Shell-Mex building.

The great fountains of Trafalgar Square are playing high, every drop glistening like a diamond in the general glow that illuminates also the National Gallery and St. Martin's-in-the-Fields, while Nelson atop his column 170 feet high basks in a spotlight of his own.

The great dome of St. Paul's is reflected in the water, which twists it into the picturesque ruins that enemy airmen tried in vain to achieve.

We pass under historic London Bridge and face the grim old Tower of London. But now it looks more fairy-like than grim under its whitewash of light and we prefer to think of it in its rôle as a palace for kings rather than as a prison and death-house.

Like a magnificent climax to all this splendour, Tower Bridge soars 142 feet into the air, the tips of its two Gothic towers lost in the mist, its twin bascules raised and opened like a pair of gigantic jaws to allow the passage of a ship.

We tie up at St. Katherine Dock and, like the people we have just been criticising for not visiting the Thames, we make straight for Piccadilly, Leicester Square and Soho.

CHAPTER 17

The Pool

We understood why we must have a licensed waterman on board as we dodged crazily through the frantic traffic of the Pool of London, made more dangerous by morning fog. We rolled and pitched violently in the wash of ocean liners, coastal steamers, tugs and barges. This was probably the most heavy river traffic anywhere in the world. London of course was built here because the Thames was here and grew because the Thames brought the world to its door.

Canals led off from the river through locks into the largest area of enclosed dock water in the world. There lay ocean liners and cargo giants by the score, row on row, mile on mile, great cranes moving over them like enormous spiders, picking off cargo or putting it on. Here approximately a thousand ships a week come and go, more than fifty thousand a year. A quarter-million passengers arrive or depart during the year. More than fifty million tons of cargo are handled, a greater tonnage than in any other port of the world except New York.

In endless warehouses are stored the treasures of far lands: marble, mahogany, mother-of-pearl, ivory, tortoise-shell, indigo, spices, quicksilver, gums, rubber, silks and perfumes, grain and timber, sugar and tea by the ton, coffee and tobacco and wine, tallow and hides, and cattle frozen stiff from head to tail.

We landed to look in at the ivory warehouse. Great elephant tusks and rhinoceros horns lay in rows. Every part of the tusk, we were told, is good for something, even the dust that falls when the tusk is sawed. The tusk is not just a senseless piece of bone; we could see the end of the nerve which makes it as pain-conscious as a human tooth. It seems that many a 'rogue' has been driven into roguery by the agony of an eight-foot tooth-ache.

Other warehouses are devoted to wild animals. Gigantic fish destined for some aquarium, a sacred white elephant from Burma, an oversize tortoise, a pair of ibises, are among the inmates. One ship brought forty-six orang-outangs, one elephant, one tigress, twenty-five rare apes, two bears and a leopard.

We heard the story of the first cargo of ice that ever came to London. This was in 1845. There was no provision for such a commodity in the charges of the custom house and officials didn't know whether to call it raw or manufactured material. At last they classified it as dry goods. By that time it had become wet goods, for it had melted and run out with the tide.

Supreme over all this colossal activity is the Port of London Authority. It is not a government agency but is made up of representatives of the various interests in the Port. The Port of London is sixty-nine miles long, extending up the river from the estuary to Teddington. The Authority owns and operates the five great dock systems, controls the loading and unloading of vessels and the storing of goods, regulates all water-borne traffic, keeps the tidal river clear of wrecks and obstructions and licenses the lightermen and watermen.

Tucked in among the warehouses were fragments of old London. Here was Limehouse, London's Chinatown. Here was an old waterfront pub. Here was Wapping Old Stairs where smugglers used to sneak their goods into London, and Execution Dock where pirates were hanged and then tied to a post until three tides had washed over them. It was here and in such fashion that Captain Kidd came to his end.

The Thames made almost a complete loop around the Isle of Dogs, so called because here were located the royal dog kennels belonging to Greenwich Palace across the river.

We were about to pass from West to East, from the Occident to the Orient. Mr. Hoolahan pointed out a vertical line on the north sea wall. "The meridian," he said. "This is Longitude zero."

On the south bank, looking quite out of place in this region of docks and warehouses, was the white grace of Greenwich, formerly the palace of kings and now the Royal Naval College, the National Maritime Museum, Queen's House, and, on the hill behind, the Royal Observatory.

From this point time is still reckoned although the various departments of the Observatory have now been moved to Herstmonceux Castle in Sussex. The smoke of giant power stations had polluted the Greenwich atmosphere. In fact it never had been an ideal spot for an observatory. Perched on a hilltop, it was exposed to strong winds which produced slight variations in readings. The positions of the stars tended to alter slightly with the wind. The Observatory is now used only as a museum.

"That's where the great lover was born," said Mr. Hoolahan.

The infant Henry was baptised in the parish church. As a King he continued to live in Greenwich Palace though spending part of his time at Hampton Court Palace, which he had accepted as a 'present' from Cardinal Wolsey. Here at Greenwich he staged exciting jousts and tournaments. It was at a palace party that Anne Boleyn first caught the King's eye. He installed her in the palace, lost no time in getting her with child, then divorced his Queen and sailed with Anne up the Thames to the Tower, where they spent the last night before her coronation.

"How like you the look of my city, sweetheart?" he asked the next day as they made their royal progress to the Abbey.

"The city is well enough," she said, "but I saw a great many caps on heads." Anne was determined to have the homage of her people, for was she not about to bear a son to the King?

Four months later the midwives were called. The royal printer set up in type an announcement of the birth of a prince, and waited. At last the news came. The printer disgustedly added two s's to the word prince. The future Queen Elizabeth had been born.

Three years passed. At a joust in the Greenwich tilting yard Anne dropped her handkerchief in the lists. A certain handsome knight retrieved it, pressed it to his forehead, and raised it to her on the point of his lance. The face of the King darkened. That night Anne was again in the Tower, in the very same room she had occupied on the night before her coronation. She left only to go to the block.

At Greenwich, Henry married his fourth Queen, Anne of Cleves.

Queen Elizabeth also loved Greenwich. Here she flirted with Sir Walter Raleigh and it is here that the incident of the cloak in the mud is supposed to have taken place. It was near here that Elizabeth knighted Drake upon the deck of the *Golden Hind*, honouring him as the first Englishman to sail around the world. And when the Spanish Armada threatened England it was at a point across the river that Elizabeth reviewed her ships, exclaiming: "Oh! My poor fleet!" Hence the present name of the place, Purfleet.

At Woolwich Ferry I took pictures of the quaint old side-wheel ferryboats. When I was done a guard said:

"You got your photos? Well then, I suppose nothing can be done about it. You see, taking pictures of the boats is forbidden by the London County Council. I don't know why. It was a war measure. There's no point in it now, but it hasn't been changed. So I usually wait till they've got their photos before I tell 'em they can't take any."

Perhaps the wariness of the authorities is due to the proximity of the Royal Arsenal. Just beyond the ferry pier, trains pull up to a jetty and unload high-explosives into lighters on the river.

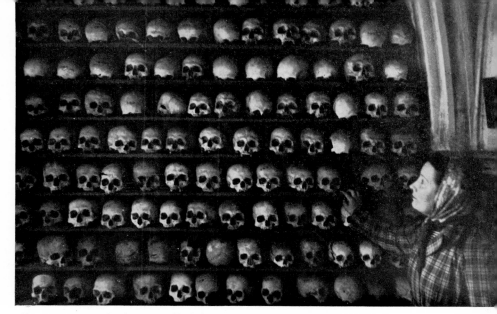

Above : experts who have studied the two thousand skulls in the crypt of St. Leonard's Church at Hythe report that the brain capacity of the 14th-century Englishman was as great as the present average and the teeth were a lot better

Below : the warming pan filled with glowing charcoal has for centuries taken the chill out of British beds. Today it is being superseded by the china pig and hot water bottle

The locomotives look rather antiquated—they are not electric nor diesel but old-fashioned steam engines. Clouds of steam belch from them. There must be a furious blaze in the fire-box, and fire should mean sparks from the chimney, and sparks in the presence of high, explosives . . . It all seemed pretty dangerous.

"Couldn't be safer," the ferry guard told us. "There's no fire in those things. They build up a big head of steam before they come into the yards. Then the fire is drawn out, the engine rolls in, couples on to a train, draws it to the jetty and gets out of the yards again before it has lost its steam. I've read they do the same thing when they build a tunnel under the Alps —run engines in on steam only, no smoke to suffocate the work-men."

On the left bank loom the Ford motor works. Since there was nothing but a mushy marsh to build upon, piles were driven sixty feet into the mud and the vast buildings erected atop the piles. Why was so unfavourable a site chosen? Because the Thames was there. It would provide the 45,000 gallons of water a minute needed by the plant. It would bring in coal from Durham, limestone from Wales, iron ore from Africa. It would make possible the loading of vehicles directly into ships to be transported all over the world.

At Tilbury there are more great docks and Gravesend across the river is in a sense Thames-end, for it is here that an out-going ship puts off its river pilot and takes on a pilot for the estuary. It is not compulsory to carry a pilot below Gravesend but the ship gets lower insurance rates if it does so.

Here too the customs officers board incoming liners. We see a ship coming up-stream flying a yellow flag at the masthead. It means she is from foreign parts and wants quarantine clearance.

Waterman Hoolahan had his theory of the origin of the name Gravesend.

"It used to be the custom to throw dead bodies into the

Thames. Then a law was passed. You could still throw in your corpses below this point, but not above it. So this became known as Gravesend."

In Gravesend there is one grave of unusual interest. Here is buried Pocahontas, who saved the life of Captain John Smith. If it had not been for her the English colony on the Chesapeake would probably have been blotted out. Says a historian: "She was the good genius of the colony at its most critical time." Supposing Smith to be dead, she married young John Rolfe and came to England with him. The English climate did not suit 'Lady Rebecca', as she was called from her new baptismal name, and she died in her twenty-second year.

We climbed to the church of St. George and saw the two stained-glass windows set up in her memory by the Virginia chapter of the Society of Colonial Dames. In the church register the Indian girl is recorded as "Rebecca Wrothe, a Virginia lady borne".

We sailed on; for although Gravesend may be considered the end of the river proper, we wanted to see the river improper, the unpredictable estuary, miles wide, sometimes savage under fierce winds, sometimes blinded with fog or chilled to almost Arctic temperatures by storms from the North Sea. Gases of various sorts drift out from the factories and oil refineries on the distant shore.

"In a bad fog," said Mr. Hoolahan, "you can *smell* your way from here to London, if you know your industries. You can, for a fact. The oil refineries have their smell, dust from the cement mills has a quite different one, and so it goes on, the soap works, the iron works, the motor works, the sewage outfall, the Royal Arsenal, the gas works, chemical factories, Chinatown, the spice warehouse, the wild animal warehouse, the fish market—each tells you exactly where you are. You don't need eyes, just a good nose."

Besides an occasional ocean liner, some strange vessels of

former times loomed up out of the mist. One belonged to that
almost forgotten species, the square-rigger. She was the ancient
ship *Shaftesbury*, now used as a training ship for poor boys who
wish to enter the Merchant Service.

We came upon a group of three spritsail barges, their great
red sails glowing in the low sun of late afternoon. It seems that
most of the fishing-boats of England used to have red sails, red
because they were treated to preserve them from the weather.
These old Thames sailing barges were used to carry grain and
other cargo down the coast and up the river. They are now
disappearing fast and a Sailing Barge Preservation Society has
been formed to buy up and preserve the few that are left as
items of historic interest.

CHAPTER 18

Holehaven or Hellhole?

It is nearly eight in the evening when we draw into Holehaven and drop anchor in a channel barely two hundred yards wide between a mud flat and Canvey Island. We are lying between two boats that are drying their very fishy nets—with the consequence that we are promptly visited by flies. These, by the way, are the first insects of any sort that have molested us during our entire trip down the Thames.

Canvey Island is a redeemed marsh. Dutch engineers, experienced on the dykes of Holland, built here a dyke to encompass eight thousand acres. This is only part of a great dyking system to protect farmland from the treacherous Thames. Even these precautions were not enough to avoid disaster in 1953 when a spring tide was pushed by a hurricane up the estuary, flooded towns and villages, burst the sea wall and devastated Canvey Island, drowning scores of people trapped in their homes.

After the men retire for the night the smell of petrol becomes so intense that we call them to look for a leak. They take up the floorboards and find the sea in the boat, water a foot deep, covered with a glossy coat of petrol. They shut off the petrol, and man the pump. But there is a constriction in the pipe and they have to go to hand-baling with can and pail.

Meanwhile the boat is doing a dance. The mud flat that protected it when we first arrived is now tided over some ten feet deep and the waves that roll across it are as high as our boat. The men stagger and stumble and would curse if they were not perfect gentlemen. Herbert does allow himself to grumble: "Holehaven! They should have called it Hellhole."

This is a new experience for Herbert. It is his first visit to the tidal Thames. He has never before had the feel of rough water. He is here only because he begged to come. His stint really ended at Teddington when Mr. Hoolahan came aboard, but Herbert explained that he had never seen the lower reaches, and since there were four bunks there was no reason why he should not come along. His experience on the mirror-like Upper Thames never prepared him for anything like this. His grin is gone and his face is green under the black mop. It takes them till midnight to bale the water and petrol out of the hold.

Then we go to rest—and what rest, tensing muscles to avoid being thrown bodily out of the bunks! It sounds as if the sorcerer's apprentice is loose in the galley. Four plates had been broken before dinner, so care had been taken to stow everything so that it could not possibly break loose. But it does, and the most weird and cacophonous medley of bangs, rattles, smacks and cracks makes the night hideous, and the morning light shows piles of crockery and tinware, milk bottles and cans, chasing each other over the cabin floor.

The day greets us with a chill winter wind, a tossing sea and a dubious captain. "We'll wait and see," says Hoolahan. Towards noon Herbert rows the dinghy ashore for petrol. He comes back reporting that there is none to be had. Too bad we didn't save the petrol from the bilges!

Perhaps the pilot can help Herbert round up some petrol, but he hates to leave the boat. It is in a dangerous spot. The flat is again inundated, we are fully exposed to the waves and the *Goshawk* is tearing at her anchor like a frightened horse trying to break away from a hitching post. To go on we must have petrol. Mr. Hoolahan and Herbert row away in the dinghy to get it.

Some time later I have occasion to step out of the cabin, and discover that our stern is within twenty feet of a lee shore under a strong gale. And the lee shore is not soft—it is the solid stone dyke.

The anchor must be dragging. Ten minutes more, perhaps five, and we shall be pounding the rocks.

Can I fend off with the boat-hook? My strength would be nothing against seven tons of boat and more tons of water. Can I haul in on the anchor chain? Ten men couldn't budge the boat against that pressure of wind and sea. My only hope is to start the engines. But an engine won't run without petrol. There may be a little left—I jump into the wheel-house and press the starter button. There is nothing but a melancholy buzz.

I try and try again. My wife reports that we are now ten feet from the rocks. Of course if we strike, the first things to be smashed will be the twin screws. Then our last chance will be gone, the boat will be broken up, and we shall be lucky if we can clamber up the steep wall without being pulped between the boat and the dyke.

One engine coughs, sputters, takes hold. I throw the lever into full ahead. The engine stalls. Mary comes running forward.

"Only five feet," she says. "What do we do?"

"Be ready to jump."

But I try the engines once more. The port engine refuses absolutely. The starboard engine starts, stops, starts again. This time it keeps going. But one engine won't be enough. We are still inching towards shore, though more slowly. I see Hoolahan and Herbert coming in the dinghy. They have observed what is happening and Hoolahan is fairly tearing his arms out at the oars. I keep begging the port engine, and it finally responds. The boat pulls away with tantalising slowness from the murderous stone dyke. The men tumble aboard, pretty well pooped, and I don't feel much better. Two anchors are put out.

"Well," Mary says when this is done, "I think you'd all like some tea." She serves it and then takes to her bunk.

The tanks replenished, we pull out and make for Southend. It proves too 'blowy', to use the captain's understatement, and after twenty minutes of furious plunging we turn back to the very dubious safety of 'Hellhole'. There the men work for half an hour to get two anchors down. Herbert loses his breakfast over the side and discovers that his two false teeth have gone with it. Mary feels so miserable that I ask Herbert to get his own and Hoolahan's tea, but he gets up and goes out into the cockpit, so I prepare tea, but do not have enough enthusiasm to share it with Hoolahan.

Herbert's lost teeth were his two front uppers and his speech is very flannelly without them.

"I'm thick," he complains, "I think I'll go to thore until the thtorm thtopth."

"Sick!" exclaims the irrepressible Hoolahan. "Oh no! Come up and help me fix the engines. That will cure you."

The lad is the very picture of misery, but manages a pitiful smile. "I didn't know it would be like this," he says.

"Perhaps," I suggest, "you'll give up your idea of a sea life and go into your father's garden business."

He shakes his head stubbornly and we know it will take more than a bout of sea-sickness to quench his ambition to become a licensed waterman.

It is as cold as Greenland all day. This is midsummer. And I am in long underwear, T-shirt, woollen shirt, two pairs of woollen socks, sweater, coat, overcoat and muffler—and cold. Mary, fully dressed, is in bed under four thicknesses of blanket, and cold.

I wouldn't say that the storm-bitten Hoolahan enjoys our discomfort, but he is remarkably cheerful as he whiles the time away with tales of his experiences at sea. He has many times sailed across Europe. When playboys of the Riviera want an English-built boat, it is cheaper and quicker to take it direct than the long way round by Gibraltar. The route runs the up Seine, through a canal, down the Saône and the Rhone to the Mediterranean. The locks make it both interesting and laborious.

"Ex-service Frenchmen are given jobs as lock-keepers—but they get themselves another job and leave the locks to their wives and children. So when you come to a lock you have to get out and help the wife or child on the lock. The Rhone is a very swift stream and you must have a local pilot. Yes, you can cross Europe in several different directions by boat. Of course the same is true in England. Have you ever looked at a canal-and-river map of the country? It looks like a cobweb, so many water routes. There are nearly a thousand miles of navigable canal and river in Britain."

By morning the wind had dropped and we were able to cross the estuary to the mouth of the Medway, last tributary of the Thames. The great oil stores of this region recall Operation Pluto of World War II, a remarkable project quite unknown to the public at the time. Millions of gallons of oil were pumped from these stores through a submarine pipeline across the Channel to supply the Allied troops landing in Europe.

A bit farther up the Medway is the ancient city of Rochester, where we spend the night in the 300-year-old Bull Inn featured by Dickens, a place of labyrinthine corridors and a great bull's head, grandfather clocks, and six-foot warming pans, one of which we gratefully insert in the bed to take off the midsummer chill.

Back across the river the next morning to Leigh, famous for its cockle-fishing and its Essex Yacht Club, which is one of the few yacht clubs in the world to use a ship as a club-house.

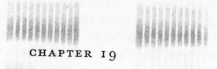

CHAPTER 19

Thames Mouth

Then to our last port of call, Southend-on-Sea, where estuary and ocean meet. It is Sunday and trippers from London have inundated the seaside resort. We part regretfully from Herbert and Denis, who will sail the good boat *Goshawk* back up-river to her berth at Wargrave.

Southend is the British Coney Island, with all manner of merry-go-rounds, ferris wheels, roller coasters, rifle ranges, Never-Never Lands, peep-shows and side-shows, boat rides, and refreshment stalls where you may experiment with cockles, whelks, mussels, prawns, shrimps and jellied eels.

At night the waterfront bursts into millions of coloured lights all the way from Westcliff to Southend and over the entire length of Southend Pier. The pier is so great that it even has its own seven-car train to transport people from the shore to the pierhead at two shillings a person. Or you may walk the mile and a third for sixpence—a moderate charge for the million gay lights and the free orchestral concert and all the other attractions of one of the gayest and longest piers in the world.

At the end you have practically a town in mid-river. The pierhead broadens to become a pile-supported island, three storeys high, and swarming with packed thousands of trippers. Here in the heart of the Thames they visit shops and shows and concerts and enjoy the bravest illumination to be found in England. They gaze open-mouthed at enormous fire-breathing dragons, a vast luminous mosaic of Queen Elizabeth I and her square-rigged ships, another of the present Elizabeth and her castles and palaces, a replica of the Statue of Liberty to please visiting Americans, a doll's theatre, Mother Goose, Little Miss Muffet, Santa Claus with his reindeer, and many other characters from fanciful fiction all blown up to gigantic proportions and blazing with colour and light. There is also an auditorium with a fine orchestra, and cafés and bars and booths where you may nibble cockles and whelks, and games of chance to suit any taste. And there are the people, with green, red or blue faces according to the colours that happen to be flashing at the moment, all struggling cheerfully to get past, under or over other people, all laughing and screaming and astonishing the grave old Thames that tries in vain to smother this gaiety with his dark, silent mantle.

And there is a place where you can get away from all the uproar at the far end of the pier projecting darkly into the river. We are a mile and a third from shore and yet far short of the middle of the mighty stream, here some six miles wide.

We stand in the dark and think of the fifty thousand ships that pass this point in a year, think of the fabulous port with but one rival on earth and the city of cities that owes so much of its greatness to this stream, think of all that the river has meant to England and the world. And it is hard to believe that this is the same Thames we stepped across at Seven Springs and took up on the tip of a finger at Thames Head.

CHAPTER 20

The Garden of England

After so long a time afloat, life on land took getting used to all over again. The crowds, the dust, the traffic, the noise, were a bit bewildering after the isolation of the river. But we must get reaccustomed to land living, and that promptly, for our next project was a journey by car through England, Wales and Scotland.

So we repaired to London, put up at a non-tourist hotel in relatively peaceful Bloomsbury Square, and set about acquiring a car.

Standard practice under such circumstances is to hire a car by the day, week or month. That is expensive if, as in our case, the car is to be used for four months. Calculations showed that the cost on this basis would be about seven dollars a day, petrol extra. Moreover, a hired car is a used car, and too often an abused car.

Diligent search turned up a reliable firm that would sell us a brand-new car on a re-purchase arrangement. That is, we would buy the car outright, but at the end of four months the firm would take it back at a predetermined price. Thus we would be out only the depreciation.

On the narrow and winding roads of the English countryside, the smaller the car the better. So we settled upon an Austin A30, though with some question as to whether the tiny capsule would accommodate six-foot passengers. We need not have worried. There were two inches of headroom, almost too much leg room, and we could have carried twice as much baggage.

The car was sparkling fresh from the factory and cost less than half the price of a used rental—three dollars a day instead of seven.

Trim, clean, and forest-green, the new car draws up before the hotel and the salesman invites us to try it. This should be a cinch. After driving big overseas cars, handling this midget will be nothing. Besides, this is an ideal place for a try-out. Bloomsbury Square is one of the quietest spots in London.

We all get in and I drive around the square. Everything goes well until we reach the east side. Here cars are parked along both kerbs leaving only a little more than enough room for a large lorry—and a large lorry chooses this moment to come along, meeting us just on the bend, where we both come to a halt and I start learning the gearshifts.

In this type of vehicle, you don't just step on the gas as in the automatic-transmission car. This car isn't built for lazy drivers. There are four shifts forward and one reverse.

The lorry-driver is very patient while I study, ,stew and experiment and grind gears and teeth and accept free, but conflicting, advice from the lorry-driver, the salesman and my wife. Finally by inhaling sharply so as to contract the sides of the car we manage to squeeze through a space large enough for a motor-cycle.

I am warm for the first time since our arrival in Britain.

Nothing daunted, or not daring to show how daunted, I go around again. It can't happen twice. But it does, and this time the lorry is larger and the driver less patient. My companions too begin to advise in a higher key than before. However, by selecting the wrong gear I snap their heads so effectively as to render them speechless and the car lurches out with only tissue-paper clearance.

I don't go around the quiet square the third time but prefer to transfer my practice to busy Charing Cross Road, where there are stop-and-go lights to control traffic.

This business of keeping to the left distorts the street so that I feel as if I were looking at it in a mirror. An invisible power, the power of long habit, keeps pulling me to the right.

But we are all sheep and tend to follow the flock. With cars ahead of me and on both sides of me, I am kept strictly in line. The inevitable begins to seem the natural. With a subtle clearing of vision, I step through the looking-glass and the cross-eyed street begins to appear almost normal.

After a few wildly careering rides by taxi we had looked forward with dread to operating our own car in the London labyrinth. But it is not so bad after all. True, there is plenty of turning and twisting to be done, because London abhors a straight line. But traffic signs are plain and all important crossings are light-controlled.

During the next few days we drove all about London, to Regent's Park, Hyde Park, the Embankment, to Soho every night for dinner, and finally to Kew Gardens and back, a thirty-mile round trip through busy city streets all the way. Still there was a lasting thrill about it, for the unexpected could always happen and often did. That we did not come to grief was due to the good judgment and skill of English drivers, for in an emergency all the carefully memorised mathematics of the five shifts were forgotten and any gear had to do. The results, especially when the gear happened to be reverse, were most surprising and brought me more public attention than a person of my modest nature would ordinarily crave.

Petrol was expensive, about sixty-five cents an imperial gallon, but we could cover forty-five miles on a gallon. It was a 'nippy' little car from 'bonnet' to 'boot' (hood to trunk) and so small and manœuvrable because of the short wheel-base that parking was surprisingly easy.

The car would turn about in one movement in a fairly narrow street, and such U-turns are not frowned upon in London, even on main arteries. You might park on your own side of the street (the left) or cross the street without turning about and park on the other side facing the traffic. The driver's seat being on the right side, it was very convenient to the kerb if the kerb was on the right, and parking could be done with precision. In quiet places such as our square the car might be parked on the street all night, provided it was locked and the lights turned off.

We stayed in London only long enough to test the car thoroughly and make sure that it had none of the ailments that usually afflict new cars. Then we took off for the provinces.

Crossing London Bridge, we paused to see Nancy's Steps made famous by Dickens, then searched through narrow alleys for the site of the Globe Playhouse where so many of Shakespeare's plays were first performed. Every moment the atmosphere became more strongly alcoholic. At last we found the bronze plaque commemorating the theatre, no trace of which remains. The plaque is embedded in the wall of a brewery which towers up on both sides of the street and connects its various buildings by over-street footbridges.

Men were shovelling something out of a lorry into the brewery interior.

"What's that—malt?" I asked.

"Yeast," and they threw me a reeking sample and apologised when it caught me full in the face.

But I reflected as I wiped it off that it was all in the best Shakespearian tradition. On this very spot many an actor mouthing the great bard's lines had been plastered, if not by yeast, by rotten eggs or dead fish or mud scooped up from the unpaved floor of the open-air pit. And perhaps this form of criticism was more wholesome than the present tendency to regard every word of the immortal poet as almost divinely inspired. The truth is that Shakespeare, greatest of dramatists, sometimes wrote a stupid line and often a dull one. We should probably be deeply grateful for the correctives administered by his audience, for without those correctives he quite possibly would have written many more stupid and dull lines than he did.

Near-by is the site of the old Tabard Inn from which Chaucer's pilgrims set out for Canterbury. We follow their trail, considerably improved since their day, better than it was only a few decades ago when I cycled over it to romantic Canterbury on a thrilling week-end escape from a print-shop job in London.

But though the roadway has changed, the fabulous county of Kent is much as it was decades ago, centuries ago. How astonishing to find this expanse of unsoiled countryside within half an hour of London! How heavily laden the apple trees, how rich the flowering shrubs, how green the grass! Everything grows with wild enthusiasm. We remember the Turkish diplomat who when asked how he liked England replied:

"England is delightful. But when I go out into the country, I have the feeling that I have fallen into a plate of spinach."

The greenness and the growth are incredible and have earned for Kent the title of 'The Garden of England'. Barely able to get their heads above the growing things appear fine old stone bridges, red-tiled Tudor houses, grey churches and ancient villages.

Across the lazy Medway towers Rochester Castle, its twelve-foot-thick walls still holding it erect after the lapse of eight centuries. The black holes which are all that remain of its windows make it look, in Dickens's words, "as if the rooks and daws had pecked its eyes out".

Almost in its shadow is The Bull Inn at which we had stayed on our trip down the Thames. We stop there again, and again use the warming pan, but this time are allowed to slip it into the actual bed in which Dickens himself slept and liked well enough to assign it to Pickwick. You will find it in room seventeen of the old Bull Inn.

We wandered down what Dickens calls "the silent High Street—full of old beams and timbers", passed the Corn Exchange "oddly garnished with a queer old clock, as if Time carried on business there", refreshed ourselves in an ancient tea-shop referred to in *Edwin Drood* as Tope's House, and reached the gabled home of Watts' Charity, a thriving institution in Dickens's time.

We knocked at the door. It was opened by a quaint little old lady who looked as if she might have been there in 1579 when the place was founded.

"Ah," she said, "you wish to see?"

We entered the low dark hall and breathed the musty odour of old walls and dubious guests. For this place has offered lodging to seedy gentlemen of the road for almost four centuries.

It all began in the mind of a boy, hungry, homeless and penniless, who curled up to sleep in a doorway, unprotected from the driving winter rain. The man of the house noticed him, took him in, fed and lodged him, and sent him on his way the next morning with fourpence.

That was the beginning of the incredible fortune built up by Richard Watts. Remembering with gratitude that night's lodging and fourpence, Richard Watts in his will provided for a building "for Six Poor Travellers who, not being rogues or proctors, may receive gratis for one night lodging, entertainment, and fourpence each".

"What is that about proctors?" I asked the little old lady.

"Proctors," she said, "were what we call solicitors, or lawyers."

"And he classed them with rogues? What did Richard Watts have against lawyers?"

"One of them had cheated him, or tried to. It happened this way. Sir Richard became so ill at one time that he was unable to see. He called a solicitor and dictated his will. But the solicitor, instead of writing it down as dictated, framed it in such a way as to convey the rich man's property to himself. 'Read it back,' ordered the sick man. The solicitor read it back as it had been dictated, not as he had written it.

"But to the surprise of everyone Sir Richard recovered his health and his sight, and upon reading his will as the solicitor had written it, declared himself the enemy of all lawyers."

Every night for three and a half centuries poor travellers gathered on the esplanade near Rochester Castle and from them six were selected, taken to the public bath, then to Watts' Charity, where three cubicles on the ground floor and three on the floor above awaited them.

The ancient lady showed us the rooms. Each was austerely provided with nothing but an iron bed, a Bible, and a large fireplace. Knowing how the English feel about heat, one may doubt whether there was very often a fire in the fireplace. Still, the occupants probably considered themselves very lucky to get two meals and a bed and fourpence, even if they had to take a bath to get it.

The Bibles are not particularly thumb-marked, and apparently did not always have the effect desired, since in the cellar it was necessary to add one more room—a dungeon for the unruly. It has a heavy oak door with iron bolts and an opening in the door only large enough to admit a plate of food.

The service was discontinued in 1947 because the supply of applicants ran out. The poor do not travel as much as they used to, and those who do travel are looking for shillings and pounds, not fourpence. The trustees might have turned the building over to commercial interests, but that would have been a violation of the will of the founder. So they took in two needy old couples, who occupy the building at a nominal rental and show visitors around.

A few streets away is a picturesque row of alms-houses, also the bequest of the benevolent Richard Watts. After these centuries it is still operated with Watts money. The boy who began his career with fourpence came to possess a good slice of the county, and as these broad lands are subdivided and sold the sums are used to continue the Watts charities.

This process is likely to go on for some centuries more, and in these pleasant houses set in gardens full of flowers old folks will live in comfort, thanks to the kindness of some unremembered man who took a boy in out of the rain.

CHAPTER 21

Canterbury

No cathedral in England is more dramatic, powerful, bloody and beautiful than Canterbury.

It bursts upon you like a thunderclap as you emerge from the shadows of the great gate and come face to face with its soaring splendour.

This is the seat of the Archbishop, Primate of all England, who does not hesitate to speak his mind to kings and queens, whether the issue be the marriage of an abdicating monarch or the romance of a princess.

From the beginning Canterbury dominated and often domineered royalty. Here Pope Gregory the Great sent Augustine with forty missionaries in 597 to convert the Britons, whom he called "not Angles but angels". Just why he thought angels needed conversion is not clear, unless he considered them fallen angels.

Augustine began at the top. He converted Ethelbert, King of Kent, then ten thousand of his people. He built a cathedral and became the first Archbishop of Canterbury.

The kings from that time on found Canterbury a mixed blessing. There was a constant struggle for supremacy between monarch and archbishop. Henry II thought he had the problem solved when upon the death of the Archbishop he nominated as the new Primate his own dearly beloved friend and loyal supporter, Thomas à Becket. Now he felt sure that the Church would bow to the authority of the State.

But whether Becket was corrupted by the lust for power or

sanctified by his new responsibilities, he now became overnight the champion of the Church against the King. He and Henry, formerly as close as brothers, became deadly enemies. For years bitter war was waged between them until one night, under the sting of new aggravations, the furious King cried to his assembled barons:

"What sluggard wretches, what cowards have I brought up in my Court, who care nothing for their allegiance to their master! Not one will deliver me from this low-born priest!"

What happened then has been told many times and too often mis-told. It is quite unnecessary to invent stories, for five witnesses of the murder of Becket wrote accounts of the event, and their accounts are readily available in the library of the British Museum.

Four knights took seriously the King's demand that someone rid him of this 'low-born priest'. On the afternoon of 29th December, 1170, they rode into Canterbury and forced their way into the Archbishop's Palace. The evening meal had just been finished and the Archbishop had left the dining-hall for his retiring-room, where he was sitting on a couch and talking with some of his monks, who reclined at his feet.

The four knights entered and, without a word, seated themselves on the floor. The monks were startled by the intrusion. But Becket was not one to be interrupted in the middle of a sentence. He continued his discourse for a few moments as if nothing had happened, then turned mildly to the newcomers and said:

"What do you do here?"

The knights broke into violent accusations. They accused the Archbishop of flouting the authority of the Crown, of taking unto himself the sovereignty that belonged to the King alone. They demanded that he bend to the King's will.

If Thomas à Becket had been a man of holy calm he might have escaped murder. He was by nature as temperamental and irascible as the King himself, and was soon trying to out-shout his accusers.

"Were all the swords in England hanging over my head," he cried, "you could not terrify me from my obedience to God, and my lord the Pope."

The knights were unarmed. It had not been their intention to murder Becket but only to force a compromise. Screaming and being screamed at, flinging epithets and receiving them from the raging Archbishop, they forgot their milder intentions and finally rushed from the palace to receive from the hands of their retainers suits of chain mail and great two-handed swords.

Some of the monks pleaded with the Archbishop to make some small concession to satisfy the knights.

"Never!" he declared.

"It is wonderful, my lord," said one, "that you never take anyone's advice."

"I am prepared to die," said Becket.

Perhaps he already had an inkling of what his death would do not only for his reputation but for the Church. However, he had every reason to expect that the knights would stop short of murder. Who would dare risk excommunication by laying hands upon the anointed one? But since his monks were already running to seek sanctuary in the cathedral, he allowed himself to be dragged along with them, commenting bitterly: "All monks are cowards."

The peace and silence of the cathedral quieted the fears of the monks. No one would dare shed blood in this consecrated place. They were protected also by darkness, the only light coming from a few tapers burning before the shrines. Nevertheless they concealed themselves in far corners and some urged the Archbishop to hide in the crypt or in the triforium. He refused. When they wanted to bolt the cathedral doors he rebuked them.

"I will not have the Church of God made into a castle."

He mounted the steps to the choir. There he stood, conspicuous and commanding, while his monks hid in the shadows.

With a clamour that echoed through the great interior, the

knights broke into the church. The one in the lead, Fitzurse, held a sword in one hand and a carpenter's axe in the other. He cried:

"Where is Thomas à Becket, traitor to King and realm?"

"Here!" came the firm answer from a figure standing alone before the Holy Altar. "Here! No traitor, but a priest of God, and Archbishop."

This reminder of his divine office fell upon deaf ears. Fitzurse ran up the steps and placed the carpenter's axe against Becket's chest.

"You must yield to us, or you shall die."

"I am ready to die," answered Becket, "for God and the Church, but I warn you, I curse you in the name of God Almighty."

This was the twelfth century, when the curse of the Church meant eternal damnation. The knights hesitated. Two of them, hoping to lessen their sacrilege, tried to drag the Archbishop away from the altar. He was a powerful man, six feet tall, and resisted strongly, beating one knight across the face and flinging the other on the floor. Fitzurse raised his sword.

"You owe me fealty," cried Becket. "You dare not touch me."

"I owe you no fealty," shouted Fitzurse, "contrary to my fealty to the King."

The great sword fell. The agile Archbishop dodged the blow, which only knocked off his skull-cap.

The knight Tracy now struck a blow that grazed Becket's head and sank into his shoulder. The Archbishop fell. Richard le Breton struck the prostrate form so heavy a blow that it severed the skull and the sword broke on the marble floor.

The remaining knight, Hugh of Horsea, perhaps thought to escape sacrilege by keeping his sword unbloodied. But the others fiercely demanded that he play his part. So he thrust his blade into the gaping head wound, scattering the brains on the marble.

The knights now fled, and a violent thunderstorm, interpreted by the people as the wrath of God Himself, broke over their heads as they galloped away.

The monks crept out from their hiding places. Mournfully, they prepared their lord's body for burial. They removed a great variety of garments, for the Archbishop had been unusually susceptible to cold. First came off the brown mantle, then a white surplice, then a lamb's-wool coat, then a pair of woollen pelisses. All this did not surprise them, for they knew that the Archbishop was fond of fine clothes. But what was their amazement to find beneath them the coarse black robe of a Benedictine monk. That the outwardly proud and ambitious Primate of all England should thus secretly humble himself touched them deeply.

"See what a true monk he was, and we knew it not!"

They were still more astonished when they found beneath the robe a hair shirt that had inflamed all the skin with its harsh fibres. They shrank back as they saw that the shirt was full of repulsive vermin. In their day this was regarded as the final humiliation of the flesh and glorification of the spirit. One more proof of the sanctity of their lord was revealed when the shirt was removed. Across the body lay the deep marks of the scourge.

Surely this man had been two men, the one proud and imperious, the other humble and self-abasing. Overnight the first was forgotten and the second was exalted to sainthood. Morning saw monks and townspeople filling the cathedral, fighting for bits of the Benedictine robe and the hair shirt and the vermin that had lived in it, and bearing them away as precious relics, capable of performing all manner of miracles. The blood on the marble floor was wiped up, dissolved in water, and the rosy water was carried away in small vials, which when placed against an afflicted part of the body would cure any ailment. Becket was canonised and 29th December appointed as the annual Feast of Saint Thomas of Canterbury. All over the

Christian world churches dedicated to St. Thomas were established. Canterbury became the Mecca for pilgrims from all England and all Europe.

And what of Henry whose thoughtless words had been taken, so literally by his four faithful knights?

He had the grace to blame only himself. Beneath all his quarrel with the Church had been his personal love for his old friend. His grief was so terrible it was believed he would die. For days he lay in his bed in a rigid paralysis, broken now and then by a storm of weeping.

In penance he donned sackcloth and walked barefoot to Canterbury. The temporary burial place of Becket's body was in the crypt. The bleeding feet of the King left a red trail as he limped down to the tomb, where he dropped to his knees, and kissed the sarcophagus. In this position he remained while his back was scourged with five strokes of a rod by every bishop and three by every one of eighty monks. The beating was very real and he lay half-conscious on the floor of the crypt all night. In the morning he attended mass, then left for London, taking a vial of the miraculous blood-water with him.

So the pilgrims came and were still coming in Chaucer's time two centuries later, "the holly blisful martir for to seke". They kept on coming in spite of the efforts of Henry VIII to discredit the miracles of Canterbury and the scoffing of the Puritans, who are said to have derived from Canterbury the word 'cant' to describe the religious jargon of pilgrims who pretended a piety they did not possess, and the phrase 'to tell a Canterbury' meaning to tell a lie. The easy gallop of the pilgrims' horses was called the 'Canterbury gallop', later contracted to canter. And the swarms of pilgrims who still come by car and bus pass through fields of charming wild flowers which, because they are thought to resemble the bells which the earlier pilgrims tied to the bridles of their horses, now appear in seed catalogues under the name of 'Canterbury bells'.

CHAPTER 22

The Disappearing Bolster

Pilgrims had packed the hotels of Canterbury. Mary vaguely remembered reading in *Here's England* that the writers of that book, finding no room in Canterbury, went on a few miles to a small village where they stopped for the night and were charmed. Mary picked out the village on the map. "This must be it." So we went on too.

We were not greatly charmed. The village was pleasing but undistinguished and the only accommodation was in the pub, which could provide a room but no dinner.

However, the country round about was beautiful, rolling, wooded, the groves interspersed with hop fields, and the river Stour meandering near-by. Sitting on a log beside it, we had dinner consisting of two bananas, two ice-cream bars and a bottle of milk luckily obtained at the tiny grocery just before it closed for the night.

In the room over the pub we lived the complicated simple life. It must be obvious to anyone who has tried it how complicated the simple life can be. Having no running water, hot or cold, in the room, nor any standing water, the room being quite innocent of pitcher and bowl, and without even the old-fashioned receptacle under the bed, it was necessary to make excursions through a creaky hall and a large sitting-room to a bathroom that might or might not be occupied and where hot water could be had only by lighting the water-heater and waiting.

"I'm surprised," I said, "that the book recommended this hotel."

"Well," Mary pondered, "perhaps this wasn't the hotel."

"But there's only one hotel here."

"Well, perhaps this wasn't the village."

Suppressing a few appropriate curses, I opened the bed and got in. It sagged like a hammock. It sagged so utterly and abjectly that my nether end bumped the floor. I got out again. We considered this new problem.

"Perhaps," I said, "we can move into another room."

"No, she said this was the only one."

"Perhaps we can sit up all night," I suggested bitterly.

Then Mary redeemed herself with a brilliant idea. Under the pillows was an enormous bolster five feet long and nearly a foot thick. She removed it and placed it across the middle of the bed. We tried it.

The effect was not quite satisfactory. With a deep valley on either side of it, the bolster bulged up like a ski jump. One would have to be S-shaped to be comfortable on it.

We got out and tried again, this time laying the bolster down the middle of the bed from head to foot. It was better that way. At least, we each had our own exclusive valley. And we did not quite touch the floor. But the central mountain range limited us severely, crowding us out towards the edge. We felt wedged as if we had been buried in coffins too narrow for us.

We got out and stood gazing at the sway-backed bed.

"How would it be," I wondered, "if we put the bolster *under* the mattress?"

It didn't seem a very reasonable suggestion, but we tried it. Miraculously, it worked. The bolster, instead of twisting the mattress up in a bulge as might have been expected, sank into the depths of the springs, leaving an almost level bed. You would never know it was there.

All this had been done by the light from the street, there being a socket in the room but no bulb. Now it was necessary to shut out the light. The curtains proved too narrow to cover the window, so we covered it with towels and shirts. The window would not open. We lived on the oxygen we had brought with us.

However, the pub redeemed itself in the morning with the best breakfast we had had since landing in England—grapefruit adorned with a cherry, two fried eggs with unscorched bottoms, three large slices of crisp, tangy bacon, marmalade, a huge plate of buttered bread, hot toast as well, and a generous pot of tea. And the modest bill made us like everything even better— twenty-five shillings for bed and breakfast for two.

We had gone many miles before it occurred to us that we had not restored the bolster to its proper place. What would the landlady think when she came to make up the bed? The familiar monster wouldn't be under the pillows where it belonged.

She would look on the floor between the bed and the wall. She would look under the bed. She would look in the wardrobe. She would look in the corner behind the wardrobe.

With her temperature rising, she would stand in the middle of the room and wonder. She would look again under the pillows. It *must* be there. But it isn't. Then she would take all the covers off the bed and shake them out. She would stare unbelievingly at the mattress. It would hardly occur to her to look under it. No one, just no one, would put a bolster under a mattress. She would look around the room again, out in the hall, in the sitting-room, in the bathroom, then she would call up her neighbours.

"How they ever got it down the stairs and out of the house without my seeing it I can't imagine. What a thing to steal! Americans! You never *can* tell about them, *can* you?"

Ten years from now if and when a bomb blows up the little pub the bolster will come to light. But it will be too late. Door-to-door gossip will have done its work and it will long since have become common knowledge throughout every shire and hamlet of England that Americans steal bolsters.

·   ·   ·   ·   ·

It should be said in extenuation that the business of a pub is to supply liquid refreshment, not lodgings. Few pubs offer overnight accommodation, and only as a service to the stranded traveller, therefore he must accept what he gets and be thankful. He would do better to go on to the nearest inn.

However, this is not quite so simple as it sounds, for it is often hard to tell whether a holstelry is a pub or a full-fledged hotel. Pubs never call themselves pubs, and often do call themselves hotels, though they may provide no lodgings and no meals. There is one subtle test that is usually reliable. If the main entrance leads directly into the taproom, it is probably a pub only. If the main entrance is into a lobby and a registration desk, it is a hotel, even though nine-tenths of its revenue may come in across the bar.

So far as I know, there is no clear distinction between an inn and a hotel. An inn is a hotel, and a hotel is an inn, with perhaps slight nuances in age and atmosphere.

An old-fashioned hotel or one that pretends to be old-fashioned may call itself an inn. A modern place or one that wishes to be considered modern may prefer to be known as a hotel.

Many a place is non-committal, its sign reading merely The White Horse or The Green Kettle, and you are left to find out by trial and error whether it is a pub, an inn, a hotel, a bed-and-breakfast house or a tea-room.

Some go even a step further into anonymity, their sign devoid of any name whatever but merely presenting a picture of a white horse, or a fox, or a crown, or a certain king or queen, and you have the mental exercise of guessing the name from the picture. This is not always easy. If the sign depicts a rabbit being chased by a dog, should the place be referred to as The Rabbit, The Doghouse, or The Hare and Hound?

CHAPTER 23

Discovering Bodiam Castle

Secondary roads are of primary importance to the visitor who wants to get close to England. We took a winding road through soft Kentish hills and super-green meadows and gentle copses and shut-away villages to the Channel coast. Once we came out on the busy coastal highway, the charm faded.

The beach towns are week-end extensions of London, crowded and noisy, serving a utilitarian purpose in getting tired office workers out into the air and the sea. They are metropolitan and cosmopolitan, not distinctively English. The traditional England is hidden in the hills.

We stopped in Hythe to see what may be the world's largest collection of human skulls. Two thousand skulls and eight thousand thigh bones are stacked in the crypt of St. Leonard's Church. They are the remains of people who lived between A.D. 1200 and 1400. Evidently the bones had been removed from the churchyard after a century or two to make room for newcomers. The practice of removing bones from the cemeteries to a church vault was common in medieval times, and is still followed in some parts of the Continent.

Experts who have examined the bones make interesting comparisons between the people of that day and of this. The medieval Englishman had excellent teeth. In the teeth of the two thousand skulls of Hythe there is hardly a sign of decay. They had plenty of exercise, for foods were coarse and hard, but exercise is good for teeth. The molars were much worn by the grinding of whole-meal bread and gnawing of bones.

Refined foods were the monopoly of the rich in those days and the relatively poor people buried here were fortunately unable to afford foods bad for the teeth and general health.

In spite of more natural foods, the life-span was shorter than now, through lack of sanitation and skilled medical attention. The great majority died before sixty. This was true throughout England. No king lived to be seventy until George II.

Not only do men grow older today but they grow taller. Calculating the height of the Hythe people by measuring the thigh bones, which are usually one-quarter the length of the figure, the men were five feet five and a half inches tall, the women five feet one inch. Today the average height is three inches taller for each sex. The same story is told by medieval armour in the museums of Britain and the Continent. It was made for short men.

In the process of evolution, physical development takes place more rapidly than mental development. Therefore it is not surprising that the English, who have improved so substantially in height, health and life expectancy, are little, if any, wiser than their predecessors. The skulls of Hythe show exactly the same brain capacity as that of the average Englishman today.

Some of the local people maintain that each of the two thousand skulls of Hythe has its attendant ghost and these may be seen any midnight walking in solemn procession around the church. During off hours they roam the countryside.

One was believed to haunt an old house called Cheriton Grange. The owners of the house saw a middle-aged woman wearing a black cap, who appeared most frequently in the kitchen, and when spoken to promptly vanished.

During the First World War some Canadian soldiers were billeted in the house. Before they turned in, the owners warned them that they might see the ghostly visitor. They did see her, or thought they did, and refused to spend another night in the house. They were quite ready to face death on the battlefield but were terrified by an evidently quite harmless little lady in a black cap. The one danger was real, the other imaginary, and the imaginary is always more frightening than the real.

Canadians are not accustomed to ghosts, but the English, or at least some of the English, have been able to get on familiar terms with them. Once convinced that the ghost means no harm, the hearty householder refuses to be scared out by it.

Even spirits regarded as evil may be allowed the run of the house, provided they leave the living alone. The Rev. Samuel Wesley, his wife Emily and their son John, destined to be the founder of Methodism, shared their house contentedly with the 'Woodstock Devil'. They objected mildly to the noise it made, gobbling like a turkey, stumbling over shoes, rattling door latches, turning a handmill, walking heavily up and down stairs, rocking an invisible cradle, and irreverently knocking about the room during family prayers for King George.

Mr. Wesley's friends advised him to leave the house, but he refused, saying that even Satan himself could not make him fly.

The ghost did not assault the family, beyond giving them a push now and then. Mr. Wesley recorded in his diary how he was "thrice pushed by an invisible power, once against a corner of my desk in the study, the second time against the door of the matted chamber, a third time against the right side of the frame of my study door as I was going in". John Wesley in later years wrote of it:

"Before it came into any room, the latches were frequently lifted up, the windows clattered and whatever iron and brass was about the chamber rung and jarred exceedingly. When it was in any room, let us make what noise we would, as we sometimes did, its dead hollow note would be clearly heard above us all. The sound very often seemed in the air in the middle of the room, nor could we ever make any such ourselves, by any contrivance."

John Wesley grew up with a firm belief in spirits, magic and witchcraft. Though a wise and gentle man, he countenanced the burning of supposed witches as being in accordance with the biblical injunction that no witch should be suffered to live. He declared that to give up belief in witchcraft would be to give up belief in the Bible. Ghosts he believed in just as thoroughly, but the harmless ones he could tolerate with equanimity and even amusement. As a boy he used to chase the Woodstock Devil from room to room until the poor thing would hide in the rafters to get away from him.

The same light-hearted attitude towards poltergeists was held by two maiden ladies who lived in a house in Enfield Chase. A gentleman whom they invited to dinner was conscious of hard breathing, a sort of shuddering, that followed him about the house and when he sat down to table was "so near that, if there was an entity connected with it, we were two on one chair". He finally felt compelled to speak of it.

"Oh, don't mind him," said one of his hostesses. "He has asthma. He's been with us for years. He never bothers us. In fact it's rather comforting to know there's a man about the house."

Of course malicious ghosts are not regarded in so friendly a fashion, and every ghost is suspected of being malicious until it proves otherwise. The attitude towards all ghosts that have not been properly introduced is one of suspicion and uneasiness, which are dispelled only by a long period of acquaintanceship and good behaviour.

"The most painted town in England" is said to be Rye. Artists love its perched-up look on a high crag above salt marshes, its cobbled streets, its leaning houses, its church clock bearing the inscription "For our time is a very shadow that passeth away". Tourists love its quaint tea-rooms and its sixteenth-century inns and its age-old peace.

Its charm captivates even those who do not quite understand what they see. Two ladies stood looking at Lamb House, once the home of Henry James.

Above: Bodiam was the last military castle to be erected in England, and profited by all the lessons learned in the castle building of previous centuries. For more than two hundred years Bodiam repelled all assailants

Below: A swan of Avon admires the Shakespeare Memorial Theatre

Said one: "I believe Charles Lamb lived here."

"Oh no, dear," said the other, "I think it has something to do with King James."

When Henry James lived there the pleasant early Georgian brick building was hidden on the garden side by a luxuriant wistaria.

"That vine," William Oliver Stevens writes, "typified his style, wandering along the sides of the house like one of his sentences, long, involved, heavy, hung with modifying clauses and phrases, corresponding to the pendant blossoms."

Henry James, American-born, lived in England for nearly half a century. He was so moved by England's struggle with Germany in 1915 that he felt compelled to become a British citizen and expressed his feelings in a private letter:

"This grand old country has found herself again, found her soul and her special store of energy, thereby really renewing her genius and her sincerity. The nation is taking it all and doing it, facing it and meeting it, worthily and splendidly. At this hour she is in a perfectly magnificent moral position, the proudest, to my mind, of her history."

A few steps away an attractive tea-shop occupies the home of Fletcher of the famous literary partnership, Beaumont and Fletcher. The place is interesting not so much because of its association with Fletcher, one of the dullest of dramatists, but because it still contains many of the things people lived with in the sixteenth century.

Everyone who visits Rye can tell you of this Fletcher, but there was another Fletcher who lived in Rye, probably a kinsman, who is not mentioned in any guide-book. This Fletcher invented the fore-and-aft rig. While the dramatist's works gather dust on the shelves, the fore-and-aft rig is seen wherever men sail. The historian Froude pays this tribute to Fletcher the sailor:

"Mr. Fletcher of Rye (be his name remembered) invented a boat the like of which was never seen before, which would work to windward, with sails trimmed fore and aft, the greatest revolution yet made in shipbuilding."

Rye was once a busy seaport and most of its men were sailors. Then the sea began to retreat and now lies a mile off, leaving Rye and its twin town of Winchelsea marooned high and dry on rocky heights with no business but the business of keeping themselves quaint for admiring travellers.

Hops are the most picturesque crop grown in Britain and they are most at home in the county of Kent.

A hop field is a forest of poles about fifteen feet high supporting a criss-cross of wires from which depend the strings climbed by the young vines. The rate of climb may be as much as half a foot a day. When the hops are ripe, the light green tassels hang in festoons against a background of dark leaves.

When the hops are picked they go to the oast-house, most curious of buildings, with a fire in its belly and a chimney like a grandmother's bonnet. Here the hops are dried in great kilns. Then they go to the brewery to be combined with malt for the making of beer.

Of course tea is the national drink of England; but, in the alcoholic category, the laurels go to beer. Yet it is not historically an English drink. The old drink of England was ale. Today ale and beer are two words for the same thing, but in the old times ale was a thick, sweet drink made from malt.

Beer was a European drink made from malt and hops. It invaded England from Holland, but the English at first regarded it as heretical and pernicious. A fifteenth-century critic wrote: "It doth make a man fat and doth inflate the belly, as it doth appear by the Dutche mens faces and belyes."

Some towns prohibited the growing of the "wicked and pernicious weed—hops" and forbade the sale of "the poison called beer".

But the common folk liked the 'poison' and the brewers and taverns were both for it in view of the fact that it did not quickly go sour as ale did. But since the English do not part easily with old memories, the word ale has been kept even though the drink itself has not been generally obtainable for the past three centuries.

Bodiam Castle! This, to my mind, was the most thrilling sight in these parts.

It was hard to understand how I could have missed it on all previous visits to England and residence of two years in the country. It is only some fifty miles from London. And yet it is relatively unknown. It is not on a main highway and does not even appear on our detailed road map. Even the winding lane that approaches it does not come close and you leave your car to walk a quarter-mile through lush pasture where sheep and cattle graze and the little River Rother flows swiftly towards the sea.

Before you rises a dream castle of noble towers and battlements surrounded by a moat so wide that it could more accurately be called a lake. Upon the sleepy water great green water-lily leaves and gorgeous yellow flowers stretch themselves luxuriously and the castle towers are repeated in the still mirror. White swans sail in the open reaches and kingfishers and dabchicks haunt the banks beneath the big drooping trees.

To reach the islanded castle we go around the lake to the north side and then follow a causeway across the water to the castle gate. This causeway in its original form did not lead straight to the gate but was cunningly angled so that invaders crossing it would expose their right sides to fire from the castle. The right flank of an armoured knight was more vulnerable than the left, since the shield was carried on the left arm.

To make things more difficult for intruders, the causeway was interrupted no less than three times by drawbridges. Arriving at the gate, the attacker would find the entrance blocked by a spiked portcullis. Even if the assaulting troops were able to raid this portcullis or break through it they would not be much better off, for they would encounter a second portcullis stronger than the first, and behind it lay still a third.

Meanwhile boiling oil or pitch or powdered quicklime or all three would be pouring down upon the heads of the assailants from 'murder holes' in the vault above.

All this was designed to give a hot reception to the French who were in the habit of sailing up the Rother, then much bigger than now, to burn and plunder English villages. It was just after Rye had been attacked and burnt by the French that the castle was built in 1386. It was the last military castle to be erected in England and profited by all the lessons learned in the castle-building of previous centuries. It had one feature not found in the older castles, gunloops, circular openings in the gatehouse wall for cannon. Still mounted here is a replica of a bombard, or fifteenth-century siege gun, which had a bore of fifteen inches and would throw a stone shot weighing one hundred and fifty pounds.

For more than two centuries Bodiam laughed at all assailants. The French never conquered it. That remained for the English themselves to do. In 1643 Bodiam surrendered to the Roundheads and Cromwell's soldiers demolished the interior and sold the contents.

And so the castle, as proud and perfect as ever on the outside, is a picturesque ruin within. Still you may distinguish the rooms, the Lord's Hall, the Great Chamber, the bower or ladies' apartment, the chapel, the Retainers' Hall, the buttery, the pantry, the kitchen, the pigeon-house, which accommodated three hundred pigeon families, the stable, the privies, the dungeon.

"To say that Bodiam is one of the most beautiful medieval castles in England," one visitor writes, "is to state the case conservatively. It lies so far off the route of travel that few Americans know it, and yet here, if anywhere, stands the perfect example of a fortress of the day of Edward III, the One Hundred Years' War, and the height of chivalry in England."

Afternoon shadows were lengthening as we climbed to the top of the south-east tower and looked out across the dreaming moat, the green pasture that may once have been the jousting field, the stream winding away towards Rye and Winchelsea on their high perches, and the Channel, highway for French marauders until they were checked once and for all by Bodiam. Feeling somehow that the old castle and all its memories had become our own, we read in a pamphlet picked up along the way Lord Thurlow's verses, *On Beholding Bodiam Castle*:

Oh thou, brave ruin of the passéd time,
    When glorious spirits shone in burning arms,
    And the brave trumpet, with its sweet alarms
Call'd honour! at the matin hour sublime,
And the grey evening. . . .
    The owl now haunts thee, and oblivion's plant,
    The creeping ivy, has o'erveiled thy towers;
    And Rother, looking up with eye askant,
Recalling to his mind thy brighter hours,
    Laments the time when, fair and elegant,
Beauty first laughed from out thy joyous bowers!

We had passed out of Kent into Sussex, and now went on through enchanting country to Battle, where was fought the memorable battle of Hastings. Before the conflict William the Conqueror vowed that if he were vouchsafed divine help he would reward the Deity with a splendid abbey. Evidently this was considered a good bargain in the courts of Heaven, for William won the battle and forthwith erected Battle Abbey on the spot. It is now a school.

Two castles in a day was rich fare. In the afterglow of the long English twilight great Herstmonceux Castle looked even larger than it is, and repeated itself in its reflection on the moat. It doesn't seem quite like a castle, for it is in red brick rather than stone, and it really is not a castle in the sense of a military fortress, for it was built not as a stronghold but as a private home.

Since the air here is free of industrial smog, the great mansion was taken over in 1948 as the headquarters of the Royal Greenwich Observatory transferred from Greenwich on the now smoky Thames.

Where to spend the night? We had heard good things said of a retreat called Smugglers' Farm, in the village of Boreham Street near Herstmonceux. We searched it out and found it a three-hundred-year-old farm-house, home of sparkling Miss Peggy Wilson and her lively little eighty-one-year-old mother. They employ a man to look after the small farm, which consists chiefly of a thriving and extensive vegetable garden and fruit orchards.

The moment we entered the low-beamed house we breathed mystery. I asked about the name, Smugglers' Farm. Did it have any historical significance?

"Indeed, yes," said Miss Peggy. "Three centuries ago much of the contraband from France was smuggled into England through this house. The place belonged to Lord Ashburnham and with him in the smuggling scheme were the local bailiff and the parson. The bailiff lived just across the street. The profits of the nefarious business were shared equally by the three."

She opened a small door in a corner alcove, revealing an ancient winch and a fresh piece of stonework where an opening had evidently been walled up.

"This was the entrance to the tunnel that led from the house a half-mile to the creek. The goods would be brought at night from French ports across the Channel and up the creek, then carried through the secret passage to this spot. Then the boxes and bales and kegs of French brandy were hauled up into the house by means of this winch."

"How did you discover the secret passage?"

"By falling into it. Men were levelling the ground in the garden to make a croquet lawn. Suddenly their picks and shovels dropped out of sight and one of the men tumbled in after them. Strange gases rose from the hole. The other men got a ladder and went down into the tunnel with electric torches. They found it open from end to end and in good condition though it probably had not been used for at least two hundred years. Bits of jewellery and Spanish and French coins were picked up."

"Is the passage still open?"

"The lower part near the creek, yes, but the part under the garden we had filled up because of the danger of cave-ins of the ground above."

There is something highly conducive to comfort in snug low beams, polished mahogany, panelled walls, giant fireplace, ancient brass, old swords and pikes, chestnut-roasters and bellows, and a great four-poster bed. We slept well, waking now and then to enjoy the exciting fancy that we could hear the creak of the old winch, the whispers of smugglers, and perhaps even the trickle of French brandy into pewter tankards as the lord, the bailiff and the parson paused in their labours for refreshment.

CHAPTER 24

Green and Pleasant Land

On through the loveliest country imaginable, always rolling, no place level enough to set a plate of soup, dotted with red-roofed villages, brilliant with buttercups, Queen Anne's lace, opulent rhododendrons, breathless cascades of Scotch laburnum, chestnuts white and horse chestnuts red, flowering fruit trees of every sort. H. G. Wells did not exaggerate:

"There is no countryside like the English countryside for those who have learned to love it: its firm yet gentle lines of hill and dale, its ordered confusion of features, its deer parks and downlands, its castles and stately houses, its hamlets and old churches, its farms and ricks and great barns and ancient trees, its pools and ponds and shining threads of rivers, its flower-starred hedgerows, its orchards and woodland patches, its village greens and kindly inns. Other countrysides have their pleasant aspects, but none such variety, none that shines so steadfastly throughout the year."

Variety and steadfastness: they would seem to be contradictory, but are not. The variety of scene is kaleidoscopic. No two stretches of road alike, no two hills alike, no two villages alike. Each change gives new pleasure, a new wine on the tongue. But there is steadfastness, the feeling of permanence, of a long past and a long future. Subtle variations through spring, summer, autumn, winter, and yet steadfastness throughout the year, the grass as green in winter as in summer, perhaps a bit greener.

Great care is taken to preserve the beauty of the countryside.

The rural scene is free of billboards (hoardings). Your view of hill and wood and river is not interrupted by pills and soaps and cough medicines. We were to find this blessedly true throughout England, Wales and Scotland.

The American road is too often lined with these shrines for the worship of the god of gadgets, and to do away with them at the behest of some rural beautification committee is regarded by Business as no less than sacrilege. An advertising agent from Chicago would be pained by British failure to use a charming landscape to frame advertisements for whiskies and beef cubes. These lost opportunities expose the backwardness and lack of imagination of British businessmen. They have no idea how much goods a flowery hillside can sell if tastefully draped around a lithograph. As for a river with a church tower and a castle in the distance, what prestige and selling power it would lend to a new back plaster! After all, if the country can't be made to pay off, what use is it?

Rural billboards are disappearing in America. Nature-loving citizens who are slowly accomplishing the change in spite of being ridiculed as unpractical dreamers would feel less ridiculous if they could come to Britain and see how practical and successful a lovingly preserved landscape can be.

A barbed wire fence is quite rare. Flowering hedges border the road and divide one field from another. These hedges are possibly the one most attractive feature of British farmland. They astonish and delight most American visitors, disappoint a few. The reaction of one of the disappointed is told in Professor Dobie's *A Texan in England*:

"An American agriculturist visiting in England recently advised against hedges as taking up too much soil space; barbed wire fences would take up less space and serve just as well to separate fields. He seemed to overlook the material fact that hedges afford protection for animals and for tender plants against harsh winds. He took into no account how hedges shelter and feed the wonderful bird life of England and how the more birds there are in the hedges, the fewer bugs in the garden. He left out the country's deep-seated and for centuries established appreciation of the charm, the graciousness and the loveliness that hedges give the landscape."

That was written by a Texan and Texas has barbed wire, not hedges. It really takes an American to appreciate England. The English don't appreciate it. They spend much of their time trying to think of ways to get away from it. If it were made easily possible, nearly half the population would move out tomorrow. A Gallup poll made in 1957 asked:

"If you were free to do so, would you like to go and settle in another country?"

Forty-one per cent of the Britons polled answered yes, and another twelve per cent said they were not sure.

The reasons, of course, are economic, and have nothing to do with the beauty or lack of beauty of Britain. The visitor, however, is not inconvenienced by Britain's economic problems and is prepared to appreciate to the full one of the sweetest and fairest lands on the planet. The Briton properly appreciates his country only after he has left it. In the scorch of India, the miasma of Malaya, the fever belts of Africa, the chill plains of north-west Canada, the tumult of American cities, his mind goes ever back to the green and pleasant land.

We think of England as crowded. Population statistics prove that it is crowded. But there is no sense of crowding here in the southern counties within fifty or so miles of the greatest city in the world. The fields and woods roll in great green billows with only an occasional red roof to give a pleasing accent. It is surprising how much forest there is. It is usually a tamed forest, more like a park, clean of underbrush and protected from fires, so that the trees have grown old and great.

The roads are a surprise. We had expected them to be good, but not perfect. The surfacing leaves nothing whatever to be desired. There are no pits, ridges or washboards. The secondary roads are delightfully free of traffic. They are all paved; we haven't found a dirt road yet. Of course the roads, especially the secondary ones, are narrow and winding and fifty miles is a good day's travel. We go less than that, since we stop so often to see and photograph.

Impish names give flavour and character to the villages. We note on the map profane-sounding Godalming, Christmas Pie, Normandy, Friday Street, Pennypot, Chobham, Tillingbourne Valley and many others equally unstereotyped.

We visited another water-girdled ruin, moated Pevensey Castle, harking back to the Roman emperors and already ancient when William the Conqueror stepped ashore. Then we drifted north through Tunbridge Wells, lush as a botanical garden, through shaded Penshurst and quaint Chiddingstone, one of the most picturesque villages in Kent, and lodged in Tonbridge at the Rose and Crown. It was a Trust House and quite good as had been all other Trust Houses we had visited.

So that you may not be as confused as we had been, it might be well to point out the distinction between Trust House and National Trust. The Trust Houses are not, as the traveller might suppose, maintained by the National Trust. They are simply hotels that have been taken over by a purely commercial and profit-making corporation, Trust Houses Ltd. Trust Houses may be found all over England. An effort is made to run them with uniform efficiency, but there are slight differences. In all, the rates are reasonable, the accommodation clean, the food good though never excellent. If one comes upon a town blind, with no knowledge of the hotels, one will not go far wrong in choosing a Trust House.

The National Trust, on the other hand, is a non-profit organisation devoted to the preservation of natural beauties and historic places. It sounds as if it might be, or should be, a governmental agency. On the contrary, it gets nothing from the Government except a kindly smile now and then.

It is entirely supported by dues, gifts and bequests from its members, of whom there are about sixty thousand. More than half a century old, it has now acquired more than a thousand properties which it holds for the enjoyment of the public. It owns many fine gardens, thirty thousand acres of woodland, great stretches of parkland adjacent to lakes and rivers, altogether about 300,000 acres, making it the largest landowner in the United Kingdom other than the State itself.

Scores of the stately homes of old England now belong to the National Trust, wholly or partly; partly, in case the original family still lives in the house which is, however, thrown open at stated times to visitors.

CHAPTER 25

Speaking of Stately Homes

One of the great privileges of the stranger in Britain is that of visiting the fabulous mansions of a vanishing aristocracy. In these splendid houses, filled with treasures from all the world, he gets some idea of the grace and beauty of a bygone age.

Less often he gets another impression—an impression that there is something to be said for the present age when unbridled extravagance is checked by taxes which distribute for the good of many the excess wealth which used to be the ruin of a few.

How tasteless, graceless and uncomfortable a home can be if one has enough money to make it so is illustrated in Knole, the palace of the Sackvilles, which we visited the following day.

The best part of it is the great and beautiful park that surrounds it. The building itself, though immense, does not tempt one to unsling a camera.

Inside the house there is an occasional thing of beauty. One of the young blades of the house brought back with him from Italy a sinuous Italian dancer, and her sculptured body, nude and recumbent, commends his good judgment. There are two fine canvases by Titian and a number of masterpieces by Sir Joshua Reynolds.

For the most part the countless rooms are floridly extravagant, over-decorated, ludicrously lavish, and must make a strong appeal to those who are awed by monumental waste.

One bed alone with canopy and spread embroidered with gold and silver thread is said by British Museum experts to have cost the equivalent of $100,000. Whether such threads have held the fabrics together any more firmly than plain cotton, or whether they made the occupant sleep better, may be doubted.

Tables encased in solid silver that tarnishes, with raised designs that catch the dust, look tawdry beside their poor cousins in polished oak.

Room after room is hung with oil portraits of members of the family, reflecting a sense of self-importance that must jar upon visitors who would consider it poor taste to cover the walls of their own homes with self-portraits.

Knole was born in arrogance. The ecclesiastic who built it aimed to impress the King with his own wealth and importance. Hence the thousand acres of park and the vast 'calendar house' containing 365 rooms, fifty-two staircases, twelve courtyards and seven great entrance doors. During the lush years, 126 people sat down to meals in the house every day.

The vastness of the house means that the average room can have windows on one side only. Some rooms are long and narrow with light only at one end, comparing unfavourably with the main room of a humble cottage which can be so designed that it may be windowed on three sides if not on four.

The result in the case of Knole is insupportable gloom. Even at noon, the sun shining brilliantly outside, ghostly twilight pervades all rooms.

It's a place to breed neurasthenics. Loneliness evidently went with the gloom, for each member of the household had his own apartments, separated by long echoing corridors from those of any other human.

"It is hardly possible," writes Morton, "that the whole of Knole could ever have been inhabited at one time. There must always have been large uninhabited areas. Even Jacobean Sackvilles must have said to their wives: 'We must make up our minds to go over and live in the east wing next year.'"

Victoria Sackville-West in her illuminating book, *Knole and the Sackvilles*, admits that "after a lifetime of familiarity, I still catch myself pausing to think of the shortest route from one room to another".

The isolated humans, separated from others by empty rooms and hollow halls, made pitiful attempts to allay their loneliness. We noticed in some of the bedrooms and sitting-rooms life-size cut-out figures of men and women. They seemed to have been made of thin board and were propped so that they stood upright. We asked the guide about them.

"Oh," he said, "those are dummy boards."

"What was their purpose?"

"Companionship. They were called the silent companions. If the person living in this room got lonesome he could always talk to his silent companion."

Some of the figures were of courtly ladies, some of fashionable gentlemen, and in one case of a humble but pleasant serving woman peeling a potato.

What a blessing to the owners that deflated income and inflated taxes have forced them to relinquish most of the building to the National Trust, reserving only one small part as their own living quarters. Here they live in sufficient intimacy to have no need of 'silent companions', and the burden of the monstrous mausoleum has been transferred to public shoulders.

The present Lord Sackville cannot be blamed for Knole, and his ancestors were responsible only to a degree. They did not ask for Knole—it was wished upon them by Queen Elizabeth I. She gave it to her cousin, Thomas Sackville. Nor was she to blame for it. She had it from her father, Henry VIII, who had magnificently stolen it.

Knole had been begun by a too-wealthy archbishop in the fifteenth century, was enlarged and embellished by later Arch-bishops of Canterbury, and was involuntarily resigned by Archbishop Cranmer to the King in the general reduction of clerical wealth and arrogance carried out by that strong-minded monarch.

The park is lovely. There are hundreds of tame deer quite evidently very happy and contented. They don't have to live in the house.

A big house can be beautiful. Going on a few miles we came to Clandon Park, mansion of the Onslows, who have given three Speakers to the House of Commons.

Clandon Park is as bright and liveable-in as Knole is depressing. Six years ago it was surrendered to the National Trust. The rooms are finely lighted and tastefully decorated—in fact any interior decorator who serves great houses could look through this one with profit.

The gardens too are a masterpiece, the work of the great landscape architect, Capability Brown. He tried to keep himself and his skill out of the picture, and achieved his effects so artfully that it looks as if Nature had done it all by herself.

The place gives one the impression of having been honestly earned, thoroughly enjoyed, and given up with regret.

The tallest man on earth is also a property of the National Trust. Standing two hundred and thirty feet high, the Long Man of Wilmington walks across the Sussex Downs with a staff in each hand.

His outline stands out in white against the green hillside. It was made by cutting away the turf surface to expose the white chalk underneath. It is the largest representation of a human figure in the world, twice the height of the Statue of Liberty measured from head to toe.

The best guess as to its origin seems to be that it was the work of the Celts some thirty-five hundred years ago and represents the god Bel or Baal, contemporary with Baal of the Bible.

Baal was the god of procreation and fertility, and there is evidence that the figure was once visibly male but was modestly emasculated by fifteenth-century monks. A similar but shorter figure, the Giant of Cerne Abbas in Dorset, has not been so mutilated. Dorset likes its giant as he is and resists all demands for surgery.

Baal did not procreate for the pleasure of it but had to be paid. It is thought that within the outline of the figure the bodies of young men were piled and burned, a holy sacrifice to gain the good will of the god, who could then be expected to reward his worshippers with fertile fields, increase of flocks, and more sons to burn.

CHAPTER 26

The Education of Leaders

"Education is class-conscious to a high degree in Britain," said George Seaton. He should know, since he is one of the masters in a distinguished and historic public school, Wellington College.

We had been spending two days with George and his wife in their pleasant cottage overlooking the fabulous park that serves this school as a campus. Imagine the pride and joy of an American high school student if his schoolyard, instead of being limited to one or two acres as is usually the case, comprised six hundred acres of hill and dale, lawn and rough, streams and lakes, playing fields for every sport, and miles of winding trails through virgin forests!

The school had an interesting beginning. When the Duke of Wellington died, a public subscription was taken to provide a suitable memorial. It was proposed that a statue of the Duke be erected in every market town in England. Then someone thought to ask the opinion of Queen Victoria's husband and consort, the wise Prince Albert.

He advised that a more practical memorial would be a school in which the principles of the Iron Duke would be passed on to new generations. So, Wellington College.

The school has an enrolment of some 670 remarkably spruce-looking youngsters ranging from thirteen to eighteen years of age. Though not a military school, it was begun as a school for soldiers' sons, and even today nearly half of the boys go into the Army, most of the rest to the universities.

But not just any universities. Parents are deeply mortified if their sons are refused at Oxford or Cambridge. It takes a far smarter than average boy and a lucky one to be accepted by either. And if he fails to pass he is inclined to dismiss the idea of a university education altogether rather than go to a university with less prestige.

"Isn't it the same in your country?" asked George. "You have your Yale and Harvard."

"Yes, but we also have our Princeton, Columbia, Cornell, Chicago, Michigan, Stanford, California and several dozen more of the same rank. Yale and Harvard may have a slight edge because of their history, but scholarship is just as high elsewhere. To the average boy a university is a university and he's as happy, or unhappy, to be sent to one as another."

"It's not so here," George said. "Education is graded according to how much it costs. Government schools that cost little or nothing are not respected. Parents scrimp and pinch to send their boys to an expensive school and then to Oxford or Cambridge.

"But it's not as foolish as it sounds. The graduate of the great universities really has something that he couldn't get elsewhere. It may not seem important to Americans—but it means a lot in England.

"He acts differently. He talks differently. There was an amusing book published recently about what the author called the U and non-U person—that is, the upper-class person and the rest. It has had a great vogue because everybody recognises the truth behind it—that English society is sharply divided into U's and non-U's.

"It described very cleverly the terms of speech that immediately classify the speaker as belonging to the one group or the other. The U's read it because they read books, but the non-U's who seldom read books read it too—because they want to become U's.

"Of course they can't do it just by reading a book. But twenty-two years of training in the right home, a good school,

169

and Oxford or Cambridge will stamp a man so plainly that any Englishman will recognise him for what he is, a product of the best education England can offer."

Having visited Eton, Rugby, Oxford, Cambridge, London University and other institutions of higher and lower learning, we had become impressed by two things: (1) the sorry lack of education; (2) the high quality of what little there is.

In America thirty per cent of the eighteen-year-olds are enrolled in universities. In Britain the corresponding figure is five per cent.

H. G. Wells once described America as the best half-educated country on earth. His observation was amusing and apt, but rather too flattering. Instead of fifty per cent, thirty seems to be the best we can do. Still that is better than five.

However, there is quality to be considered. Too many American colleges are little more than social and athletic clubs. Education is not taken seriously. The high privilege of going to college is not appreciated. Americans don't count their blessings, they have too many of them. It is too easy to go to college. Family incomes are large, college fees are low, there is not much struggle and sacrifice involved.

In Japan a farm boy's parents and sisters will endure the bitterest toil and privation to send him to college, and if he fails in his studies he will feel the disgrace so keenly that he may commit suicide rather than come home to face his family and friends. In Germany, in Scandinavia, in Britain, going to college is a serious matter. Students really study.

Brilliant American students picked to be sent to Oxford as Rhodes Scholars find the work very difficult in spite of the fact that they are four years older than their classmates. But the English student begins college with an already well-packed head. In public school he has had to carry six major subjects. In the average American high school four or five are considered enough.

Nor are the English schools content to pack knowledge into the skull. They go after the heart and spirit as well. This is particularly true of upper-class education.

For there are two fairly distinct educational systems in England, one for the rich, one for the rest. Children of the rich go to a private preparatory school where high fees are charged, then to a public school (don't be misled by the word 'public'; the so-called public school is more private, exclusive and expensive than any other), then, if they can pass the entrance examinations, to Oxford or Cambridge.

The rest attend free or largely free State schools until the compulsory age limit of fifteen years, when most of them drop out. Those who continue may go to one of the civic universities. Chief of these is London University, which has a larger enrolment than Oxford and Cambridge put together.

Religion is the privilege of the rich. Religious instruction is available in State schools, but is the very core of the matter in independent schools, many of which operate under Church auspices. Every college of Oxford and Cambridge has its chapel. The moulding of character and toughening of moral fibre is considered to be the school's most important job.

The toughening process begins with the body. English schools have not forgotten their ascetic past, when education was in the hands of the monks. Comfort is a snare of Satan and to be avoided at all costs. In many a reading-room the windows are high and small and the boys study in eye-taxing gloom. They wash in cold bathrooms and sleep in cold dormitories. The stone floors are conducive to chilblains and there is so much coughing and sneezing in the classroom that it may be difficult to hear the teacher. A graduate of a young ladies' boarding-school says she was almost never without a heavy cold during the school term. In one school a midwinter test of hardihood is to run naked through a stone hall and jump into a pool of cold water. (However, the water is probably not as cold as the hall.)

Fagging and flogging are not what they were in *Tom Brown's Schooldays*, but they still persist in modified form. The new boy spends his first term as fag for a senior student. He must run errands and do menial chores for the older boy no matter at what inconvenience to himself or what cost to his studies. It is of no use for him to rebel, for the orders of the senior will, unless unreasonable, be backed up by the headmaster. When the senior is a tyrant, the way of the youngster is hard.

But he does learn discipline and obedience, and sometimes humility. He learns how to take orders, which is a necessary preparation for giving them. If he is lucky enough to be assigned to a wise and sympathetic senior, he benefits immensely by the arrangement.

Seniors used to be allowed to flog disobedient fags. That is not permitted today and any beating a fag gets from his young master is carefully kept off the record. But there are headmasters who still believe in the *argumentum a posteriori* administered by cane or birch.

The sportsmanship of the English is proverbial and it is largely the product of the playing field of the public school. Underdogs are favoured by educated Englishmen, partly because they themselves have been underdogs in their fag days and know how it feels. The American loves a winner, the Englishman sentimentalises a failure. Says an Englishman, C. V. R. Thompson:

"This means that almost anyone can make a career out of losing in England."

The discipline of public school develops self-control. The student meets criticism with silence and carries the same technique into later life. He is inclined to understatement. He is famous the world over for his reticence. A classic example is cited by Frank Dobie, visiting professor at Cambridge:

"In the eighteenth century two brothers of the Cavendish family, 'famous for dignity and reticence', stopped one night at an inn and were ushered into a bedroom with three four-poster beds. One of the beds had the curtains drawn around it. Before getting into his own bed, the older brother went over to the drawn curtain, held his candle up, and looked inside. He redrew the curtains and said nothing. Presently the other brother walked over also, drew the curtains, looked in, closed the curtains and said nothing. Then they blew out their candles and went to sleep. The next day on the road each remarked to the other that he had seen a corpse in the curtained bed. This is English reticence."

The monastically trained Englishman is honest even if it hurts. Of course it is a peculiar kind of honesty. He is honest when he is compelled to speak. He prefers to keep his mind to himself and let you suppose anything you please, no matter how mistaken. Classroom discipline under dogmatic and sometimes bigoted masters has taught him to disagree in silence.

"The English hardly ever lie," someone has said, "but they would not dream of telling you the truth."

The greatest blessing and the greatest curse to come out of upper-class education is superiority. The graduate of this educational mill is superior and he knows it. At best, he has acquired a high sense of responsibility. At worst, he has become an insufferable snob.

He has been trained for leadership. The destiny of the nation is in his hands. The destiny of the world will be profoundly influenced by him. The rise of America to world power is apt to make us forget that the British Commonwealth of Nations still girdles the globe and comprises a population of 640,000,000.

The chief spokesmen for this quarter of the human race will be products of the English public school and Oxford or Cambridge. No wonder they feel their responsibility. No wonder it sometimes goes to their heads.

"It does not take long for a foreigner to observe," writes William Oliver Stevens in *Forever England*, "that though England has travelled far on the road towards democracy in political life, even towards socialism, it has clung to its feudal distinctions far more than any other nation in the world."

The schools themselves are aware of their drawbacks. And one headmaster admitted:

"The public school is the chief bulwark of the caste system in England."

The problem for the future would seem to be the preservation of the merits of upper-class education and their extension to the lower classes to the end that in time every educational opportunity will be open to all without distinction based upon wealth or pedigree.

England is moving steadily along this path. She still has a long way to go.

CHAPTER 27

Do the English Speak English?

At a stationer's we picked up the book George had mentioned.

It was *Noblesse Oblige*, edited by Nancy Mitford, and its principal feature was *U and Non-U: An Essay in Sociological Linguistics* by Professor Alan Ross of Birmingham University.

George had described the book as amusing, but Professor Ross was quite evidently not amused. As a philologist, he had with admirable detachment made a sober and scientific study of the differences in speech between the U's (members of the upper class) and the non-U's (the generality who have never darkened the door of a public school or either of the two venerated universities).

It is perhaps the first critical analysis that has been made of a well-known phenomenon—that an Englishman has only to open his mouth to be classified at once as aristocrat or plebeian. He can scarcely say good morning without revealing himself. England is rent in twain by English. That is what gives such sparkle and contrast to a play like *Pygmalion*, in which the two Englands are juxtaposed.

No other European nation is so affected. In France the upper and lower classes, if there can be said to be upper and lower, speak essentially the same language. There are regional differences of course, and some speak more grammatically than others, but there is no distinction based on social standing.

A playgoer saw *Journey's End* in London. Then he went to Paris and saw the same play, this time translated into French. "I was struck by the fact that the speech of the mess-orderly or the ranker-officer was indistinguishable from that of the public school men."

The class distinction that had given the original its acid tang had been lost. All the players used the same words and the same intonation. Much of the social equality of France is due to language uniformity, and social inequality in England is maintained by language difference.

Getting down to cases, Professor Ross painstakingly parallels U and non-U usages.

The U says *témporarily*. The non-U says *temporárily*. The U says *fórmidable*; the non-U *formídable*. The U, *int'resting*; the non-U, *interésting*.

The U pronounces *either* as aye-ther; the non-U, as eether. The U rhymes *forehead* with torrid; the non-U pronounces it as spelled.

The non-U tendency to pronounce words as spelled is a source of great amusement to the U's. The non-U's actually say *medicine* and *venison* instead of *medsin* and *vensin*. They seem unaware that nice people don't say *motorist*, *secretary*, and *military*, but *mertrist*, *seccertry*, and *miltry*. They seem to have an unreasoning respect for their dictionaries, which specify that these words should be pronounced as spelled.

Sometimes the U word is distinctly simpler and better than the non-U, which is inclined to be pretentious. The non-U may say "I was ill on the boat". The U would say "I was sick". The non-U will ask "Shall we wear evening dress?" The U version will be "Do we change?"

In a hotel dining-room I asked for a napkin. The waitress did not seem to understand. I groped on the table where the napkin should be and spread an imaginary something over my lap.

"Oh," she said, "you want a *serviette*."

So *serviette* was the word. Later, entertained by friends, I asked for a serviette. My hostess smiled tolerantly and turned to the maid:

"Bring a table napkin."

Professor Ross clears up the mystery. *Serviette* is non-U. *Table napkin* is U.

The non-U has *dinner* in the middle of the day, while the U has *lunch*. The non-U eats *greens*, but the U prefers *vegetables*. The non-U ends the meal with a *sweet*, the U with a *pudding*.

In delicate matters there are delicate distinctions. Sometimes the U expression is more straightforward than the non-U. The U will call the chamber pot the *pot*. The non-U will refer to it as the *article*. However, non-U mothers in the privacy of their own home may use the expression *to pot the baby*.

If you stay long in a non-U house your host may ask you if you want to go to the *dub*, meaning the W.C. or lavatory. The U will try to show a little more finesse and will say something like, "Let me show you the geography of the house."

Incidentally there is no *toilet paper* in an upper-class home. It is *lavatory paper*. That seems rather cumbersome. Perhaps the battle will be won by certain manufacturers of this paper who call it simply *tissue*.

But entirely aside from choice of words, the U-man can be spotted by the tone and timbre of his voice. Even if he were speaking an unknown language his intonation would give him away. This manner of speech is not at all the monocled 'bah-Jove' caricature which passes in America as the speech of Englishmen. The Oxford accent (curiously enough one never speaks of the Cambridge accent though the speech there is almost identical) is characterised by a slight drawl, precise articulation and an easy and smooth flow accompanied by an unassuming, casual or offhand manner. On the tongue of the cultivated Englishman, English is a delight to hear. Says an American writer:

"It is pleasant to listen to the modulated, low voice, the broad a's, the full value of the consonants. No wonder the American woman's all-too-frequent nasal whine and flat vowels give English people the shudders."

In defence of Americans it must be said that the speech of cultivated Americans (if the English will admit that there are any) does not differ so much from that of the U-Englishman as the latter's speech does from that of the English non-U. The American visitor in London attending church or a play has no difficulty whatever in understanding cultivated English speech but is completely baffled by the H-eliding Cockney or the dialect of Yorkshire, Lancashire or Cornwall.

An American clergyman occupying a London pulpit is perfectly understood, though the tone of his voice may be slightly trying, causing one old lady to protest:

"I was shocked to hear the Lord's Prayer in American. It seemed almost like sacrilege."

Some English folk not born and bred to the Oxford accent go to great pains to put it on. The result is the unbearably affected caricature which amuses both Americans and English U's. This bogus substitute is apt to be aggressive. The speaker is trying to impress you with his culture and therefore inevitably loses the unassuming manner of the genuine U. This fraudulent speech has been called Morris-Oxford (after the manufacturer of cheap cars who has invaded the city of learning). In its worst form it is described as "blah-blah". It creeps into American films and provides as much fun for English as for American audiences.

On the whole, there are probably more snobs among the non-U's than among the U's. The U's do not need to put on airs. What they are speaks for them. The non-U's are under the constant strain inevitable in a class-divided society.

Trying to avoid errors, they fall into worse ones. Having heard that *me* is common and *I* is polite, they carefully and correctly avoid *Me and you will* . . . and say with bland assurance *Between you and I*. They struggle to avoid ending a sentence with a preposition despite the fact that the Bible and Shakespeare bristle with examples of such usage, but they cheerfully split infinitives to bits.

Their labour unions, political parties and social welfare bureaucrats are afflicted with a malady known also in America, where it is called gobbledygook—the substitution of high-sound pseudo-scientific words for simple ones. Thus in America there are no longer any *poor* people. They are *under-privileged*. In England the *slums* are now *depressed areas*, the *idle* are *a redundancy of workers*, the *removal van* has become a *pantechnicon* and the *rat-catchers* have decided it would be more dignified to be known as *rodent operators*.

Affectation finds an outlet in the creation of private words, words that cannot be understood by anyone who is not in the know. The harder they are to understand, the more they are prized. Note, for example, the rhyming slang of the Cockneys. Two Cockneys conversing in the secret code can feel quite smug and smart in the knowledge that what they are saying is above the head of any eavesdropper not acquainted with the code.

The trick of rhyming slang is to say not what you mean but something that rhymes with what you mean. These rhymes are standardised, you cannot invent your own. If you wish to say *stairs* in code you say instead *apples and pears*. *Suit* becomes *whistle and flute*. *Tie* becomes *reason why*, *hat* is *titfer* (*tit for tat*), *feet* changes to *plates* (*plates of meat*), *wife* is appropriately *trouble and strife*. *Tram* is *veal and ham*.

The expert educated in rhyming slang would not think of saying, "My wife went on the tram to save her feet" when he can mystify listeners with "My trouble and strife went on the veal and ham to save her plates".

Schoolboys in Britain, and the world around, for that matter, delight in inventing jargon that their elders cannot understand. Students of Winchester have to master a vocabulary known as 'notions' that has persisted for four centuries. It now shows signs of weakening and at Eton there has been a marked decline in the use of school slang during the past fifty years.

The delight of provincial people in the use of words that make outsiders stumble and look ridiculous is painfully evident in

English place names. I don't believe we are so addicted to this vice in America. We don't require that the stranger visiting our town should make a fool of himself when he tries to pronounce it.

But the people of Beverley have a good laugh when visitors show their ignorance by saying Beverley instead of Babingley. Visitors to Foulis make themselves look foolish by pronouncing it Foulis whereas every Foulish citizen knows it should be Fowls.

Each town is a sort of private club and the test for membership is the pronunciation of its name. Only a rank outsider would call Wormegay, Wormegay. Of course it is Rungey. Methwold is Muell. And anybody should know that Mountnessing is pronounced Moneyseen.

Of course Launceston and Leominster are really Launston and Lemster.

Even strangers from overseas may be aware that Buccleuch is Buckloo, Wemyss is Weems, Cholmondeley is Chumley and Hertford is Harfud.

But who would guess that Figheldean would come out as Fyaldean, Colquhounie as Coohooney and Wyrardisbury as Wraysbury?

Thornhill in *Explorer's England* tells of an inspecting officer who asked his yeomen how many of them had come from Mayfield.

"Not a man replied. Surprised that there seemed not to be a single Mayfield man in that large assemblage of South Downs' soldiery, the officer inquired a second time. Still no response. Then a Sussex-born member of his retinue whispered that the inquirer might try calling the place Mearvel. At once a score of men loudly shouted assent."

This points up the fact that even the people who live in a place don't recognise its name if pronounced as spelled. Eye and ear have become so estranged that neither can understand the other.

This is a great pity. One of the most precious features of

English is that it is, or can be, an eye-and-ear language. Chinese takes ten times as long to learn as English because it is not an eye-and-ear language. That is, the written ideograph gives no hint whatever as to how it should be pronounced. Indeed, a given ideograph may mean a dozen different things represented by a dozen completely different spoken words.

When one cannot tell from the look of a word how it should sound, learning is slowed down to a snail's pace. A phonetic language such as English and the Latin tongues correlates eye and ear so that each may help the other. If you hear an Italian word spoken you know how to write it. If you see it written you know how to say it. English is not so nearly perfect in this respect and users of English are to blame because it is not. If we grant that the purpose of language is to convey thought, not to conceal it, we must concede that the more transparently phonetic we can make it, the better.

I am quite aware that there are historical associations involved in the pronunciation of place names. I venture to guess, however, that in nine cases out of ten the historical reasons for the distortion have been forgotten. Even where they are not forgotten, I should suppose that easy communication in the future would be more important than some pleasant memory of the past.

It isn't just the tourist who suffers. He comes for a few weeks or months and goes home again. But for Britons the problem is a lifelong obstacle race. This is very well illustrated in the questionnaires filled in by youths reporting for national service at the Army Recruiting Centre in Brighton late in 1955. They spelled one fairly simple place name in twenty different ways. Army education authorities declared nearly a quarter of the applicants as "educationally backward" and six per cent of them "illiterate".

The problem is not limited to place names. There are hundreds of words such as *seccertry*, above-mentioned, which Britons manfully refuse to pronounce as their own dictionaries say they should be pronounced. To the extent that we allow this divergence between the written and the spoken word we are spoiling a simple and beautiful language and imposing unnecessary handicaps upon those who try to learn it.

This is a book on Britain, not America, therefore I am not taking space to detail American offences against the English language. Suffice it that they are many, though different from the British.

One problem, not nearly so acute in America as in Britain, is diversity of dialect. To be sure, we have our Brooklyn accent and our Southern accent, but on the whole a Californian speaks much like a New Yorker and it is impossible to tell by his speech whether a man is from Cleveland or Denver. There are villages ten miles apart in Britain that are more distinct linguistically than those three thousand miles apart in the United States.

In Britain there are nearly as many different accents as there are counties. Surrey has trouble in understanding Lancashire, which finds Yorkshire peculiar which, is mystified by the brogue of the Scot, who can't converse easily with the man of Devon; and none of them can make head or tail of the Cockney. Large numbers of Welsh speak nothing but their national tongue and Gaelic is still heard in the highlands of Scotland. And there are considerable numbers of cinema-corrupted young people who speak American!

"In the dialects of England," says Edith Olivier, "you can call a man a fool in thirteen hundred ways."

That is not as great an advantage as it seems, for the man you called a fool would understand only one of your thirteen hundred ways. The remaining 1,299 would be wasted breath.

There is too much wasted breath in Britain, too many messages that fall on deaf ears, too many obstacles to concerted thought and action. Britain needs one language.

Perhaps she is slowly getting it. The schools are bringing it. Cinema and television are bringing it. The press is bringing it.

The British are among the world's greatest book readers, and the books are not in dialect. Perhaps even America helps—for American tourists cannot be addressed in dialect. The day may come when the English will speak English.

CHAPTER 28

A Channel Islands Queen

Guests of the ghost of Tennyson, we stay a night in his poetry-soaked home, now the Farringford Hotel, in the Isle of Wight. The island is easily reached by a half-hour car-ferry trip from Southampton.

Quite off the tourist's beaten path, the Tennyson mansion should be the Mecca of travellers who want not only the best of lodgings and the finest of food but the charm of a great house so lovingly preserved that it still seems to breathe with the presence of one of England's most beloved poets.

It is said that the poet still haunts the dark little spiral staircase which he had built so that he could reach or leave his study unobserved. The study is a large room, designed to accommodate his extensive library, and some thousands of his books are still in the house, not in locked glass bookcases but on open shelves where anyone may enjoy them. Or purloin them—but the guests in this hotel do not seem to be the predatory sort.

The furniture and furnishings are mostly as the Poet Laureate left them and include many inlaid pieces of exceptional beauty, Oriental cabinets, splendid vases and fine paintings.

The drawing-room enjoys a superb view of park, woods and sea. In fact it was the view from this room that decided Tennyson to buy the mansion. The same view can be had from the study, which was added later.

On the other side of the house, the bedrooms, including the one we occupied, look out over country sweet enough to make any man a poet. Yonder is the Solent, separating the Isle of Wight from the mainland.

It was this outlook that inspired, "Sunset and evening star . . ." Looking from our window we saw the same setting sun and perhaps the same evening star, and fishing boats "crossing the bar".

The house is set in a beautiful estate of 235 acres of parkland and copses of oak, ilex, pine, cedar and magnolia. The nearest village is Freshwater. Near-by is Totland Bay, where Ellen Terry and her husband spent their honeymoon.

The Isle of Wight is a perfect honeymoon island, if the honeymooners wish to feel that they are out of the world in a near-paradise of rolling downs, flowering groves and smooth beaches protected by white cliffs. Time may not quite stand still here but she does drag her feet.

We took a night boat from Southampton to the Channel Islands, so close to France and so influenced by her that they constitute a little French England.

Landing at St. Peter Port on the island of Guernsey, we taxied up the steep hill to the Old Government House Hotel for breakfast.

Then we hopped the morning boat for Sark, first telephoning the famous Dame of Sark, monarch of the island, as we had been advised to do by Lady Diana Avebury. The Dame, Mrs. Hathaway, was most cordial and invited us to come to the seigneurie for tea.

Sark is a rockbound hideaway strongly reminiscent of Pitcairn, South Sea refuge of the *Bounty* mutineers. After an hour's trip from Guernsey, we pulled up to a forbidding cliff and climbed cement steps to a high jetty where carriages waited. No motor traffic is allowed on Sark lest its primitive charm be disturbed. The carriages take visitors around the island, returning in time for the five o'clock boat back to Guernsey.

Our three-thirty appointment at the manor house would not

work into this plan, so we by-passed the carriages, walked up the long hill to the village, lunched at the Pavilion, walked through the rain over unpaved roads fortunately too hard to become very muddy, up a lovely flower-hedged road to the manor house deep in a gorgeous garden.

In a magnificent drawing-room looking out into blooming laburnum Mrs. Hathaway received us. She proved to be a very charming and lively lady, perhaps in her sixties, full of good talk, and with enough appreciation of American ways to serve tea with lemon—our first in Britain.

"Oh, I know something of America," she said. "My husband was an American. I went on several lecture tours through your country from coast to coast, telling about Sark and its feudal system."

"In what way is it feudal?"

"In a very literal sense. I have the island from the Queen. I pay her £1 15s. 9d. a year. The island is mine. The people pay me ground rent. This is supposed to be paid in kind, in grain or livestock, but when this is impossible I take payment in money. No tenant may sell his land without my permission, and I take one-thirteenth of the sale price.

"Otherwise the people are not taxed. There's no income tax whatever. As you know, it's quite different in England, where as much as half of a man's income may go in income tax. Here all a man earns is his own."

"Don't they have to pay for social security, old-age benefits, socialised medicine?"

"We have none of these things. The people take care of their own aged, and we don't believe in socialised medicine."

"But you have to pay public officials."

"We expect every citizen to give public service without payment when called upon. Our constable serves on a voluntary basis. He really has very little to do—Sark is law-abiding and there are less than six hundred people on the island. The prohibition of motor traffic means that road maintenance is not difficult. We have given the island a parliament in which all the members serve on a voluntary basis. There are practically no poor on Sark, the people are well off and can afford to give their time. Most of them are quite willing; Sark citizens are very patriotic. Many of them never leave the island."

"Not even to get wives?"

"That brings up something very interesting about Sark. Sark boys marry Sark girls, and since there are only a few different families it means very close blood relationships, yet anthropologists tell us that the people of Sark are a distinctly superior breed. Their ancestors had the right qualities, so the descendants are good stock. It's only when a Sark boy or girl marries an outsider that the children are apt to be inferior. Sark is quite self-contained—so much so that the language of the people who immigrated here from France centuries ago is still the common speech."

We had already heard this *patois* spoken in the pub at the Pavilion. It sounded like nothing else in the world, certainly very little like French.

"It's a very ancient form of French," the Dame said. "French people can't understand it. But when I was in French Canada I found that the people could understand me perfectly when I spoke the Sark *patois*. So did people of French derivation in Louisiana. For a while our young people were ashamed of their *patois* and insisted on speaking English only. Now the *patois* is coming back. I see no prospect of its dying out. We are rather proud of it."

The Dame's daughter and grandson and his wife joined us later. The grandson is a good-looking young fellow in his twenties. He will be the Seigneur when the Dame dies.

On both Guernsey and Sark we saw many of the Guernsey cattle, light brown and white. No other breeds are allowed on these two islands. Only Jersey cattle are permitted on Jersey. At the Pavilion we were served butter that looked atrociously artificial, a brilliant orange colour. But it appeared unreal only because it was so real. "Because the grass is so rich," said the proprietor.

We took the afternoon boat back to Guernsey, spent the night on this delightful island, took the morning boat to Southampton, where, believe it or not, we had to go through customs, quite as if the Channel Islands were foreign territory.

We picked up our car, drove to Salisbury, and were thrilled to the marrow by the heavenly cathedral spire which Morton calls "the finest in all England". We stopped at the Old George Inn and tried to visualise life as lived when it was built in 1320.

We went on the next morning with a sense of high anticipation to Stonehenge, and were not disappointed. On the bleak upland stand these mighty monoliths, some of them rising twenty feet above ground and sunk eight feet into it, weighing many tons, and challenging man to guess what breed of giants put them there.

"The origin and purpose of Stonehenge are still moot points," says Muirhead. "The open part of the horseshoe faces the sunrise at the summer solstice and the fact that the sun on midsummer's day rises over the Friar's Heel, on the axis of the avenue, has long been used as an argument that Stonehenge was a temple of the sun. Astronomers, on the assumption that this stone was erected in the exact line of the sunrise, contend that the slight deviation now visible places the date of the structure at about 1700 B.C."

We crossed Somerset and came to rest near Honiton in the county of Devon at a good country inn by the name of Monkton Court.

All day long we had been passing through country so fine that if the writer of a tourist folder should call it ravishingly beautiful he would be guilty of understatement. It had been a succession of sweeping views from incessant hills.

And never a billboard!

On the waterfront at Plymouth we read a sign marking the

site of the Mayflower Hotel where passengers of the first *May-flower* put up the night before leaving for the new land. Across the road from it is the dock from which the ship sailed. A Salvation Army band was playing on the dock. Noting our interest, one of the officers came over to talk with us.

"An ancestor of mine was a porter here at the time," he said. "He helped the passengers get their things aboard."

On through exquisite, green, rolling country, unscarred, no bare cuts through hills, no wire fences, rarely any poles in evidence, charming hedgerows full of flowers along the road and winding away between the fields, many patches of wild woodland, green tunnels through which the road passes, quaint Devon villages, low-browed thatched roofs . . . Never in our lives have we seen a prettier countryside than here in southern England.

It has the intimacy of the Japanese landscape but a more finished look. The roads are always well paved—in Japan they are quite likely to be dirt roads, rough and stony or muddy. The houses here are of stone or plaster and look permanent, those in Japan are of wood and paper and look as if the first fire would pick them off, which is just what happens. The churches here are of stone and some are a thousand years old; Japanese temples, being of wood, must be restored frequently. England is full of solid rock castles that have stood for a millennium and will probably remain for another. Japan has only a very few of her fine old wooden castles left.

I shall never go back on Japan, loveliest country in Asia, but the loveliness of England is more well-groomed and ordered.

And so to Dartmouth on the fine Dart River, where excursionists enjoy the scenic boat trip up-river to Totnes. And we have the dish of Devon—strawberries with clotted cream, delicious.

We stop for the night at a rather dreary little hotel in a Cornwall market town. This is Sunday night and you get cold supper on Sunday night in English hotels. The crabmeat salad reacts upon us violently in the middle of the night. Since it is sinful to cook on Sunday, the salad had probably been prepared the day before and had undergone normal processes of putrefaction.

Beware of Sunday night in England.

Cornwall is not as soft and gentle as the green-velvet counties we have been passing through. This spur of land projecting into the harsh Atlantic is affected by that severity. Salt winds stunt growth. The fences are not hedgerows, but walls made of stones gathered from the fields. Cornwall is a cousin to Brittany across the Channel. The people are similar and so also are their houses and their mode of life.

The Cornish language has almost died out but the people still regard themselves as Cornish, not English, and anyone from another county is as good as a foreigner. The county actually has a unique status for it is a duchy, its lord being Prince Charles, Duke of Cornwall.

Tradition reaches back a long way in Cornwall. There is a firmly-believed legend that Christ as a boy was brought here with his great-uncle Joseph of Arimathea, who was engaged in the tin trade between Cornwall and Phoenicia. These visits of Joseph are believed to have culminated in the building of a mud-and-wattle church at Glastonbury, the first place of Christian worship in Britain.

In later centuries Cornwall was highly cultured because it was the first landing place of saints, monks and scholars from Ireland, then a centre of learning. Perhaps England today does not particularly care to remember that much of her civilisation came from Ireland, just as Japan's history books are inclined to make light of the fact that the greater part of her ancient culture was imported from Korea.

Customs antedating Christianity are still observed in Cornwall. One was a festival in honour of Flora, Roman goddess of fertility and flowers, during which every house was decked with flowers, the doors left open so that everyone might pass in and out freely and the women of the house were expected to give themselves to strangers. The custom persists but with an important difference. The women give cakes and drinks rather than themselves.

The beaches of Cornwall are warm, some almost sub-tropical, and the coastline is dramatic and picturesque. One of its most striking features is St. Michael's Mount, an islet nearly three hundred feet high crowned by a castle and con-nected with the mainland a quarter-mile away by a causeway which is uncovered only at low tide. At other times the islet is reached by boat from Penzance or Marazion. The castle is still occupied by its owners, but the grounds, chapel and armoury are open to visitors. St. Michael's Mount is almost an identical twin with the more frequently pictured Mont St. Michel off the French coast.

Caught in a dense fog while walking the moors behind Penzance, we took refuge at a farm-house and, thanks to Cornish hospitality, stayed the night.

From the outside this lone house on the vacant upland looked pretty bleak, another Wuthering Heights, or haunt of Jane Eyre, where any sort of strange and weird thing might happen.

The square, unadorned stone structure appeared to have been a sort of afterthought of the barn which came first and must be circumnavigated to reach the back door of the house—the road never did reach the front door.

But our room was pleasant, with a thrilling view, when the fog cleared, across the high downs to the sea.

In so isolated a place we might have expected to find only a man and his wife. Instead, eleven of us sat down to dinner. Four grown sons had stayed on the farm, and today three neighbour boys had come in to help dig potatoes.

"But we're just about ready to quit," said the farmer,

"because the price of potatoes has . . ." He made a dropping-out gesture with both hands.

"What do you raise—besides potatoes?"

"Wheat and barley. But we aren't allowed to sell them."

"Why not?"

"The Government pays us not to. We feed them to the animals."

"What animals?"

"About a hundred head of cattle. Also we raise chickens and turkeys. Just now we're having a hard time with the chickens. The crows, you know."

"What about the crows?"

"They pick up the eggs and fly off with them. Put them down in a field, crack them open and eat them. The foxes bother us too—always after the chickens. We've got to shoot the crows and foxes."

"When you get ready," said one of the neighbour boys eagerly, "let us know. We'll help you. It'll be fun."

"Do you work back and forth this way all the time?" I asked.

"All the time," the farmer said. "Not for money. Nobody gets paid. They help me dig potatoes, I lend them my dung spreader—we just trade back and forth. It's better than hiring. Hired men think of nothing but their pay, they don't want to work."

It was a farm of two hundred acres, larger than the average. Eighty-five per cent of British farms are under 150 acres. Half the farms of Britain are under fifty acres. And yet tractors and combines are used.

Any agricultural theorist knows that small farms are un-economic, if worked with machines. It is said that a farm must be of at least six hundred acres to be machine-operated success-fully.

Actually it doesn't work out that way in England. The large farm is operated by indifferent hired labour, the small farm is worked by people who care. The output falls off proportionately as the acreage increases.

The truth appears to be that British small-farming is highly efficient. For example, Britain produces thirty-six bushels of wheat to the acre, compared with thirteen bushels in Canada. As for cattle, the entire western hemisphere is stocked with cattle derived from famous British breeds—Herefords, Durhams, Aberdeen Angus, Guernseys, Jerseys and Shorthorns.

CHAPTER 29

Land's End and Scilly Isles

Before us the land narrowed to a point and dropped off into the sea.

An inn bore the inscription "First and Last Hotel in England". A grocery announced itself as the first and last grocery. A garage was the first and last garage. A tea-room was the first and last tea-room.

Then we came to the first and last cliffs, a hundred feet high, cut into fantastic shapes by the surge of the Atlantic.

This is Land's End, the westernmost point of England. The flood of ozone is exhilarating and the view is breathtaking. Rocky spurs jut out to challenge the sea. Offshore great rocks tower like prehistoric monuments and carry such imaginative names as the Irish Lady and the Armed Knight. Two lighthouses gleam white against the blue-green water. Beyond them is the archipelago of 150 big and little scraps of land known as the Scilly Isles.

But the most romantic feature of the scene is visible only to the mind's eye. Buried forty fathoms beneath the sea between Land's End and the islands lies the fabled land of Lyonesse where many of the incidents in the life of King Arthur are supposed to have taken place and Tristram loved Iseult. It was a rich and flourishing land, according to the legend, until one day it suddenly disappeared beneath the sea.

Nor is it all pure fancy. "The legend may be a greatly exaggerated version of some actual subsidence of inhabited land," states the *Encyclopædia Britannica*. "There is a very ancient local tradition, apparently independent of the story of Lyonesse, that the Scilly Islands formed part of the Cornish mainland within historical time."

There is enough substance to the legend to interest a party of twenty-four experienced aqualung divers, archæologists and geologists known as the Archæological Diving Group. These underwater explorers have already found unmistakable evidence that lands now covered by the sea were once the home of man. Remnants of ancient walls and villages have been found and artifacts dating from pre-Christian times.

From Penzance we take the motor ship *Scillonian* for the Scilly Isles.

It is disturbing to find everywhere deep, foot-wide plastic pans lying on the deck awaiting contributions. A better way to induce sea-sickness could hardly be imagined. As soon as a slight roll is felt, the pans are in use.

Perhaps because these seas are shallow, this can be a very rough passage. The waters that drowned Lyonesse still have a nasty temper and have taken a large toll of life among fishermen. However, for those who do not care for the three-hour sea trip, a plane hops to the Scillies in twenty minutes.

The Scillies are worth the trip. Imagine an archipelago of 150 rugged islets rising out of waters that bear no comparison with the dull, opaque stuff to be found along most English coasts. This water is a brilliant tropical turquoise as transparent as glass. Birds love such seas and the air is alive with gannets, gulls, roseate terns, razorbills and shearwaters. Their colours blend and clash with the colours of the islands, for the Scillies are England's greatest flower garden.

We land on St. Mary's and take a bus trip through endless acres of flowers—marguerites, gladioli, marigolds, mesembryanthemum, gorse, heather, stocks, anemones, violets, iris, ixias and freesias. The geraniums and fuchsias are enormous. Cactus and aloes attest the warmth of the climate. There are even some palms.

In a good season the islands dispatch to the mainland some sixty million cut flowers, or twelve hundred tons. The ship *Scillonian* alone carries thirty to forty tons of flowers a day. The daffodils of Scilly are famous. There are ten thousand varieties of daffodil and Scillonian flower farmers are always breeding new ones.

The Scillies have another claim to fame. This is said to have been the first place in Britain to have compulsory education. How the authorities persuaded parents to send every child to school was explained to us by a young Scillonian schoolteacher.

"They charged a penny if you went to school, twopence if you didn't. So everybody went."

The Cornish north coast is rich in traditions of King Arthur.

We come to the valley village of Camelford, which is (not very authentically) claimed to be the Camelot of King Arthur. It takes some searching in the lush country behind the village to find Slaughter Bridge, so named because it is supposed to be here that Modred was slain by King Arthur. We found masons apparently skilled in the old stonework repairing one wall of the bridge where a lorry had broken it.

"If you follow the lane that parallels the stream," one of them said, "and go through the first gate on the right you will find King Arthur's grave."

We did as directed, opened the pasture gate, crossed a pathless meadow, climbed a barbed wire fence and scrambled down through thick woods to the river.

A monolith lay on the edge of a flower-choked stream half hidden by the cliff and a large tree that sent its horizontal trunk over the diminutive Camel River. Some acrobatic leaps and drops were necessary to get down to the stone, and ferns and nettles had to be cleared away before we could get a good look at it.

Completely neglected, the stone quite evidently has some significance, though whether it is actually the tombstone of the King, who can say? It is some twelve feet long by four by four and bears an inscription in Roman letters cut into the stone. Some of the letters are very plain but others are so worn that they cannot be deciphered.

Of course the monks of Glastonbury claimed that they found the remains of King Arthur and Queen Guinevere in their cathedral, and thus started a stream of pilgrims that still continues. But since this was only one of a number of fantastic claims which proved commercially profitable, one is inclined to favour the very non-commercial and almost inaccessible monolith beside the woodland stream.

Tintagel!

What a castle, and what traditions it cherishes of King Arthur and his knights!

A mile walk across the moors is necessary to reach it, then a steep climb up several hundred stone steps cut into the face of the cliff to the castle which is perched atop a dizzy crag above the surf of the Cornish coast.

The fortress crowns two hills which were once connected by a bridge. Now the buildings are roofless walls, some rising twenty feet high. The oldest are the remains of a monastery reduced almost to the ground, for according to archæologists they have been taking the rough Cornish weather since about A.D. 350.

King Arthur, the real rather than the fictional King Arthur, is supposed to have lived about A.D. 500, therefore the castle was already old when he first saw it.

According to the traditions of Malory, turned into poetry by Tennyson, the infant Arthur was thrown by the waves upon the beach near the cave known as Merlin's Cave.

We walked through it—a natural tunnel penetrating a cliff from one beach to another. Sheer above it rises the giant spur that bears Tintagel Castle, and looking up one sees people there too, dwarfed by distance, appearing no larger than seagulls against the sky.

Whether or not Arthur actually grew up here and here held his Court, certain it is that such an impregnable stronghold must have been fortified from a very early date and was the scene of many battles of Saxons and Britons and perhaps Romans as well.

The culture of the Romans is evident in the monastery, which boasted heated floors, hot air being conveyed under the paved floor from a firing chamber. The experts identify this as "an obvious survival of the Roman hypocaust".

In another spot are traces of fire and deposits of wood ash indicating that certain small chambers were used as sweat-houses. "By heating the interior to a high temperature and pouring water on the stones, steam was produced and the resulting vapour bath was considered beneficial against rheumatism and similar ailments."

Walking over the wind-swept crest one comes suddenly upon a slanting tunnel about five feet in diameter which plunges steeply down until it is choked with débris. The excavators have yet to clear it to the end, but it is believed to have led to the seashore far below and may have afforded a means of escape if the castle was too hotly attacked from the land side.

According to the earliest historian of Tintagel, Geoffrey of Monmouth, who wrote his *History of the Britons* in 1145, the infant Arthur was not thrown on the beach but was born of a *mésalliance* in the castle. Quoting from the Ministry of Works document:

"Tintagel first appears in this work as the impregnable town of Gorlois, Duke of Cornwall, where his wife Ygraine was placed for safety when Uther the British king invaded the country. While Gorlois was shut up in a neighbouring castle, Uther, with the help of Merlin's magic, disguised himself as the duke and was allowed to enter Tintagel. The seduction of Ygraine and the subsequent death of Gorlois were followed by the birth of Arthur."

Tintagel emerges from legend into proved history in the twelfth century and its story from that time on is well known. For centuries the Kings of England took a keen interest in it, doubtless because of its value as a fortress, and assigned it to successive Earls of Cornwall. Cornwall was always a special gift, not regarded as a part of England proper, and, as I have said, remains a duchy under the eldest son of the reigning sovereign. Along with Wales, it is the particular domain of the Prince of Wales.

Of course the present child Prince couldn't care less, but some day he will climb Tintagel's height and probably agree with Winston Churchill that no matter whether the Arthurian legends are or are not true, they are a precious heritage.

"Will you have tea or cream tea?" we were asked in a Tintagel tea-room.

"Cream tea," we replied, under the delusion that, for the first time in England, we were to have cream instead of thin milk in our tea.

In ten minutes the girl reappeared with a pot of tea, a number of scones cut in half, a couple of cakes, a dish of jam and a dish containing a generous quantity of clotted cream sufficiently solid to stand up like a monument.

We looked doubtfully at these ingredients. Mary put a shy question.

"Do you put the cream in the tea?"

"Oh no!" the girl said, and made a wry face.

I didn't want the girl to think I was as ignorant as my wife.

"You just eat it like ice-cream," I said.

The girl writhed in horror.

"No, no," she protested. "You do it this way." She cut off some of the cream with a knife as if it were butter and spread it a quarter-inch thick on a scone, then topped off with a spread of jam.

It was delectable (and indigestible, in my case).

Clotted cream is a Cornwall and Devon institution. We saw later how it is made. A pan of whole milk is placed over a pan of constantly boiling water and kept there for hours. The cream is skimmed off as fast as it comes to the surface. The result is an off-white substance as thick as butter and rich as the fare of the gods on Olympus. It is put on strawberries, ice-cream sundaes are topped with it, toffee is made of it, it is spread on bread, scones or cakes, a dab of it will turn a commonplace sweet into a superb confection.

Walled in with flowers, we ride through eastern Cornwall and Devon between two continuous rock gardens.

Solid banks of foliage rise on either side of the road. We naturally suppose them to be banks of soil and it's only after many miles that we discover that the banks are actually stone walls. In the course of decades, or centuries, dirt has blown in between the stones, seeds have taken root, and now the walls are so completely covered with grass, flowers and shrubs that not a stone of the wall is visible.

The effect of course is very lovely, especially when the green is interspersed with bluebells, buttercups, dandelions, valerian, violets, Queen Anne's lace and big pink or purple rhododendrons.

The growing wall is often twice as high as the stone wall within, and to ride between two vertical rock gardens ten feet high is an experience. Just at the moment when you begin to feel that they are shutting out too much scenery, one wall or the other drops to two or three feet for a mile or so, or may rise and fall with delightful lack of uniformity.

These winding walls of grass and flowers probably began by accident but now are often the result of design. We saw a new stone wall being completed and on top of it had been carefully spread a continuous layer of dirt, ready to receive any seeds the wind might care to bring. Within a few years the wall will be buried in greenery.

It's not just for looks. The tangle of roots binds the stones in place so that they can't fall away. Instead of disintegrating with the passage of time, the wall is renewed and reinforced every year by the thickening mass of twigs and roots.

Clovelly, the village that stands on end, is a fishing hamlet in a crack in the cliffs running down steeply to the north Devon coast.

The drop of four hundred feet means that no two houses are on the same level but descend like steps, and the main street has such a tilt that nothing on wheels can make it. You must leave your car at the top and climb down, and up again. The 650 people of the village must bring everything in pick-a-back—or donkey-back.

Time was when visitors were returned to the upper level on donkeys, but it was found to be too hard on the animals, and now there is a regulation that no Clovelly donkey shall carry a load of more than nine stone and three pounds. Since this is only 129 pounds, the rule bars all riders except juveniles and jockey-light adults—the very persons least likely to need a lift. To make the footing more difficult, the way is paved with cobbles.

But Clovelly is as quaint as a daguerreotype and well worth the scramble.

CHAPTER 30

Island of Pirates

Believe-it-or-not Ripley would have found plenty of material on Lundy.

This incredible island lies twelve miles off the north Devon shore. It is the least known of the forty islands or island groups that fringe the coast of Britain, for until recently it was inaccessible. Its owners were pirates and did not welcome visitors, except rich ones who could be dropped into the dungeons and held for ransom.

Now a plane makes infrequent trips to Lundy from Barnstaple. From the air it looks like Gibraltar, but more picturesque since it is crowned by a seven-hundred-year-old castle. The island rises abruptly from the sea to a plateau four hundred feet high, and when the edge of this plateau and the castle itself bristled with cannon the stronghold was considered impregnable. It was so self-sufficient that it declared itself a separate kingdom and still claims to be virtually independent of Great Britain. Its claim is buttressed by ancient charters which gave its owners sovereign rights and privileges.

The island has always been privately owned, the present 'king' being Martin Coles Harman. The forty inhabitants are vassals and tenants of the lord of the island.

The present owner is not a pirate—in fact he is the very respectable president of the Lundy Field Society, for the island is now a wild life sanctuary swarming with sea birds, rabbits, deer, goats and half-wild ponies.

But it is only of late years that the lord of Lundy has been so peaceably inclined.

Henry II granted the island to the Mariscos, and was sorry when he saw what use this turbulent clan made of it. Standing in the middle of the Bristol Channel, the island was in a position to control all shipping passing up and down that great waterway. The Mariscos saw their opportunity. They stopped every ship of value, demanded heavy tolls, confiscated precious cargo, held important passengers for ransom, hanged the unimportant and displayed their dangling bodies above the shore. They raided both England and Wales. When warships came to punish them, they were beaten off with heavy losses by Lundy cannon.

A long line of piratical chiefs succeeded the Mariscos. There was a Captain Salkeld, who was no captain, and an Admiral Nutt, who was no admiral, but was so stout a buccaneer that it took twelve warships to halt his activities. But soon the pirate gang had another leader, a Moor from Barbary. He was followed by a Spanish privateer, then a professional pirate from France and finally a clergyman, the Rev. Hudson Heaven.

He does not seem to have made full use of his piratical opportunities but planted gardens and made other improvements and turned this nest of hellhounds into what became known as 'The Kingdom of Heaven'.

The island gave up some of its feudal privileges, adopted British coinage, but still issues its own stamps, which are valued not in pennies but in puffins, in honour of the most common bird of the island. Lundy is now considered nominally a part of Devon, but Devon authorities wisely refrain from any practical interference in the affairs of this 'free island'.

Grim and dramatic, Marisco Castle still towers over the Bristol Channel, its nine-foot-thick walls showing no sign of decay, its dungeons full of tragic memories still laying a clammy hand upon the heart. On one side of it is the precipice over which were hurled ordinary captives who were not considered worth the trouble of hanging. Muzzle-loading cannon poke their long noses seaward, and beneath the castle, opening to the seashore, is a cave used for storing smuggled goods or the booty from pirated ships.

Back to the mainland and on through Woolacombe and Ilfracombe, pleasant beach resorts, and across Exmoor of romantic *Lorna Doone* associations, the mysterious fog-swept home of red deer, horned sheep and wild ponies, coming down finally into the lovely age-old village of Dunster, hugging the feet of a beautiful castle.

"How does it feel to live in a castle?"

"It would seem strange to live anywhere else, since this has been the home of our family for nearly six centuries."

By way of a friend's introduction we were calling upon people who actually live in an ancient castle and don't mind the fact that there are dungeons beneath with grim memories, narrow windows set in walls five feet thick that exhale the damp, stony breath of a crypt, arrow slits in the walls, apertures to pour boiling lead upon the heads of unwelcome guests, ghosts that wander noisily through scores of unused rooms and corridors and towers and turrets in this vast mansion many storeys high and covering an area as large as a generous city block.

Set on a hill, Dunster Castle overlooks country so heavenly that one inspired guest wrote a hymn about it, a hymn now included in every Anglican hymnal. Across one deep valley, the green slope rising to the woods is a deer park where as many as thirty or forty of the wild red beauties may be seen at a time. On another side, beyond the roofs of the many outbuildings of the castle and the castle wall and gate, lies the charming medieval village of Dunster, tucked in a lush valley below foggy moors.

The hill-top around the castle has been landscaped into an extensive garden where every century has added exotic trees and vines from the tropics, the Antipodes and the Orient. And as far as eye can see are lands owned or once owned by the Luttrell family.

"No, we didn't build the castle," said Mr. Luttrell. "We have lived here only since 1376. The castle was built by Mohun, Earl of Somerset, about 1070. Of course we have made many changes and additions."

"Has the castle ever been attacked?"

"Indeed yes. In fact we lost it for a year. It was besieged and taken by Cromwell and his Parliamentarians in 1645, and Cromwell built those stables. Then we got it back along with the stables, so we lost nothing and gained a little."

"Your family supported the Royalists?"

"Not particularly. We never mixed in politics more than we could help and have not held official position. We are just farmers."

That was putting it mildly. The Luttrells were at one time feudal lords of much of the great shire of Somerset. They are still great landholders, though their relationship to those who till the land has been modernised. They love the land and everything that grows upon it.

Mrs. Luttrell, white-haired, attractive, charming, set a brisk pace up and down garden paths accompanied by three highly decorative dogs on leash. Thousands of roses were in full bloom. Purple and pink rhododendrons as big as cabbages vied with magnificent poppies. Aged but vigorous wistaria and magnolia climbed the castle walls to the third storey. Almost unbelievable was a yew hedge, *forty feet high*. We stopped in amazement before some orange trees ten feet high growing in wooden planters.

"Of course they are nothing compared with California's," admitted Mrs. Luttrell. "But we are pretty proud of them. Naturally we have to take them in when cold weather comes. They spend the winter in the conservatory."

There were trees from China and Japan. There were even a

few date palms. We were struck by the number of Australian varieties, including bottlebrush and eucalyptus.

"You see, I came from Australia," explained Mrs. Luttrell.

"It must have been quite a change."

"It was, of course, and it took a bit of getting used to. But with many of my old Australian plant friends around me, and all the hundreds of new flowers and trees that grow here but never would in Australia, I am quite at home. After all, when Australians come to England they are coming home, aren't they? I imagine that Americans, at least those of English descent, feel rather the same way."

The medieval monks were romancers of a high order and they outdid themselves at Glastonbury Abbey.

We walked through these amazing ruins, great and beautiful buildings open to the sky, and remembered the wondrous tales that the lively imagination of the monks had originated. Yet who knows what grains of truth there may be in the tales?

That someone built here the first Christian church ever erected in England is fairly probable. But that the builder was St. Joseph of Arimathea, contemporary of Jesus, that he brought with him the chalice of the Last Supper filled with the blood of the Crucifixion, that when he buried the Cup there gushed forth an eternal spring of blood, by drinking which pilgrims might cleanse themselves of sin, that when Joseph, tired from the climb up Wearyall Hill, leaned on his staff it took root and grew into the very same sort of thorn tree from which the crown of thorns had been made, that the said tree or the root thereof is immortal, and that the remains of King Arthur and Queen Guinevere lie buried here—these tales may be products of monkish imagination, yet they were exciting and glamorous enough to take us to Glastonbury this day. They were what took countless other pilgrims to Glastonbury during the Middle Ages, with the result that the institution became so rich that no architects and sculptors were too good for it to employ in the

construction of a magnificent abbey, and the Abbot of Glastonbury became the premier abbot of England.

So the gods reward those who have the courage to tell tall
stories and stick to them.

The thoughtful visitor who feels that religion should be something more than a magic formula is likely to be unhappy at
Glastonbury. Here was the cradle of Christianity in England.
The cradle was rocked by magic and miracle. The pilgrims did
not come because of their veneration for the teachings of Jesus.
They knew little or nothing of those teachings. So far as they
were concerned, Jesus might just as well have saved His breath.
They came because this amazing new prophet who had turned
water into wine, walked on the sea, and raised the dead, was
continuing to perform miracles through the monks of Glastonbury. They came to see the wonders. They came to be healed
of their diseases by drinking from the Bloody Spring, and it
would have been useless to tell them that the water ran red
because of a heavy impregnation of iron. They came to get a
phial of dirt from the spot where the Holy Grail was said to be
buried. They came to get a splinter of the Cross, guaranteed
to bring good fortune, they came to pluck a sprig of the Holy
Thorn which, if buried with them, would be a certain passport
to Heaven. They came ready to pay for these miracles. The
rapid growth of the churches was for centuries directly attribut-
able to the supposed wonder-working powers of the Church
and churchmen. That Christianity ever survived this stultifica-
tion is itself a miracle. That it has entirely survived it is
doubtful.

It is still the miraculous that draws visitors to Glastonbury.
Some come out of mere curiosity, believing none of the tales of
wonders. Many come tingling with the thought that 'it just
might be true' and they furtively rub a bit of iron-red mud on
an ailing stomach or painful sciatic nerve, look for the ghosts
that are said to haunt the ruins, and steal a twig of the Holy
Tree 'just for good luck'.

About the tree, an attendant told H. V. Morton:
"See that bush? That's the Holy Thorn! The original one was hacked down by a Puritan who got a splinter in his eye from it and died. There are several offshoots around Glastonbury, and you'd be surprised at the number of slips we send away. One is going to a big church they are building in New York. We sent one to America not long ago for the tomb of President Wilson."

It has been a highly profitable business, this sanctified leger-demain of Glastonbury. The lush living and overweening power of the churchmen of Glastonbury brought down the heavy hand of Henry VIII and in 1539 much of the abbey was destroyed. For centuries it was used as a stone quarry for building local houses. It was not until 1908 that the ruins were acquired by the Church of England and measures taken to preserve them.

These rich old walls, arches and towers are well worth a visit, and all the more interesting because of the legends that entwine them. If you can think of these legends merely as pleasant flights of fancy, you will be all right. But if you understand them as deliberate and venal devices to deceive the credulous, you will come away heavy of heart that this bed of superstition had to be the birthplace of Christianity in England.

CHAPTER 31

Everybody Goes to Stratford

All tourists who get outside London make a bee-line for Stratford-upon-Avon. That is sometimes held against the place, on the theory that anything that is very popular cannot deserve the attention of the discriminating.

The truth is that tourists flock to Stratford because it offers as much as or more than any other village in England.

We were impressed by it although we had come to it by way of a path of wonders. At lovely old Wells we had seen the beautiful cathedral and slept in the Ancient Gatehouse. At Bath we had walked through the Roman baths dating from the fourth century and had been charmed and amused by the streets of houses with fine old façades but with modern appurtenances such as bathrooms and pantries boxed on to their rears, thus making them appear to one witty visitor as "Queen Anne in front and Mary Ann behind". We had seen the famous 'White Horse of Westbury', an immense equine figure carved into a mountain-side, and had visited the four-thousand-year-old Avebury Circle, a huge earthen embankment that has excited and puzzled antiquarians for centuries.

But Stratford has very special gifts for the traveller.

First, it has the Avon, a river with a peculiarly deep and dreamy quality as if it were stored with memories. Especially in the shade of the Shakespeare Memorial Theatre, the river is a velvet black that makes the swans appear whiter than they are. The Swan of Avon was so named because of the stately birds on his favourite river. The comparison is good so far as it goes;

the birds have grace, beauty and power. But their brains are not equal to a humming-bird's.

Stratford has half-timbered Elizabethan houses. At every turn it has a lovely park or flower garden. Best of all, of course, it has Shakespeare—not his ghost, but the living presence.

After you have visited the girlhood home of his mother, Mary Arden, then his own birthplace, then the home of his sweetheart, Anne Hathaway, New Place where he lived out his married life with her, the church where he is buried, the home of his daughter Susanna and that of his granddaughter Elizabeth, the garden of flowers mentioned in his works, the riverside haunts he knew so well, the woods and fields about . . .

And after you have capped it all by seeing three of his magnificent plays magnificently acted, it is impossible to escape the feeling that Shakespeare is alive—almost as alive as when he lived.

We saw *Othello*, *Love's Labour's Lost*, and *Hamlet*. *Hamlet* was splendidly played by Alan Badel, *Love's Labour's Lost* was colourful in scene and costume and bright in repartee, but *Othello* was really tremendous. That play alone, provided it could always be produced with Harry Andrews as Othello, Emlyn Williams (competent playwright as well as fine actor) as Iago and Margaret Johnston as Desdemona, would establish Shakespeare's fame.

The theatre itself makes the plays more enjoyable. The outside reminds some people of a factory; but the inside leaves nothing to be desired. It is modern, yet warm and human as too much modern architecture is not, the seats are soft beneath you and firm to your back, there is plenty of room for latecomers to get past your knees, and the man with the cough behind you is a foot farther away than usual.

As we found eighteen years ago when a round-the-world trip had drained us and we wanted the cheapest seats, it is possible to hear perfectly well in the farthest part of the auditorium. This time we had the best seats because only the best were left, and they were returns. But the best cost only 14s. 6d. and prices range down to 2s. 6d. That's remarkably cheap Shakespeare.

An added attraction is the theatre restaurant on the terrace overlooking the Avon. It is in a sense part of the show. You book a table in advance, surrender half of your theatre ticket at the door of the restaurant, take dinner from six to seven-thirty, pass directly from the restaurant into the theatre. Not that the price of the theatre ticket covers the dinner, but the charge is moderate for so good a meal. It's with a sense of deep contentment as well as anticipation that you take your seat before the stage.

These plays that seem so ancient when played in skyscraper New York don't seem nearly so old here because the town is in tune with them. Many buildings are quite as they were in Shakespeare's time. Trinity Church was old when he was baptised in it, and the chapel across the street from his house was there three hundred years before he was born. His house no longer stands (irascibly torn down by a later owner because too many people came to see it), but the chapel remains, three hundred and more years after the poet's death.

Many of the old houses still contain the things he wrote about, unused now, but treasured. We have seen several of the old-time rush candles. The common rush that still grows beside streams was dipped in grease and clamped between two iron jaws, where it would burn for a little more than half an hour. It was quite smoky, hence Shakespeare's "base and unlustrous as the light that's fed with stinking tallow". Sometimes, to increase the light, both ends of the rush were ignited, and that is how we come by the phrase "burning the candle at both ends".

The old houses here, as elsewhere in England, still have their enormous fireplaces, though in many cases a tight little coal stove or an electric heater now takes the place of the logs. Some of these hearths are so great that from four to six persons could sit in the ingle-nooks without being scorched. In the fireplace at Mary Arden's home is the old weight spit, ancestor of the *rôtisserie*. It is a great iron shaft some five feet long and was turned, not by electricity, but by a weight like that in a grandfather clock.

Our ingenious forefathers had another way of turning a spit, and the contrivance remains in some Stratford chimneys. An iron fan in the chimney was revolved by the hot air rising from the fire, and the power was geared to the spit, which turned accordingly.

Household articles mentioned by Shakespeare are still to be seen: the trencher or wooden plate that did for two courses, being turned upside down for the second; the pewter dishes that gradually superseded wood; bone bobbins used for making lace by "the three maids that weave their thread with bones".

There are many reminders of sixteenth-century customs in the home of Shakespeare's mother. The walls are of "wattle and daub"—a screen of hazel twigs plastered with a daub of clay, horsehair and cow dung, the whole weather-proofed with a smooth coat of plaster.

Ale was drunk from a great wooden mug called a pigon and 'pig and whistle' is a corruption of 'pigon whistle'. When the boy was sent to the cellar for a pigon of ale he was expected to whistle all the way back to prove that he was drinking none of it.

Bread was baked in wholesale quantities and the 'bread ark', so called because of its resemblance to Noah's or perhaps the Ark of the Covenant, was a huge box six feet high. Even this vast supply of bread did not last long, for there were many to eat it, a dozen in the family and twenty servants. Servants were not hard to get in those days, but hard to shut out, and worked for their keep alone.

The problem of sleeping so large a number of persons was solved by putting all the women in one large bedroom at one end of the house, the men in another at the opposite end. All slept on the floor. No air was admitted lest it might bring in evil vapours. Windows in bedrooms were almost unknown until 1597.

The women's bedroom was reached by a ladder and after all had ascended to their rest the ladder was removed. This was meant to protect female chastity. But just how any male inter-loper could have found his way in complete darkness to the side of his lady love over fifteen or more sleeping forms without disturbing the lot is hard to understand.

Only outer clothing was removed at night. Heavy inner clothing was put on at the first frost of autumn and kept on until Easter. If the room became odoriferous, sweet herbs were burned in the warming-pan, so Shakespeare speaks of "smoking a musty room".

Behind the Mary Arden house is a great dovecote in whose interior wall are 657 holes for nesting doves. Apparently these were multi-family homes, for there were commonly from three thousand to four thousand doves in the cote.

Only a lord of the manor, such as Mary's father, was per-mitted to have a dovecote, and indeed this rule still prevails, though dovecotes now may be so small as to be merely symbolic. But in Shakespeare's day doves were an important item in the food supply of the nobility. They ravaged the crops of the tenants, who dared not kill them except at the risk of severe penalties, even death. Shakespeare was a landlord but he felt for the tenant. Whether or not he was ever fined for poaching, as the story goes, he rose in defence of the poacher and con-demned the selfishness and rapacity of landowners.

And if you are annoyed by the fact that other people want to see what you see, you can readily escape by hiring a canoe and paddling up the lazy Avon. This is the land that Shakespeare knew and loved. You see what he saw. No road or railroad has intruded upon the river and there is no sound but the dip of your paddle. Weeping willows kiss the stream. Woodland and thicket alternate with green pastures that rise in billows towards the castles of Kenilworth and Warwick. Now and then there is a house half concealed by greenery. The winding river approaches it as if in timid curiosity but shies away before reaching it. It's an introspective river, a river that loves to be alone, a river of flowers and dreams and sleep.

We probably have the Avon and Avon country to thank for much of the gentle beauty which the poet so artfully infused into even his most powerful passages of action. Without Avonland, we should still have had a great dramatist, but not Shakespeare.

Within easy reach of Stratford, Kenilworth "flings its tattered walls to the skies, and its once grand stairways end in thin air". A romantic but empty shell, Kenilworth contrasts with near-by Warwick, complete and in perfect repair, and full to bursting with treasures of art. Only a little farther afield is Sulgrave Manor, which no American will care to miss, since it is the beautifully restored home of the ancestors of George Washington.

Thinking to enjoy another series of great plays, this time by Shakespeare's modern rival, we went to spend Shaw Centenary Week at Malvern.

The results were rather disappointing. There was only one production, *Cæsar and Cleopatra*, and it played to a half-empty theatre. Shaw is at a discount in England. His social, religious and political views were unorthodox. He trod on too many toes. So did Shakespeare, but the owners of the toes died off and later generations acknowledged the genius of the bard of Avon. Stratford took no notice of him until he had been dead almost a century and the increasing stream of visitors forced the village to appreciate its greatest son and cash in on his memory. It is not impossible that Shaw will grow in stature as time passes, but there was no sign of it at Malvern.

This charming village in the hills was for many years the workshop of Shaw productions and the annual Malvern Festival drew admirers of Shaw from all England and abroad. The patron of the Festival was Sir Barry Jackson, who spent on encouragement of the drama the money his father had made on margarine. Sir Barry founded also the Birmingham Repertory Theatre, which inspired many others—so he is actually the father of repertory in England. The Malvern Festival failed financially some years ago—this centenary celebration was an effort to revive it.

We met Sir Barry at tea and found him quite undiscouraged by his small measure of success.

"Will you try again?" we asked.

"Of course. But it doesn't matter too much whether we succeed or fail. Shaw doesn't need us. He can make his own way."

Sir Barry had many stories to tell of his personal friendship with Shaw.

"It amused Shaw to enrage people by pretending that he was a great egotist. Actually he was a humble man and very critical of his own work. After a first performance of one of his plays I took him to my home for the night. He was in very low spirits. As we opened the door we were met by my small dog. Shaw bent down to it and said: 'How sensible you were to stop at home, Lulu. It was a rotten play.' "

Leaving Malvern and its lovely hills, we journeyed to Hereford.

In magnificent Hereford Cathedral we stood before the tomb of the boiled bishop.

"If you think this cathedral is rich and gorgeous," said the guide, "this is what made it so."

It seems that in the late thirteenth century the Bishop Thomas de Cantilupe of Hereford had a quarrel with the Archbishop of Canterbury. He went to Rome to appeal to the Pope. While there he died.

The chaplain who had accompanied him refused to bury him in Rome. He had a better idea. The Bishop had been a great man in his own country. For many years he had been Chancellor of England. His dispute with the Archbishop of Canterbury had been widely publicised. If his body could be laid to rest in a transept of Hereford Cathedral and miraculous powers could be ascribed to it, many of the pilgrims who flocked to the tomb of Thomas à Becket at Canterbury might be diverted to that of Thomas de Cantilupe at Hereford. Thus the Bishop, though dead, might still put the Archbishop's nose out of joint.

But to transport a corpse so great a distance was not easy in the days before refrigeration. The chaplain solved this difficulty by securing a man-size kettle in which he folded his Bishop and boiled him down. Then he carried the bones home and enshrined them in the north transept of Hereford Cathedral.

The plan worked perfectly. The bones at once began to work wonders and so many miracle-seeking pilgrims were drawn to the shrine that the church became rich and powerful and a grateful Rome placed the name of Cantilupe in the catalogue of saints.

One should pause in Leominster long enough to see the old ducking stool in which common scolds were strapped and plunged into the nearest pond or stream. A placard above the stool bears this notice and verse:

"The latest recorded use of this instrument in England was at Leominster in 1809 when a woman, Jenny Pipes alias Jane Curran, was ducked in one of the adjacent streams.

"Down in the deep the stool descends
But here at first we miss our ends,
She mounts again and rages more
Than ever vixen did before.
So throwing water on the fire
Will make it burn up but the higher.
If so, my friends, pray let her take
A second turn into the lake;

And rather than your patience lose
Thrice and again repeat the dose.
No brawling wives, no furious wenches,
No fire so hot but water quenches."

It is also stated that this was the remedy not only for scolds, but for butchers, bakers, apothecaries and others who gave short weight or sold adulterated food.

Make another brief pause in the village of Much Wenlock to see two other old-time instruments of justice, the stocks and the whipping post.

Ludlow Castle looks like every schoolboy's dream of what a castle should be. It stands high on a hill staring haughtily across the Tame River. If you stand in one of its watch-towers and peer through the arrow slits you can see the blue hills of Wales.

This was the chief castle on the English side of the border between England and Wales. Norman barons took their swords to the table with them, for there was no knowing at what moment the turbulent Welsh might attack.

The Normans subdued England in seven years. It took them two hundred years to conquer Wales.

The fiercely independent Welsh could even put patriotism before love. There is the story of Marion, beautiful maiden of Ludlow Castle, who fell in love with a prisoner. The prisoner was a Welsh knight called Arnold de Lisle. She loved him so much that she helped him escape from his prison tower by means of a rope.

Then she was lonely when Ludlow's baron went on a journey. She sent word to Arnold that he might safely come to her.

The postern gate was left ajar. Through it Arnold entered and climbed to Marion's window. In the morning her lover slept, but Marion wakened to mysterious sounds in the castle. She went to learn the cause and discovered that her Arnold had brought a storming party with him and Welsh troops were now in full possession of the castle.

She returned to her room where her lover still slept. His sword lay on the floor. She seized it and plunged it deep into his body; then with a wild scream she leaped from the window and died on the rocks below.

CHAPTER 32

Don't Miss Wales

The winding Wye, a beautiful and swift river among splendid
hills, more dramatic than any we have seen, carries us into
Wales—if Monmouthshire is in Wales, a question upon which
there appears to be some doubt.

On official maps it is in England, but according to the *Blue
Guide for England* it is "still reckoned with Wales for most ad-
ministrative purposes".

The Welsh inhabit it, and we have heard plenty of Welsh
spoken today. A beautiful, beautiful county, thanks to its hills
and valleys, rivers and woods.

We stop for the night at a guest-receiving farm-house near
the village of Mitchel Troy. Farmer Farrington and his wife
have their own chickens, cows, vegetable gardens, twenty apple
trees, a raspberry patch, and TV.

"Price is a Welsh name," said Mrs. Farrington.

"My ancestors—those in the male line—were Welsh," I said.
"But they married English, Scottish and French girls, so Heaven
knows what I am."

"There's a Price family up the hill."

Curious to learn what we could about my Welsh forebears,
we went up the hill and knocked at the door of the neat white
farm-house. Merely on the strength of our name, Temperance
Price and her little daughter Ann entertained us for tea, gave us
parsnip wine (strangling stuff!), a fine dish of red raspberries
and blackcurrants topped with ice-cream, buttered bread,
scones, cakes, jam and tea, plus a good thumping of the piano

by six-year-old Ann. Their younger son had gone to farming in Saskatchewan. Mr. Price was in the house but did not join us. He was very shy, Temperance said, and anyhow he knew little about the Price tribe because his parents had died when he was five years old and he had been brought up by an aunt.

We had better luck in Brecon, stronghold of the Prices and site of their castle—for they took an active part in the border wars. Brecon is a mountain city in beautiful billowing country rising to a climax in the Black Mountains and the Brecon Beacons. The landscape is not merely charming, but magnificent, the Wyoming of Wales, a land of long views and soaring heights. The towering Brecon Beacons, grassy and treeless, send dozens of waterfalls tumbling into the lush valley, where cattle and sheep graze.

We pursued Prices about the town and in the cathedral records, learned matters of interest to us but of none to the reader, climbed to the ramparts of the last remaining castle and looked across a land so lovely, fertile and kindly as to make us wonder why anyone should care to leave such a haven to dare the chances of a new world.

During the weeks that followed we completely circled Wales by way of Tintern Abbey, Cardiff, Pembroke, St. David's, Harlech, Caernarvon and Conway, with many a side trip into the mountainous interior.

Mountains are the chief feature of Wales. They have played the leading part in Welsh history. They furnished a retreat for the Britons fleeing from the Angles, the Saxons and the Norsemen.

For it must be remembered that the Welsh are not Welsh. They are the real Britons. If anyone should feel at home in Britain, they should, for they were there first.

They were also the first Christians. While the ancestors of Englishmen were still worshipping pagan gods, the Britons were listening to Christian missionaries from Rome.

They lived at peace and had no occasion to cultivate the arts of war. So they were caught unprepared by invading hordes and were pushed westward till they found refuge in the mountains. There they withstood attack for centuries.

Why were these Britons called Welsh? They did not choose the name. It was given to them by their Saxon conquerors. It was the Saxon word for foreigner or barbarian. To the Teutons *wälschen* meant to talk gibberish. Any language the Teuton could not understand was to him gibberish and nonsense and the speakers of it were Welsh. So to the Teutons Italy was Walschland, Bulgaria was Wallachia, the Bulgarians were Wlochi and the Celts of Flanders were Walloons—all these words being born of the same Teuton conviction that anyone who did not speak as they did was pretty ridiculous.

The Britons in the western mountains naturally did not like the name that set them down as jabbering barbarians. They called themselves Cymry, meaning comrades. During the centuries that have elapsed they have resigned themselves to the name Welsh and are even proud of it, just as followers of the Nazarene became proud of the originally scornful title of Christians.

The old language of the Britons is still spoken in Wales. It has changed only superficially. If King Arthur were to return today he would understand and be understood.

A century ago the Welsh language showed signs of dying out. Young people were ashamed to be heard speaking Welsh. They aped the English in speech as well as in manners. But with the world-wide passion for nationalism that has grown up since the First World War, a passion that has become almost a fanaticism, the Welsh have developed new pride in their own customs and language.

It is well that people should be keenly conscious of their own merits, but not at the cost of appreciation of the world about them. In many Welsh homes Welsh only is spoken. The children must go to school to learn English. Welsh also is taught in the schools and the double burden steals time and energy that might be spent in other branches of learning.

We heard Welsh in the streets and in the stores and pubs. According to the last census there are forty thousand persons in Wales who cannot speak English. We attended the national Eisteddfod in Aberdare. In all the events of this week-long festival nothing but Welsh may be spoken. All speeches, all songs, are in Welsh. And how the Welsh can sing! But I have no doubt they would sound just as well in English.

True, every people has traditions it would like to preserve. But the loss of those traditions is not as great a tragedy as we sometimes imagine. The Welsh who came to America left their traditions behind, and their descendants now take pride in American traditions. That meant a loss, but also a gain. The sacrifice made by Germans, French, Poles, Italians, Danes, Swedes and Swiss when they gave up their own *mores* to become Americans has not been in vain. They have benefited and so have Americans.

One wonders if the real interest of Wales does not lie in closer integration with the British Commonwealth. The Britons should take pride in being British.

Welsh boys and girls find their own language hard to learn. There is even less relation between pronunciation and spelling than in English. Moreover there are singsong intonations that must be mastered. Many words are staggering in their length and complexity. The longest word in any language is said to be the Welsh place-name, Llanfairpwllgwyngyllgogerychwyrndrobwllllandysiliogogogoch. It is the name of a village in North Wales. When dismembered and translated it means: Church of St. Mary in a Hollow of White Hazel near to a Rapid Whirlpool and to St. Tysilio's Church beside a Red Cave. At the village railway station the name stretches out to a length of fifty yards.

Naturally, the time that is given to one thing cannot be given to another. The student who spends a large proportion of every

Above: the coracle, probably the lightest boat in the world and consisting of nothing more than a basket covered with tarred cloth, was the craft of the ancient Britons and is still used on the rivers of Wales

Left: a single tower of vast Pembroke Castle, one of the most impressive ruins in Wales

school day on Welsh and English has little time or energy left for Latin or Greek, French or German. Not for him are the far horizons that come from the study of such languages.

Still more important, because his attention is divided, he does not even acquire a thorough mastery of English. The primary school graduate can read an English newspaper but is apt to be completely baffled by a literary magazine or book.

Of course some English books are translated and published in Welsh. At the Eisteddfod the Welsh publishers had their books on display. The effect was quite overwhelming. One might imagine that there was no English book that had escaped Welsh translation. But when you begin to inquire for this book or that, you get a shake of the head.

"Of all works in English, what percentage would you say have been translated into Welsh?" I asked one publisher.

"Hard to say," he answered. "Possibly one in a hundred, perhaps one in a thousand."

It means that the bulk of English literature as well as world literature is unknown to the great majority of the people of Wales. This is true even though it is also true that some of the finest scholars have been Welsh. On the whole a separate language is like a mountainous terrain. They both make for provincialism, limit the long view.

There's no question about the native intelligence of the Welsh. Said Baring-Gould, who had served as a country parson in both England and Wales:

"No one can fail to be impressed with the intellectual superiority of the Welsh peasant to the English country bumpkin. The Welsh of the labourer and small farmer class are brighter, quicker, keener than those occupying the same position in England."

The Welsh make quick-witted and courageous soldiers. They proved that against the Normans long ago, and the famous Welsh troops in the British Army such as the Royal Welch (not Welsh) Fusiliers, the South Wales Borderers, and the Welch

Regiment have time and again signally distinguished themselves in Britain's wars.

Southern Wales is *How Green Was My Valley* country. The mountains are terraced and gouged by open coal cuttings. The miners live in houses attached on both sides to other houses extending for a half-mile or so, each unit exactly like another, so that where there are no numbers a man must count the doors to find his own. There is not a tree in these villages. There is no pother about flowers. Black hills of tailings stand round about.

Outside the villages the country is wild, high land with few trees, and as we went through it the wind, fog and rain swept over it in most desolate fashion.

Swansea is a great manufacturing centre and the cup of land that holds it is so crowded with belching chimneys that it might well be called the Valley of Ten Thousand Smokes.

South Wales is worth visiting not only to see how Welsh miners work and live; it is of interest because of its magnificent ruins. The broken arches of Tintern Abbey are like stone lace against the sky. Chepstow Castle stands on a steep platform of rock with a living moat, the River Wye. Raglan Castle, called "one of the most superb ruins in Britain", is all the more picturesque because it was destroyed by Cromwell's troops in 1646. The castle of Brecon, or what is left of it, stands in the grounds of the Castle of Brecon Hotel and the manager will give you a key half a foot long with which you may penetrate its mysterious passages and climb to the battlements for a grand view of the Usk River and the Brecon Beacons.

Pembroke Castle is another in the superlative class, the *Blue Guide* calling it "one of the most imposing ruins in the kingdom". The walls of the great central keep are nineteen feet thick. Beneath the castle is a natural cavern through which escape could be made by means of a water gate to the river. Despite all its strength it was conquered by Cromwell in 1648, but only by cutting off its water supply.

Again a superlative is needed for Caerphilly Castle, which is the largest in all England and Wales except Windsor. "Three castles fayre in a goodly ground" is an old-time chronicler's description of White Castle, Grosmont and Skenfrith. The castle in the great and beautiful city of Cardiff, largest city of Wales, is fascinatingly strange and alien in appearance as if it had come out of a Never-Never Land.

And as you leave the coal mines behind and pass into the wild beauty of North Wales with its abrupt mountains, rushing streams, dense woodlands and precipitous sea-coasts, the castles reach a towering climax in Harlech, Caernarvon and Conway.

The curious thing about most of these castles is that they are not Welsh. They were built by the English to control the rebellious Welsh. How hard a job that was is made plain by the size and strength of these castles.

It is too bad that the authorities I have quoted have spent their superlatives on the castles of South Wales, since we need them for Harlech, Caernarvon and Conway.

The mighty upthrust of Harlech, soaring from a rocky promontory overlooking lowlands and the Irish Sea, cleans every bit of film out of your camera. From every angle it is magnificent. Edward I thought he had built it so solidly that it would never be taken. But the Welsh took it and their valiant defence of it is immortalised in the stirring song, 'Men of Harlech'.

And how can we speak of Caernarvon without seeming too lavish? We shift the responsibility to Doré Ogrizek:

"There are the remains of over one hundred stone castles in Wales, but Caernarvon is the queen of them all. This castle is considered to be the finest piece of medieval military architecture in the British Isles." Caernarvon, though an empty shell within, is perfectly preserved on the outside. Its mighty walls, its gatehouses, its towers and turrets, are reflected in the once bloody waters of the Seiont River.

According to mixed history and legend, it was in Caernarvon

Castle that the first Prince of Wales was born. The Welsh had demanded that the ruler of Wales should be a native of Wales and speak no English.

"And will you pledge yourselves to peace and loyalty if I give you such a ruler?" inquired Edward I.

"We will."

Edward's Queen was expecting a child. She was sent post-haste to Caernarvon and there gave birth to a son. Triumphantly Edward presented the infant to the Welsh chieftains.

"This is your ruler. He was born on Welsh soil, he speaks no English, and his first words will be spoken in Welsh."

True to their word, the chieftains accepted their new ruler and since that time the eldest son of the British monarch has been designated Prince of Wales.

The historic town of Conway is girt about with a high wall punctuated by twenty-one towers. As if this were not enough to satisfy the tourist in search of medieval romance, above the town rises Conway Castle, so tremendous a pile of masonry that the railway that passes through one part of it is hardly noticeable. The castle walls are a veritable rock garden and between the great stones all sorts of wild flowers nod their colourful heads.

The sometimes crimson, sometimes purple valerian is most common. It has bloomed riotously all over North Wales since the Roman governor, Caius Valerius, built a villa near this spot and brought seeds of the plant from Rome to scatter in his garden.

We drove up the dreaming Vale of Conway to Bettws-y-Coed and Swallow Falls and Capel Curig, places as delightful as their names, then through truly magnificent Alpine scenery to Beddgelert.

The village of Llangollen on the shore of the Dee was considered by Ruskin "the most beautiful and delightful little town in Wales or anywhere else".

While we would not put it quite so strongly, we could understand why the 'Ladies of Llangollen' chose this as their home when they eloped with each other and sought a place where they could get away from the world. These two eccentric, high-hatted, long-cloaked gentlewomen who had formed a romantic attachment for each other must have had unusual intellectual qualities, for the great of England made pilgrimage to their fantastic house in Llangollen. Among their visitors were the Duke of Wellington, Wordsworth, De Quincey, Madame de Genlis and Sir Walter Scott. Each visitor contributed something to the furnishing of the house and it became almost a museum of quaint and sometimes beautiful objects. The ladies had passed on, but the house is still open to the public. On its outer wall are engraved Shakespeare's words, "There is no darkness but ignorance."

Perhaps our most interesting experience in Wales was our water-adventure in a type of vessel that has not changed in two thousand years.

The coracle was the boat of the ancient Britons. It may be remembered that I mentioned it as being used on the Thames before the advent of the Romans. It is no longer to be seen on the Thames but it is still in daily use on some of the hidden rivers of Wales.

The coracle is one of the most primitive boats in the world. In something of the sort Moses was set afloat among the bulrushes of the Nile. I believe it is now to be found nowhere outside of Wales except on the Tigris, where it is called a goofah.

It is simplicity itself—just a round basket covered with hide. The goofah is some ten feet across and will carry half a dozen passengers. The coracle is only four feet in diameter and is built to carry one person. A wooden plank across the middle serves as a seat.

The first coracle we saw lay on the bank of the Teifi River near the little village of Cenarth. It was bottom up, and looked like a big black turtle, or the huge iron pot in which cartoonists boil missionaries. Inquisitively, we walked about it.

A woman came out of a near-by cottage. She addressed us in Welsh.

"Is this a coracle?" I ventured in English.

She replied with an English yes.

"Is it just on exhibit or do you actually use it on the river?"

"Of course we use it. In fact that's how we make our living. We have three of them. We use them to fish for salmon."

We looked down at the big, black-bottomed basket.

"Is it covered with hide?" I asked.

"They used to be—but now we just use canvas, and tar it over to make it watertight."

"Is it heavy?"

She stooped and picked up the little boat with one hand as easily as if it had been a kitchen chair. She passed it over to me. I judged that it weighed about twenty-five pounds—one third the weight of the average canoe. Until someone produces evidence to the contrary, I am inclined to believe that this is the lightest boat in use anywhere in the world today.

"Would you show us how it works?"

The woman flipped the basket-boat right side up and slapped it down upon the waters of the River Teifi. She picked up a paddle, stepped into the boat and sat down on the plank.

The Teifi, having just tumbled over a waterfall and through a series of rapids, has a very strong current at this point. The coracle began to float swiftly down-stream. It rode as light as a leaf on the foaming water. It was tossed from wave to wave and we began to be anxious for our Welsh friend, who had perhaps been too willing to demonstrate an art usually left to the men-folk.

But before the bouncing black bubble could disappear around the first bend, the woman began to use her paddle. Astonishingly, she put it into the water not beside the boat or behind it

—but in front! She leaned forward and began to paddle over the bow, if a round boat can be said to have a bow. The roundness was only approximate and the 'bow' was even blunter than the rest of the craft, so she had not far to reach.

She waggled the paddle from side to side in what appeared a very futile gesture, but the little tub halted in its plunge towards the sea and then actually began to glide up-stream against the powerful current. It slid to the bank where we stood, and the woman stepped out.

"You see," she said, "it is very simple."

It didn't seem so simple, but I itched to try it. I suggested as much to the coracle-woman, but she discouraged me.

"I promise to stay within three feet of shore," I said.

She was not convinced. "You may promise for yourself, but you can't promise for it," indicating the coracle. "It has a mind of its own. If you will wait until my husband comes . . ."

It was worth while waiting to meet Evan Jones. He was a brawny fisherman, expert coracle man, and spoke English well. When I commented on this last fact, he said:

"We should all know English. Some Welsh nationalists in North Wales insist upon teaching Welsh only in the schools— no English. I think that's a great mistake."

He was quite willing that I risk my life in a coracle. But he advised me to leave ashore anything that might be spoiled by a ducking.

Following instructions, I stepped into the basket just where strong withes crossed, sat down in the exact middle of the one seat, braced my feet apart so as to control balance, took in hand the primitive paddle and pushed off. Mr. Jones followed me closely in another coracle.

I promptly discovered the futility of paddling alongside as in a canoe. That set the boat spinning like a top. The river, the hills and Mr. Jones were a whirling blur. Pressure on the paddle not only stopped the spin but started the boat revolving in the opposite direction. Again I checked the spin, but more gently.

This little craft was as responsive as a racehorse. The least persuasion got immediate results.

We were drifting down-stream at an amazing rate. Black rocks stuck their heads above the white water. If I was going to learn how to paddle a coracle it would have to be within the next ten seconds.

"This way," said Mr. Jones. He plunged his paddle into the water straight before him and oscillated it from side to side in an S motion.

I tried it and suddenly felt at home. For this was old stuff; it was exactly the motion used in drawing a canoe to one side. In that case the paddle is not removed from the water between strokes but is drawn back and forth in a sort of figure 8 and turned every time so that the blade presses against the water at an angle like a propeller blade. The only difference was that now the paddle was used over the bow rather than over the side.

My cockle-shell immediately began to edge forward in the direction of the paddle. To beat up against that current would have meant hard work in a rowboat or canoe. The coracle, riding atop the river rather than in it, slid up-stream with amazing ease.

Through the canvas bottom I could feel the river humping and bumping against my feet. I found myself breathless, not from paddling, but from trying to preserve my balance in this very tippable eggshell. We crossed the river through rapids and returned without mishap. But when we stepped ashore I still felt as if I were walking a tightrope.

Then Mary, equally familiar with the use of a paddle without withdrawing it from the water, was persuaded to try the coracle—which she did with complete success.

"It's the nearest thing to flying," she said.

Mr. Jones put on a show of his own to demonstrate the coracle's speed and manœuvrability. His powerful arms zipped it across the surface like a skipping stone. When it was necessary to turn, the least touch in one direction would send the 'bow' whirling in the other. In this respect the coracle is much more easily handled than a canoe or even a keelless punt.

In fishing from coracles, two of them are used, Mr. Jones explained, and a net is spread between them. When the net is drawn up, the salmon are clubbed to death with a 'priest', much like a policeman's club. Salmon-fishing is good on the Teifi.

The coracle can easily be hoisted on to the back and carried around rapids or from one lake to another. Imagine how pleased we would have been in the old days up Canada way when faced with a mile-long portage if we could have packed a twenty-five-pound coracle instead of an eighty-pound canoe.

Of course the two craft are not equal in carrying power. The coracle is built to carry one person, two at the most. But for solo water travel it is hard to beat.

Tip for beach-resort owners whose guests are tired of surf-boards, water skis and paddle boats. Try coracles.

CHAPTER 33

Lure of the English Lakes

You don't shake off Wales easily. Chester is well across the border, but the Chester phone book contains seventeen columns of Joneses. Evidently the Welsh have turned the tables on their invaders and are now invading England.

They could not have invaded a lovelier town. Chester is rich in fine half-timbered houses, unique because of its 'Rows' (elevated galleries by which you may do your strolling and shopping ten feet above the street), and the only city in England to keep its medieval wall complete.

I say medieval, but Chester's city wall was first laid down by the Romans. The Normans only built it higher. From its battlements you may look down on the remains of Roman villas and baths. Walking along this rampart, some twenty feet above the ground, you may completely circle the old city. That is an experience not to be duplicated anywhere else in England.

Boring under the River Mersey by way of the world's largest underwater road tunnel, two and five-eighths miles long, we emerged in Liverpool.

This being Sunday, traffic was light in the city. Yesterday's newspapers blew about the streets. The fine public buildings were black with age and soot. The place looked rather like a burnt-out planet, deserted by all its inhabitants. At last we spotted a human being and drew up to ask directions.

"Sorry," he said, "I don't know the city well. I'm not a Liverpudlian."

It sounded like a new and distasteful occupation, this puddling of liver. The word seems to be constructed by the deft substitution of a puddle for the pool in Liverpool. A pool is sometimes attractive, a puddle never. Why the pool should have been abandoned for the puddle is not clear, for surely it is no easier to say Liverpudlian than Liverpoolian. The second is, if anything, a shade less painful than the first.

The residents of English towns take a peculiar delight in this sort of thing. You might suppose that a resident of Manchester would just be a resident of Manchester or, at worst, a Manchestrian, but no, that's too easy—he must call himself a Mancunian.

A man from Glasgow is a Glaswegian; from Birmingham, a Brummie; from Galloway, a Gallovidian; from Chester, a Cestrian.

Of course an Oxford man is an Oxonian and a Cambridge man is a Cantabrigian.

If you are from Shropshire you are a Salopian. And a resident of Newcastle-upon-Tyne comes out a Novocastrian.

Our chief objective in Liverpool was the cathedral, which, when completed, will be by far the largest in England, and with St. Peter's in Rome and St. John the Divine in New York will rank as one of the largest cathedrals the world has ever known. Its site is lofty and its architecture imposing.

We went in to attend service. We found the interior as big as night and as dark, made more gloomy by the use of dull reddish-brown sandstone instead of grey.

The central tower is finished and much of the nave. The nave is staggering in its immensity, but funereal and remote. God seems very far away. None of the warmth of Christianity is felt here. The stained-glass windows have jumbled images. Nothing stands out distinctly and the colours are not decisive.

The organ is splendid. Reverberating acoustics help an organ, but ruin a voice. The preacher's words echo for five seconds, so that, when he particularly wishes a word to be heard and understood, he pauses five seconds before pronouncing it to allow the echoes of old words to beat themselves to death against pillars and arches.

The English Lakes are completely satisfying. I hazard the guess that no lovelier lakeland exists outside of Northern Italy.

No wonder Wordsworth found inspiration here. Circling beautiful Lake Windermere, we visited the church at Ambleside which Wordsworth helped build and in which are stained-glass windows to him and other Wordsworths, then went to his little Dove Cottage at Grasmere. Wordsworth, resisting all forces that would have drawn him to London, spent fifty-one years of his life in the exquisite Grasmere country.

And so to Coniston Water, where big, black Coniston Old Man weeps into the lake, seven cataracts streaming down his hoary face.

High in the hills near picturesque Keswick (pronounced Kezzik) we found lodging in a farm-house. It was a place of staggering views, howling winds and thumping rain, so cold that the farmer's wife herself suggested bottles in the bed. There was no electricity. We retired by the light of tallow candles.

"The weather will be bad today," said the farmer's wife the following morning.

"How can you tell?"

"When the sheep go up on the hill we know it's going to be fine. When they seek shelter down in the valley, we will have bad weather."

It was bad, but there was a pleasant wood fire on the hearth in the sitting-living-dining-room. It was an agreeable room with a grandfather's clock in the corner, geraniums in pots, and 'God Bless Our Gracious Queen' on a sampler above an embroidered Westminster Abbey.

There were three other guests, all English. The most gay was a young lady who had a lover in the barn. So devoted was

234

he that he had been walking seven miles daily to see her—but finally got permission to stay and sleep in the barn. The nights were very cold, but he got along because he was in with the farmer's three dogs. He didn't eat with us. While the young lady dined in comfort and chatted merrily with a young B.Sc. from Hull, he prepared his own meal—just how, is hard to see, since the farmer would not let him make a fire in the barn and the rain and wind certainly would not permit a fire to be made outdoors.

Whether by demeaning himself for love's sake he could win his love, was an open question.

The next day was fine and we journeyed to Ullswater, a big lake with bare brawny mountains, very imposing; and to Aira Force, a waterfall in a deep cleft, scene of Wordsworth's 'Somnambulist'. The field near-by is supposed to have been the scene of his host of daffodils.

Over fascinating mountain roads, narrow and steep, to Buttermere, shadowed by towering High Stile, from whose cliffs tumble cascades a thousand feet high. To Crummock Water, crowded by rolling mountains, and Loweswater, small and little visited but worth seeing for its improbable mountains.

The Lake District is the name applied to this region, but it might just as well be The Mountain District, for the mountains are quite as fine as the lakes—in fact the lakes would not be very important without them.

The mountains, believe it or not, are quite as impressive as the ten-thousand-footers of the American West, though they rarely go above three thousand feet.

But the impressiveness of a mountain depends not upon its height but upon the distance from which it is viewed. Most American mountains are separated from the low land by ranges of foothills, so that you can seldom get closer than ten miles to a high peak. In England the mountain springs straight from low ground and when you come within half a mile of a hill three thousand feet high the effect is far more striking than a mountain three times as high viewed from ten or twenty times as far away.

The mountains here are spectacular, breathtaking, quite illogical, springing suddenly with no apparent reason, not prepared for by gradual steps as most mountains are. And when they leap up from the edge of a lake and throw their reflection deep into it, they are as completely satisfying as any mountains could be.

CHAPTER 34

Land's End to John o' Groats

Anyone who can cross the border into Scotland without a tingle of excitement may as well find himself a grave, for he is dead.

Romance lies just over the line in the blacksmith shops of Gretna Green, famous for marriages more speedy than the horses of angry fathers.

Romance lies knee-deep over the countryside of Robert Burns and Tam O'Shanter.

Romance that has enmeshed a certain distinguished American hangs over Culzean Castle, a magnificent fortress-mansion looking down rocky slopes to the sea. The owners have set aside the top floor as a private residence for Dwight D. Eisenhower in gratitude for his services as Supreme Commander during the war.

The songs of Scotland ring in the mind's ear as we follow the east shore of Loch Lomond, a handsome be-mountained and islanded lake with cloud-capped Ben Lomond dominating the scene.

The poems of Scotland throw over the Trossachs a veil of romance as thick and deep as the purple heather that carpets the mountains. The Trossachs Hotel is turreted like a castle. From our room in one of the towers we look out on lovely Loch Achray, backed by 2,300-foot Ben Venue. We walk a mile or two along the shore of Loch Katrine, lake of *The Lady of the Lake*, under cliffs covered with blooming heather. The real Ellen's Isle is as beautiful as imagination made it. In the background Ben Venue is like a black giant with a green velvet coat worn through in spots so that the black shoulders, elbows and knees of the monster appear. A little steamer, S.S. *Sir Walter Scott*, takes visitors on a cruise to the other end of the lake and back.

Even Edinburgh is in a romantic mood, for she is holding her annual international Festival. There is a feast of operas, concerts, plays, colourful events culminating in the exciting Military Tattoo, a thrilling performance of Scottish bands with illuminated Edinburgh Castle serving as a backdrop. The Queen, the Duke of Edinburgh and Princess Margaret enter the Royal Box. The Queen wears a tiara on her head, a white ermine stole over her shoulders. Eight thousand of us get to our feet and the bands strike up 'God Save the Queen'.

But, alas, how badly the audience sings it! Not one in twenty opens his mouth. Those who do sing pipe but feebly. Such a pitiful contrast to the way the Welsh at the Eisteddfod sang the Welsh national anthem!

But there are bound to be flaws in the romance that is Scotland. A whipping may be dramatic, but hardly romantic. Hazel, sweet thirteen-year-old daughter of the proprietor of a small hotel in which we stay, is quite a talented violinist, but not so smart in other studies. She is twenty-eighth in her class of forty-four at school. Occasionally she gets the 'belt'—that is, she is whipped on the palms of the hands, which she takes care to curve so that they are concave: curved the other way, the whipping hurts a lot more. One boy who got the apostrophe in 'man's house' after the s instead of before it "got six of the best", said Hazel, three on each hand.

It seems harsh punishment for the misplacing of an apostrophe. And yet, who knows, perhaps we need a little 'belting' in America to get us out of the barbarous misuse of this little mark. With more stinging palms as a reminder, we would not put so many name-plates outside front doors with such inscriptions as *The Smith's*.

Driving north through Perth we kept an eye out for 'Mac-

Above: in the mountains of northern England and the Highlands of Scotland, cottages are small. There are no TV aerials or neighbours, and winter piles snow to the eaves

Below: 'The Monarch of the Glen.' Mountain cattle seem in need of a hair-do, but their coat is none too heavy to withstand the chill storms of the Scottish Highlands

beth's Castle'. It was mentioned in the *Blue Guide*, page 278, and clearly located on the official road map. At the village nearest the spot indicated, we inquired of a man with a scythe.

"I've lived here fifty years," he said, "and I've never seen any such castle."

We repeated the inquiry at a petrol station.

"A lot of people ask for it," said the attendant, "but there's no such thing."

Mary suggested that they build it, since there was so much demand for it.

But there was nothing elusive about Glamis Castle, also associated with Macbeth. With its towers and turrets, bartisans and embrasures, merlons and crenels, its high square keep with walls fifteen feet thick, Glamis is one of the finest and most picturesque of all Scottish castles. Though open to the public, it is still inhabited and was the birthplace of Princess Margaret.

British royalty loves Scotland. After visiting the Edinburgh Festival the Queen and Prince Philip immediately repaired to their Scottish residence, Balmoral Castle, to spend two months. As we looked down from a high hill to the fairy castle set in the beautiful valley on the banks of the Dee we could readily understand why they might prefer Balmoral to Buckingham Palace.

The country became wild and high as we climbed into the Grampian Mountains. The most exciting bit is the 'Devil's Elbow', a twisting ascent that seems as steep as the roof of a house and is introduced by the sign: "Water. Caution. Allow engine to cool." The more daring travellers stop part way up, get out and take photographs of their cars sitting up on their rear ends like begging dogs. We went up in second without trouble, but the engine smelled in protest.

The high country is bare—that is, bare of trees, but richly robed in purple heather. We look out on hundreds of square miles of purple, furnishing an effective background for white sheep and black cattle. The mountains are steep but always

239

rounded, with no points or bumps. Streamlined and flowing, they look like so many great purple whales. The few small stone cottages are overwhelmed by their surroundings.

In winter this purple land becomes pure white and the road would be hard to find were it not that at intervals of five hundred feet posts have been placed tall enough to keep their heads above the winter drifts.

And so we reach the tip end of Britain. The British equivalent of "from Dan to Beersheba" or "from the Statue of Liberty to the Golden Gate" is "Land's End to John o'Groats".

Here at the farthest point from Land's End we stay at the John o'Groat's House, a hotel with an octagonal tower on the site of the octagonal house of John, who made it that way so that each of the eight Groat families might have its own door and sit at the head of the table.

It is cold, nipping cold, and our ears ache as we walk along the beach. There's a fire in the lounge of the hotel, but none in our room. Great piles of black peat bricks stand outside the houses. We have seen where they cut them from the bogs.

A great red moon rises over the North Sea and the castle-like towers of John o'Groat's House loom black against the sky where the Northern Lights begin to play.

CHAPTER 35

Scotland's Farthest North

We travel along the north coast westward. The snug, tight little stone houses are further protected by a high wall to shut the north wind out of their gardens.

A miniature black mountain stands outside each house. In this bleak land no house is a home without its pile of peat. There is comfort just in the look of it, and in the thought of how much warmth there is in it. Today, 25th August, is stinging cold. What must winter be!

There are many abandoned houses falling into picturesque ruin. Young people evidently consider this a good country to get away from.

All the way across Scotland and well down the west coast it's a 'single traffic road', that is, wide enough for only one car. But suppose one car meets another? The problem is solved after a fashion by white-and-black posts labelled *Passing Place*. There a small turn-out makes it possible for one car to 'lay by' while another passes. When two cars come within sight of each other the one nearer a Passing Place will presumably turn out. If they come upon each other suddenly around a blind turn, the matter is considerably more difficult. One of them must back, and if the road twists and squirms along the edge of a thousand-foot cliff, the backing is done with some reluctance and trepidation.

The courtesy of the road is unfailing. There are no arguments, only a competition in politeness. Most considerate are the lorry-drivers. You come up behind a slow, cumbersome vehicle and have a moment of despair, but the lorry pulls out at the first opportunity and the driver sends you by with a friendly wave of the hand.

We are really in the Highlands now. The road is like a bucking bronco, doing its best to throw us off into a black canyon or a glistening loch. We are still riding on metalled road, but the 'metal' consists of two asphalt strips a foot wide with a strip of grass between them.

This is the most magnificent country we have seen in Britain and the worst road. The road is red on the map, signifying that it is in the first category. Yet it is far inferior to any green road we have followed in the last four months. But in this wild northland what else can be expected? We go forty miles without seeing a house. There isn't enough population to maintain good roads.

The scenery makes up for the road. Norway could do no better. Tremendous fjords are bordered by dozens of mountains. We are seldom out of sight of a loch or a lake and sometimes look down on three or four. This county of Sutherland has more water than any other in the British Isles.

We come on a block. A car and trailer half-way up the hill can't do more until half a dozen of us get out and push. The trailerites are East Indians, the ladies in thin, fluttering saris. How did people of so warm a land happen to choose northern Scotland for a holiday?

On Loch Assynt, where a ruined castle crowns an island and fantastic mountains look down, we stop at the hotel in Inchnadamph after 150 splendid miles over the roof of Scotland—and go to bed in thankfulness that we are all of a piece instead of in fragments at the bottom of any one of a hundred abysses that have yawned up at us today as we picked our way along the tightrope of a 'single-traffic road'.

The Highlands give us another surprise the next morning. We come upon a sign, 'Gate Ahead'.

It seems unbelievable that the gate mentioned will be across our road but, as we round a turn, there it is—the sort of gate one would find to a pasture or a hayfield, but here it stands squarely across the highway. Perhaps the farmer insisted that the road could not be laid across his property unless it was gated to keep in his stock. We have to get out, open the gate, drive through, and close it. Within a mile or so there is another gate and the performance must be repeated.

The road continues one-car wide with pull-out places, and we follow the green line, the strip of grass down the middle. There is not a house to be seen for many miles until we get to beautiful Loch Broom, which, after the desolation, seems thickly populated with a house to almost every mile. Then a cluster of houses on a point projecting into the lake is identified as the village of Ullapool. In the protected valley grow thousands of rhododendrons, and rowan trees (mountain ash) with their gay clusters of red berries.

Up again to the treeless moors. Scores of cascades and waterfalls tumble down the mountain-sides. We pause for lunch on a breathless pinnacle looking down to birch-embroidered Loch Maree.

Our gipsy lunches are the best meal of the day, though the simplest. We make out very well with a can of hot soup (thanks to canned heat), a few cream crackers, cheese or ham, an apple or orange or banana or pear, some milk chocolate or raisins. The view always helps make the meal a great success.

On the shore of Loch Carron severe women in Sunday black, Bibles in their hands, walk the long lochside street of the village. Many of the houses have Gaelic names and the inscription on a monument is all in Gaelic. We stop a man on his way to church to ask about Gaelic. He says it is still spoken by the adults, and understood, though not so widely used, by the young.

We talked with a family who had just come in with their house trailer, or caravan as it is more pleasantly called in

Britain. They were happily settled in Gairloch this morning, but their two children began to bat a ball about and the citizens objected, this being Sunday. So the caravaners thought best to move on.

As we talked with them the two children went down to the edge of the loch and began to throw stones into the water.

"Stop that," called their father. "Do you want us to be thrown out of here as well?"

Highlanders do not permit anyone to forget that Sunday is the Sabbath. A clergyman from the Lowlands was invited to preach in a Highland church. He rose bright and early Sunday morning and prepared to shave.

"I wouldna do that," said his host. "If ye shave on the Lord's Day in this town ye'll never preach here again."

The minister went to the pulpit unshaved.

H. V. Morton tells of finding himself without hypo to print some pictures. He went to the shop of the Highland chemist. It was closed, for this was Sunday. Morton knocked. The chemist looked through a slit in the door.

"Weel?"

Morton explained. A stern voice answered him.

"D'ye no' ken it's the Lord's Day?" And the slit was closed.

Morton went to church. After the church he encountered the chemist dressed in Sunday black with black gloves. Morton, feeling guilty, tried to sneak by, but the chemist detained him and said in a low voice:

"If ye still want the hypo come roond tae the back door!"

Hot water bottles are taken for granted in all Highland hotels. The maid offers to fill them with *very* hot water in the kitchen, but often the water in the room is hot enough. In fact the tap water in the room has been satisfactorily hot in ninety per cent or more of all the hotels we have visited in England, Wales and Scotland.

Luxury is carried a step further in the Inchnadamph Hotel.

Instead of a hot water bottle, they furnish a brightly decorated china pig to warm the bed.

I never realised what a heaven-kissing land the Island of Skye is until we approached it today on the car ferry from the mainland. It seems to be nothing but mountain peaks. This is one of the Hebrides.

For a few miles on Skye the road is wide and fine, then we get on a road that is red on the map, but very rough, and with four gates as obstacles. It leads through wild mountain scenery to Elgol on Loch Scavaig, across which we get a magnificent view of the Cuillin Hills, bare, black and devilish.

Returning to the mainland, we skirt fine Loch Alsh and then perfectly stunning Loch Duich with its picturesque Eilean Donan Castle.

There was no room for us in the Kintail Lodge on Loch Duich, so they put us in a knotty-pine cabin a quarter-mile down the beach.

The place was haunted and the spirits played tricks with the door of our room. When we left to go to dinner at the hotel, we closed the door. When we came back it was open. When we went out again we closed it. When we came back it was not only closed but locked.

Three big keys hung in the outer hall. None of them would turn in our door. We gave up—but before leaving for the hotel to register a complaint we gave the knob a final twist. The door opened.

Later I wished to leave the room to search for the bathroom. Our door was locked. No amount of knob-twisting would open it. We were definitely locked in.

But there was the window. It would not open more than ten inches. I squeezed through with the greatest difficulty, fell sprawling in thorny bushes and crept around the house in the dark, encountering a cow on the way. I entered the outside door, found the bathroom, then, before circling back to the window, tried our door. It opened easily.

From somewhere came a low laugh. We have all heard of ghosts in castles but this is the first I have ever known in a knotty-pine bungalow.

It is still a single-traffic road through lovely Glen Shiel and along Loch Cluanie. At a petrol station we ask how this name is pronounced. The young man says visitors usually call it Cloonie.

"Rightly in Gaelic it's Cloo-ah-nee," he says, "but most of these names get 'Inglified'."

But it is our impression after a week of mountain travel that it will be a long time yet before the secluded and exclusive Highlands of Scotland become too much 'Inglified'.

CHAPTER 36

Loch Ness and the Monster

We come out beside Loch Ness on to the first two-lane road in seven hundred miles.

It seems strange not to have to retreat into a passing place when another car approaches. Now we even have a white line, not a green one, and cat's-eyes. Cat's-eyes are not known in America but should be. They are small reflectors placed at intervals in the white line and are a great help in night driving.

The road along Loch Ness is beautifully graded and surfaced and so wide that you may pass a car coming in the opposite direction without even slowing down! But it soon becomes monotonously easy and we regret the loss of those high moor roads, leaping to heights to get magnificent views, plunging into hollows, dizzily twisting down steep slopes, offering an accident at every blind turn.

Loch Ness is splendid, however, not surrounded by flat, tame country as I had expected, but trenched between mountain ranges with the road half-way up the slope. Perched-up houses command extravagant views. But the road is usually too far from the loch edge to see any monster smaller than a whale.

A man tells us that he fishes Loch Ness frequently and has never seen the Loch Ness monster.

"Then you don't believe it exists?"

"Oh, I am sure it does. So many trustworthy witnesses have seen it."

"Does Loch Ness communicate with the sea?"

"Yes, by a canal, but there are locks in the canal."

I suggest the possibility that the young of some marine animal might have come up through the locks, then grown to considerable size in Loch Ness.

"But," he says, "Loch Ness is fresh water. A sea animal could not live there."

I tell him of the fresh-water lake in Nicaragua inhabited by sharks, and of the sharks, manatee and porpoises that live a thousand miles up the Amazon. Loch Ness would make a good home for a deep-sea animal, since it is nine hundred feet deep. And as for the stories that the 'monster' looks like a dragon, swims with its head out, and has several humps behind, might it not be an oarfish, which is a snake-like creature some thirty feet long? Though it prefers the depths it sometimes comes to the surface, and then swims with its dragon-like head elevated and with the undulations of its body emerging from the water, so that they might easily be mistaken for humps.

Most monsters must be taken with plenty of salt, and a few grains may be advisable even in the present case, yet it is not at all impossible that a deep-sea animal may have taken up residence in Loch Ness.

We leave Loch Ness and plunge into country where the monsters had human form. How grim are the tales of these lovely lochs and glens! Loch Oich has its monument to seven murderers, Fort Augustus is remembered for a bleeding head. Glencoe is famous as the "glen of weeping", scene of the famous massacre of their hosts by a visiting clan. It's a wildly picturesque glen between bare giants and any deed could be imagined here.

And lest all the trouble be relegated to the past, modern malcontents have painted in huge white letters on the face of a great rock the demand: "Home Rule for Scotland."

Revisiting Loch Lomond, we stop at the Colquhoun Arms (pronounced Cahoon), a very comfortable place with a view of the loch from our window and heat in the room!

Picturesque mountains admire themselves in the smooth surface. We commandeer an old rowboat, use the broken stub of an oar as a paddle, and go out on the still mirror, the late sun picking out patches on the bonnie, bonnie banks of Loch Lomond.

This quiet uneventful paddle on a dreaming loch is one of the high points of our British journey. We can understand Smollett, who after reviewing the names of the lovely lakes he had seen in Europe concluded: "On my honour, I prefer Loch Lomond to them all."

In the lounge we meet a young man who is making a bicycle tour of Scotland. We ask him why so many cyclists carry two bottles strapped to the handlebars.

"One contains water," he says, "the other, a mixture of water and oatmeal, or sometimes orange juice. We can slip a tube into the bottle and drink without stopping."

He works in London on a desk job for the P. and O. He has only two weeks' vacation. He took the train to Edinburgh, is cycling through Scotland at about seventy miles a day, and will take the train back to London from Glasgow.

He belongs to the C.T.C., Cyclists' Touring Club, and the Youth Hostel Association. The hostels are pretty good, he says. The C.T.C. puts out a handbook of accommodation, and young cyclists from abroad may take advantage of their services.

He complains that motorists treat cyclists without consideration, racing by at fifty miles an hour and splashing mud on them.

"There should be a red line within five feet of the edge of the road and that space should be reserved for cycling. No cycles should be allowed outside it and no motors inside."

We rode down the west shore of superb Loch Lomond, up again to the Trossachs, Loch Achray, Vennachar, past Stirling Castle to Edinburgh, on to Melrose to see the ancient and beautiful ruins of Melrose Abbey and stay at the fresh and beautiful George and Abbotsford Hotel.

This is the first new hotel we have seen in Britain. Struggling through the aftermath of war, Britain had other things that must be built first. However, newness is not the most important thing one can ask of a hotel. Some of our best hotels have been the oldest.

And so, concluding our Scottish journey with a visit to Abbotsford, home of Sir Walter Scott, we cross into England without an official or a sign to mark the point of transition.

CHAPTER 37

England's Far East

It takes a little searching to find the famous Roman Wall. The moat (vallum) and wall that once stretched across Britain as protection against the barbarians of the north are still to be seen, especially the trench, and a fine section of the wall at Winshields Crag.

Here we walked for miles along the top of the wall. We could see far to the north and the south, for the Romans chose a high ridge for their wall. It contrasts strongly with walls around the same fields built by farmers with rough stones used as nature left them. Every stone in the Roman wall is carefully squared off and neatly fitted.

Near Chollerford is a museum packed with Roman artifacts picked up along the wall, and in the adjacent field are the excavated ruins of a Roman fort and elaborate bath-house. How particular the Romans were about their bathing may be deduced from the types of rooms in the bath-house. Besides the room of the cold bath and the room of the hot bath there is a hot dry room or *sudatorium*, warm moist room or *tepidarium*, oil massage room or *unctorium*, cold laver or *frigidarium*, hot moist room or *caldarium*.

A unique side trip takes us across treacherous sands to the holy isle of Lindisfarne to visit an old priory and castle. The island can be reached by car across the sands only at low tide. At high tide the road is buried under twelve feet of water. Posts are placed to mark the road when covered by the sea. Cars that deviate from the track may be caught in soft sand. There are a few platforms built high enough to escape the tide. The traveller who is trapped by rising water may find refuge on one of these and wait six hours for the ebb. Travellers are discouraged from using their own cars and make the trip in a gaseous old wreck of a taxi whose driver tells so many harrowing tales of past disasters that we are delighted to pay him fifteen shillings for getting us back to the mainland alive.

We are coming into Robin Hood country. The road drops down a steep toboggan to Robin Hood's Bay, a picturesque fishing village on the North Sea.

Sherwood Forest, though smaller than it was when Robin Hood and his men may have roamed here, is fascinating, with its great old half-dead oaks, contrasting white birches, carpets of bracken. It is a lovely place for a long walk. Well inside it we come upon the fourteen-hundred-year-old 'Queen Oak', really a monstrous shell with a hole inside it large enough to hold twenty-eight persons. Its huge branches are cabled up, its sores are covered with metal caps, and the tales it could tell of Robin Hood are probably not half as good as the ones that have been invented.

York is a fascinating old-time city, interlaced with quaint and lovely streets, girt about, but not completely, by a high wall, and dominated by huge York Minster.

The cathedral did not impress us greatly except by its size. Its stained glass is extensive but lacks clear images. We attended Sunday service and enjoyed the music of the great organ and of the male choir of thirty. The congregation was also in the choir, less than a hundred of us all told in a church that would hold several thousands.

There was a short sermon and a fourfold prayer: for the Queen, for world peace, for industrial peace—and for good weather.

We visit Byron's home, Newstead Abbey, and are not surprised that he lived there only off-and-on over a period of ten years, for it is as uninhabitable as a mausoleum or railway station. But the estate is lovely, with its lake, waterfalls, brook, woods, lawns, flower gardens, and monument to Boatswain, Byron's dog, on the face of which appears Byron's touching tribute in verse to his 'only friend'.

Byron appears to have needed and wanted friends but did not have the temperament to win and hold them. He was married for only a year. He became involved in a scandal which forced him to leave Britain for the Continent, never to return. He died at thirty-six.

To the famous Fen District and the Norfolk Broads.

We had thought of the Broads as marsh intersected by waterways, but it appears that a 'broad' is merely a broad place in a river where it widens to form a lake. This is a land of shallow lagoons among expanses of reed, fen and farm.

We hire a boat and follow the bewildering meanderings of the Bure, Ant and Thurne Rivers. Occasionally the river expands into a 'broad' and some of these lakes are exquisitely beautiful. In this region as a whole there are some three dozen broads and these, with the rivers, provide about two hundred miles of navigable water. Naturally it is a favourite vacation land for Britons. Thatch-roofed summer homes and boat-houses hug the shores and multitudes of yachts, motor-cruisers, wherries and sailboats make for exciting navigation.

It reminds one of Florida. It is England's Florida or Venice. Or Holland, for it has both tulips and windmills. George VI used to come to Salhouse Broad to shoot and it is said that Queen Elizabeth II learned to swim here. Fishing is phenomenal and no one quarrels with travel posters that proclaim this to be the sportsman's paradise.

More cathedrals. Lincoln is one of the most satisfying of cathedrals because of the splendid variety of its architecture without and the wealth of glorious stained glass within. What lively imaginations must have been its creators'.

Norwich Cathedral is well worth seeing, but is eclipsed by superb Ely Cathedral with its magnificent stained glass and the remarkable and lovely interior view of its octagonal tower.

That the residents of cathedral towns have something else besides cathedrals on their minds is hinted by a poster announcing the next event in the Hippodrome at Norwich:

"Come and See Britain's Loveliest Star without a Bra, Peaches Page, the Girliest Show of Nineteen Fifty Sex. Take a Journey into Spice and See this Heavenly Body."

Students in Cambridge are peculiarly blessed.

They have a beautiful city as their three- or four-year college home, even more pleasant than Oxford because it has not been industrialised. Cambridge is still a university town. The colleges, many of them, are quite as fine as those in Oxford, and the 'Backs', the green stretches along the Cam behind the colleges, bring the open country to the college door.

Since Cambridge is stronger in science, one supposes that there may be a little less academic ceremony here, although we have to smile at the pompousness of a notice on the bulletin boards:

"The attention of persons *in statu pupillari* is drawn to the edict regarding the wearing of academical dress."

The notice goes on to point out that the gown must be worn over a jacket, never over a sweater or pullover, and concludes solemnly:

"Gentlemen *in statu pupillari* are reminded that the wearing of the gown is a privilege which has been jealously guarded by undergraduates since the earliest times."

We stopped at the much-better-than-average Garden House Hotel on the river-bank. We rented a canoe, went out on the Cam, and paddled lazily down along the 'Backs'. It was as charming a little journey as one could ever make by water.

The river mirrored the towers of King's College Chapel and the ivy-covered walls of St. John's College, and the Wren-built library of Trinity.

The Cam is no child of nature like the wildwood Cherwell of Oxford. It flows between close-clipped green lawns, flower gardens and noble trees, and even its weeping willows weep with restraint and grace, thanks to careful trimming.

Dignified statues of kings and scholars look down upon it. It is a highly civilised river. Its banks are not disorderly but brick-walled like a Venetian canal. At times college buildings rise straight from the water just as in Venice, their rich old walls aged with lichens, moss and ivy. Oriel windows lean out to peer down upon lovers in canoes and punts.

As in Venice, graceful bridges span the stream: the single stone span of King's Bridge, the intricate wooden arch of Queens', the finely sculptured Clare Bridge, and, most Venetian of all, the enclosed Bridge of Sighs connecting two buildings of St. John's.

The only thing definitely non-Venetian is the weather. Black clouds sweep across the sun and every voyager has taken the precaution to bring along a raincoat, just in case. But in the sunny intervals the scene has a snap and brilliance that even an Italian sun could not improve upon.

John Harvard was educated here, later went to America to found Harvard University. It would be interesting to know to what extent he was influenced in his choice of a site by his memories of Cambridge and the Cam. The Charles is another Cam. In both cases the river is a real part of the institution and must have its effect upon the character of those who look out to it from college windows, lie on its grassy banks to study and to dream, or fall in love in a boat for two under the moon. I know our own mental image of Cambridge will always include the river.

CHAPTER 38

Driving in England

Back to London.

Our very irregular circle through England, Wales and Scotland had put 6,280 miles on the speedometer. Excursions by boat had added another 1,800 miles.

The little car had given us no trouble. The gearshift (low, second, third, high, reverse, and neutral) was an unmitigated nuisance. But the starter never failed to work, the wheel could be turned as easily as the handlebar of a bicycle, manœuvring into a parking space was never a problem, windows could be pushed up or down in a flash, you could reach all corners of the car from the front seat and yet the car was large enough to accommodate the two of us and all our baggage. We became as fond of it as if it were a member of the family and gave it up with regret.

Driving in England is tricky and we are pleased to have got through six-thousand-plus miles without accident—or almost, our only accident occurring when the car was standing still and a lorry backed into it.

It's a two-lane country and, for seven hundred miles in Scotland, one-lane only. Near big cities there are snatches of four-lane road, or, as the English call them, "dual carriageway roads".

There's a flexibility of operation in cities, undreamed of in the States. A U-turn is allowed anywhere, and you may park on either side pointed with or against the traffic. There have been threats to introduce the parking meter, and it is being tried out in London, but on most streets where parking is allowed you may stay as long as you please.

Private drivers are not as courteous and patient as in America. The car that is a bit slow in moving out of the way will be honked at. On the other hand, the heavy transport men driving slow lorries and vans are remarkably thoughtful in waving you on if they see that it is safe for you to pass, or checking you if there is danger ahead. And if the car breaks down it is the transport driver who is most likely to stop and lend a hand. They are the "gentlemen of the road".

Helpful too is the motor-cycle corps of the Automobile Association and the Royal Automobile Club who patrol the roads. Their duty is to help their members if in trouble, but they go well beyond the call of duty and come to the rescue of non-members as well.

Petrol is expensive, roughly double the cost in America. If one uses an English car this expense is offset by the additional mileage obtained. Except in hilly country or in the cities, our Austin A30 made forty-five miles to the imperial gallon (slightly larger than the American gallon).

Petrol station attendants are not expert, many of them women with no knowledge of what goes on under the 'bonnet' and unable to make any repair or adjustment. The attendant, whether man or woman, will consider his work done when he has filled the tank, and will not look at the water, oil, battery, clean the windscreen or check the tyres unless expressly asked to do so—but when asked, he will respond readily enough. Garages are numerous and their mechanics well trained.

The surfacing of British roads is remarkably good. Not only are all roads metalled, but the metal seems to have been laid on only yesterday, its condition is so close to perfect. Only in remote and uninhabited regions of the Highlands of Scotland did we find badly worn surface.

These fine roads seem to keep themselves in shape, for we never saw but once any extensive road repair going on. I mean the sort of thing one is used to at home when anywhere from a mile to five miles of road may be shut off for repair and all traffic re-routed through dubious back roads where the car must pick its way through ruts and mudholes or clouds of dust.

In 6,280 miles of Britain we were not detoured once. Frequently there appeared the sign 'Road Up' but it usually meant that only a few spots were being patched and traffic was not impeded. When a stretch of road was due for repair, the work would be confined to one half at a time, allowing traffic to pass in the other half. In all cases there was scrupulous regard for the convenience of the motorist and an almost fanatical zeal to keep traffic moving.

Just once we were brought to a halt. This was on a Highland road that was being resurfaced; since the road was only one-lane wide it was impossible to follow the usual system of limiting the work to one half and allowing traffic in the other half. But here we were held up for only twenty minutes. One twenty-minute delay in a four-month journey must be something of a record. Our respectful salute to those who build and maintain British roads.

CHAPTER 39

On English Food

Cooking as commonly practised throughout Britain (London excepted) suits the stomach better than the palate. And, after all, the stomach deserves first consideration. The cooking is plain, and the stomach approves. There cannot be much of a market for antacids in England as compared with the Continent or the States.

Take potatoes.

You will take them, for they come with every dinner and in two forms, 'roast' and boiled. A 'roast' potato is simply a browned potato. Why these two forms should be favoured above all others is an occult mystery, or why both should be served when either one would be quite sufficient. But at any rate they agree with the stomach, as 'French fried', so common in the States, may not.

Mashed potato, whether in its watery form or made rich with cream and butter, is practically unknown in the provinces.

The term 'baked potato' is not understood. Waiters suppose it to be another name for 'roast' potato. When I explained the American use of the term my waiter said:

"Oh, you mean jacket potatoes."

In five months of travel we have not seen one 'jacket potato' and we dream of a big Idaho the size of a boxing-glove, broken open, filled with butter and salt, sprinkled with paprika, and good down to the last scrap of skin.

The egg-cup still reigns supreme as the throne of the boiled egg. The idea of opening and emptying two eggs into a dish

259

where they can be thoroughly mixed with salt and butter before eating is not appreciated.

The egg after being set up in the egg-cup is decapitated and a little salt is placed on top of the yolk. This is supposed to sink down by some mysterious process unknown to science and impregnate the entire yolk and white of the egg. If butter is added, and it seldom is, it also is placed on top. The result is that the first spoonful has too much salt and butter and the rest have none, unless both ingredients are reapplied each time.

But English taste is too ascetic to require butter in egg, and as for salt, it is noticeably and rather painfully absent in all English cooking. We have come to know that the first thing to do with any hotel main course is to salt it thoroughly before taking one bite—for the first bite unsalted may spoil the meal.

In a way, the cooks may have logic on their side. If the food is salted some people may find it too salty, but if unsalted each may season it according to his taste. The flaw in this reasoning is that no food is properly seasoned unless the seasoning is *in* it, not on it.

The none-too-good reputation of English cooking is due more to lack of salt than to any other one factor. Outside Britain one may attack a dish of meat and vegetables without first dosing it with salt and pepper. This procedure at the British table results in condemnation of all British cooking.

There is usually a good reason for human behaviour. Could the reason for the low intake of salt in England be that the English, living in a cool climate, lose little salt through perspiration, and therefore demand little? People from warm countries who rapidly lose their salt and must replace it have become accustomed to well salted food and, having developed a taste for it, demand it even when they don't need it, as on a British tour. Could be.

Breakfast is a severely stereotyped meal. The waitress will ask whether you want fruit juice *or* cereal. Not once has the 'or' been missing.

It was not until some three months had gone by that I plucked up the courage to say that I would like fruit juice *and* cereal. This produced only mild consternation and I was put down as a peculiar fellow who must be humoured. Since then I have frequently asked for both, and have been served without question or extra charge.

But still the 'or' never disappears from the formula, even when the waitress knows very well that my answer will be 'and'. It's as if she were gently reminding me that I am getting both only through her intervention and I am really a bit of a glutton to want both.

The 'or' implies that the two are equivalent, but how can a fruit juice be a substitute for a cereal or a cereal for a fruit juice?

The fruit juice is always out of the can, never produced by squeezing an orange or a grapefruit. The canned grapefruit juice is not bad. The orange juice is to be avoided whenever possible. It can be good and it can be execrable.

As for fresh fruit, it is taboo. Not once in five months have we been offered an orange, apple or pear. Twice only we have had fresh grapefruit to begin breakfast, but it was small and bitter. The grapefruit on the English market is no larger than an orange.

Very rarely 'stewed fruit' appears on the menu. This usually means prunes, occasionally figs. But if one orders figs with a mental image of fat, round, smooth fruits, one is disappointed. The figs are dried figs, puckered and leathery.

The cereal is usually cornflakes. Sometimes it is 'porridge'— oatmeal quite innocent of salt. In Scotland the porridge was good. In England we understood why most guests prefer cornflakes. No cream is served with the cereal—milk only, and that too often thin.

The variations mentioned occur only over a period of many months. Ordinarily there are no alternatives except a choice between fruit juice and cereal and there is only one kind of fruit juice and one cereal.

The hotels do rather better with the second course. It also is strictly formalised—the menu has no room for such nonsense as waffles, pancakes or steak. You may have an egg with bacon or, sometimes, with sausage. The egg is usually fried, but may be boiled or poached if you prefer. The English have found no way of de-salting bacon and its saltiness saves both itself and the egg from insipidity. One gets to enjoy this course thoroughly and to be rather glad it is standard practice.

The same thing happens in regard to marmalade. After the first half-dozen marmalade mornings you begin to long fiercely for a change—for blackberry jam or blueberry or currant or grape or plum or fig or strawberry, raspberry, boysenberry, pomegranate, date . . .

But no, it's against the rules. Jam belongs with tea, not breakfast. You *must* want marmalade for breakfast.

Rebelliously, you buy a small jar of jam and take it to the breakfast table every morning. At first you relish it exceedingly, but after a few mornings you furtively slip back to the marmalade, and like it. You are a marmalade convert.

The tang of the stuff is just what you need to start the day. And no people in the world make better marmalade than the British. Ninety per cent of it is orange marmalade, ten per cent is the more delicate and mild lemon marmalade, which does for toast what a cool morning breeze does for a morning-after head.

The toast *needs* to have something done for it. It is really in a desperate plight. It does not know its own mind. In some areas it is brown as toast should be, in others, white, in others, black as a cinder.

Remember, I am still speaking of hotels outside London, though these comments would apply to many inside as well. In London you may get an evenly browned piece of toast; in the shires, don't expect it.

It isn't that the electric toaster is unknown in England. One sees it in the windows of electric-appliance stores and on the tables of private homes. But a hotel must produce toast in wholesale quantities, therefore it is apt to be made on a broad pan covering a number of gas jets with blanks between them and the uneven heat means uneven toast.

This thing of spots and patches is then placed in a toast rack and so borne triumphant to the table. The toast rack is a sort of aerator or ventilator in which each piece of toast stands on edge well separated from its neighbours and the breeze of transition from kitchen to dining-room ensures that the toast will be stone-cold by the time it reaches the table.

What this does to a self-respecting and well-intentioned piece of toast can only darkly be imagined. The toast rack demoralises toast as the rack of Inquisition days used to break down the morale of human victims. The toast, already humiliated by finding itself piebald, now discovers that it will not even be permitted to be hot. And is toast toast if it is not hot?

A thousand times no, says the American hot-toast addict. But yes, say the English. Toast does not need to be toasty to be toast. It is not necessary that the butter sink into it and become one with it. There is no objection if the chilled butter lies in ridges and humps on the resistant surface.

Pity spent on the English is pity wasted so far as their cold toast is concerned. They like it that way. Said an English friend:

"We prefer our toast cold."

Thinking this might be just a regional idiosyncrasy, I asked another Englishman three hundred miles away.

"Ah, but you see," he said, "it's better cold. It brings out the flavour."

Perhaps he is right. At any rate I have since been conscientiously trying to appreciate the flavour of cold toast, and have had reasonable success. Whether this success is due only to a sympathetic imagination or to the superior virtues of cold toast, I don't know. Anyhow it makes for inner contentment to stop expecting something you can't have.

Tradition and custom affect the taste of toast. On our boat my wife served hot buttered toast. The pilot and Herbert attacked it with knife and fork, supposing it to be some sort of fried bread, a common English delicacy.

"This fried bread is great," said Herbert, gulping it down. "Fried bread!" said my wife. "That's toast."

Herbert would have no more of it and the pilot laid down his knife and fork and turned to his tea with the look of a man who has been cruelly betrayed.

Hot buttered toast, sternly excluded from breakfast, is sometimes admitted to afternoon tea, though it never attains to the rank of the scone or the tea cake. Then, in the best places, every precaution is taken to keep it hot. It is served on a hot plate, there is no breathing space between slices, and the whole is covered by a metal or padded cosy.

"Why is it served hot?" I asked a head-waiter in Chester.

"Why not?" he answered. "It just tastes better that way."

"The heat brings out the flavour," I slyly suggested.

"That's it," he agreed. "That's just it."

So there you have it. The heat brings out the flavour that is wanted at afternoon tea and the cold brings out the flavour desired with bacon and eggs.

It may not be as fantastic as it sounds. Perhaps English taste buds are more highly discriminatory than ours and the rigid rules that allocate certain flavours to certain meals and prescribe which foods may be used together and which may not are the outcome of a longer gustatory history than our own. They may also be due to influence from across the Channel.

But there is some excuse for the freedom with which Americans throw together apparently conflicting foods into a single meal. They are compelled to do so by the fact that they have only three meals a day.

If they allowed themselves from five to seven meals, as many English do, they might distribute and group taste patterns more properly. The fact is that the English eat so often that they must vary the menu or die of boredom. With a seven-stringed harp to play upon they can achieve variations and nuances that we find impossible on our three strings.

To the visitor it seems that the English are for ever eating or thinking about eating.

Morning tea served in bed does not impair an appetite for a breakfast that would choke a *café-au-lait* Frenchman. But the generous breakfast fades fast and must be supplemented by 'morning coffee' at eleven, and, two hours later, a dinner-sized lunch.

This is no sooner forgotten than the most indispensable gastronomic event of the day, afternoon tea, stops all work and play. Factories grind to a halt, office desks are deserted, tennis matches take a recess, the lock-keeper on the Thames lets the boats wait, for "a man must have his tea".

The tea may be 'plain', with only a three-storeyed rack of some dozen sandwiches, scones, buns, tea cakes, biscuits, jam-filled rolls and iced cakes. Or it may be 'high', with all the aforementioned together with eggs or meat and sweets, a young dinner. This 'high' may be pushed so late that it serves instead of dinner.

But if the tea be 'plain', dinner follows at about seven. In a hotel it consists of three or four courses: soup, main dish of meat and vegetables, sweet (dessert), cheese and biscuits and small coffee. In a hotel this is the last chance to eat, but in the home there is quite likely to be a late light supper or bedtime snack with tea, cakes and any leftovers from the day's engorgement.

At that, the British do not compare with the Germans or the French as gourmands, nor even with themselves before the two Great Wars. The wars, particularly the second, so severely restricted the diet that I have heard more than one Englishman complain that now he simply can't eat the meals he used to. His habits have been changed by years of war, perhaps his stomach has shrunk.

However, according to statistics of *per capita* food consumption, the stomach is now re-stretching and will soon be back to its old capacity. There is no dearth of food, good food, in Britain today. The visitor will never go hungry. His only anxiety may be that, tempted by the world's best baked goods, he will put on too much weight.

The seven feedings already enumerated do not satisfy some Britons. In the trains, on the beaches, in the parks, in the theatres, you will find a constant re-stoking going on regardless of meal-times, and advertisements such as this appear in Tube stations and on buses:

BRIDGE THAT GAP WITH CADBURY'S SNACK
Real nourishment between meals

The gap is also bridged with millions of chocolate bars, lollipops, sandwiches, hot dogs, biscuits, nuts, sweets in a hundred forms and, for ever, tea.

There are some who must nibble their way through everything, whether a cricket match or *Macbeth*. Even grand opera is not immune; ladies and gentlemen in evening dress ladle ice-cream into themselves from small paper cups and La Tosca plunges from the battlements to a tinkle of spoons and cups. During one intermission a group of fashionably dressed guests in the third row of the stalls happily passed around slices of cold boiled ham.

Some philosopher should explain all this. Is it a British reaction from the deprivations of war? They are so happy to eat again that they cannot stop? If another war pops in on them they are determined not to start it hungry?

But no, the multi-meal system far antedated the great wars. My own explanation, tentatively offered, is simple enough. It is that Britons need, and have always needed, frequent replenishment to fend off the cold.

Britain is a cold country. Even the British summer is not as warm as the Californian winter. It is true that New England is much colder in winter than England. But American homes, offices, trains, are heated. The British indoors is heated very lightly, or not at all.

This leads the Briton to congratulate himself that he is more hardy than his American cousin. It is not so. What the American does with fuel, the Briton does with food and, more specifically, tea.

Instead of using gas, electricity or coal, he keeps himself warm by liquid heating. In the morning chill he fortifies himself with hot tea before he faces the rigours of dressing in a cold room.

But the effect of hot tea wears off and must be renewed frequently. Therefore he must have more hot tea at breakfast, tea or coffee at mid-morning, tea at noon, tea at mid-afternoon, tea at dinner, tea again before he dare crawl in between the cold sheets.

It is a way of escaping reality and perhaps as good a way as any other. Not only the heat of the tea but the theine makes him forget the cold, and the frequent taking of food serves the same purpose.

It may be said in objection to my theory that Britishers living in the blazing tropics, where they obviously do not need liquid heat, demand their tea at the same intervals as at home. But that is sheer habit. Customs a millennium old will not be upset by a few years on the Equator, no matter how ill-suited they may be to the equatorial climate. The Englishman has long since lost track of why he must have his tea. He only knows he must have it. In the fires of hell—if Englishmen go to hell— he will want his tea. The ball, once rolling, continues of its own momentum. But I suspect it began rolling because the Englishman was cold.

The tea is good. The English know how to make it. Coffee they are not so sure of. Housewives often make excellent coffee, but hotel coffee sometimes tastes as if the boy who does the boots had inadvertently dropped one or two into the pot.

This would not be so bad if the boots were boiled fresh every morning. But one day's coffee too often lies over till the next.

A Colombian whom we happened to meet in Stratford had his own explanation of the taste of English coffee. According to him, England relies chiefly upon inferior coffee from her own African territories because it is cheap, and flavours it with a small percentage of Brazilian coffee which costs twice as much, or Colombian coffee which costs three times as much. Chicory is added. This unsatisfactory blend is made less palatable by delivery to the hotels in paper bags rather than tins and does not lie long on pantry shelves before the flavour has disappeared.

However, bad coffee can be mitigated by hot milk. If you order coffee the waiter will ask:

"White or black?"

He is jesting of course, for he is not prepared to give you either. The 'black' is brown and the 'white' (half milk) is the colour of the Mississippi in flood.

There is a third category, 'all white'. Coffee that is 'all white' is hot milk with no coffee.

But now you are toying with taboo. If you go a step further and ask for a glass of cold milk you have overstepped the line.

English hoteliers seem to share the attitude of certain primitive tribes who regard the drinking of milk as obscene. It is even more degraded than drinking water, and what waiter would serve a glass of water unless pressed? But milk!—it may be all right for sucking babies and cats, but that an adult human should drink it!

We subsided in shame and confusion and thereafter contented ourselves with buying a bottle of milk, concealing it in the car, making a noon stop at some desolate and lovely spot where there was no one to see, and there furtively drinking the milk with our gipsy lunch.

It is not easy to buy milk. The search for it is comparable only to Jason's quest for the Golden Fleece. Groceries are not allowed to sell it. Only the dairy is qualified, and the nearest dairy is usually in the next village but one and at the end of a remote alley with no sign out. You may or may not encounter a milk cart on its rounds to regular customers—and the milkman may or may not have a bottle to spare.

The housewife has her order in for a little milk daily to go into the tea and coffee, but if she suddenly wants more she can't step over to the shopping centre and buy it. She must use tinned milk. If she dislikes the taste of tinned milk, she goes without.

The authorities defend the ban on the easy sale of milk on the basis that the dairy must be protected—even if there is none in the town or it is so hard to get at as to discourage all but the most milk-minded.

The result of such restriction is of course much lower consumption than there might be of the most nutritious liquid known to man.

The meagre consumption of milk is indicated by the fact that it is mainly available only in pint bottles, whereas in some other lands milk is commonly sold in quarts or half-gallons. Pint-size milk makes for a pint-size man. Not only the quantity of milk consumed is inadequate but English nutritionists complain of the quality as well.

Cream is hard to come by in the English hotel. In our hundred hotels—which were always the best to be found in the places visited—we were served cream but once. We frequently inquired for it but the word did not seem to be understood. The waitress tapped the jug of skimmed milk. When we hinted that this was not what we meant by cream:

"Oh, you mean thick like in Devon. Oh no, sir, not here."

But we didn't mean thick like in Devon, where it stands up as stout as library paste under the strawberries or is spread a quarter-inch thick on scones. That is not cream in the ordinary sense, but a confection.

Cream, light cream, is sold in the dairies, but not to the hotel, except when needed to make whipped cream for tarts or trifles. Cereal is served with thin milk. If there is any absolutely flat taste in the whole range of gastronomy it is the taste of saltless porridge with thin milk.

Because of the British emphasis on tea, the baked goods are uncommonly fine. Bakeries are not only competent but ingenious and their window displays of fancy breads, scones, buns, tea cakes, biscuits, cookies, rolls, iced cakes, tarts and pastries of every description would make an American baker feel like a raw amateur.

This delightful carbo-hydrate debauchery is a survival from a richer age. There was a time when the whole British *cuisine* was almost as Continental as the Continental. Look back at Tudor recipes and marvel at the garnishes, cloves, oils, paprika, garlic and whatnot with which they ruined the character of honest English beef.

The English have gradually come to the conclusion that good meat does not need sauces and disguises. Their meat is better than may be found in most parts of the Continent and its natural flavour can hardly be improved upon by the application of any creams and cosmetics. The American appreciates this point of view in so far as meat is concerned, but he does feel that the English vegetable falls between two stools. It is so cooked that it is not allowed to retain its natural flavour, and no other is substituted.

In all this I have been talking about the provinces. London is another story. London cooking is not English cooking.

The *cuisine* is cosmopolitan. In no other city in the world can you dine better than in London. Every meal can be different. You can enjoy infinite nuances. Without stirring from London you can eat your way around the world: through England, France, Spain, Portugal, Germany, Italy, Greece, Scandinavia, Hungary, Turkey, Russia, Israel, Persia, India, China, Japan, the South Seas and the U.S.A.

London is a gourmet's delight and a gourmand's debauch. Of course it is easy to find bad food in London but it is also easy to find the best. If you do not keep a close rein on your appetite you will eat too much and too richly. The stomach will protest and you will welcome a chance to get back to the plain and not unduly tempting fare of the provinces.

CHAPTER 40

For Love of London

The most striking characteristic of London is its infinite variety.

An American city is homogeneous. Everything in it is mass-produced. One building looks like another; and all belong to the same general period.

In London, modernistic post-war business blocks rise alongside fine old residences of Georgian days and they in turn nudge relics of the Middle Ages.

In America we set a style and then all conform to it. Every house built in my California home town in the last ten years has been almost indistinguishable from any other house built in the same decade. The same is true in the new housing developments of England.

But in London proper the changing ages have left so much variety that there is no norm to conform to. The architect is free to express his own or his client's individuality—and he does so. Londoners complain that the result is a hodge-podge. So it is, but a delightful one.

Looking down a street you do not see two monotonous walls of uniformity. There are gables and towers and gates and columns and setbacks and pushforwards, broad windows and windows made of scores of small leaded panes, balconies with beautiful iron grillwork, church steeples of many designs, streets that refuse to go straight, streets that send off twisting lanes, no two of them alike.

The multiplicity of ideas expressed in all these forms of architecture gives you the feeling that a lot of people have been thinking for a long, long time and each has come up with something of his own. It is intellectually stimulating, this tremendous variety of ideas.

Of course one man's idea is apt to conflict with another's. London is a city of fierce conflicts and a muddle of winding ways that make no sense at all and are more fascinating because they do not.

Fresh, green parks pop up in the most unexpected places and make a detour necessary. Two churches stand plumb in the middle of London's main street, the Strand. Roads meet in a 'roundabout' or 'circus' like the spokes of a wheel, a giddy wheel with not a single straight spoke. Fine monuments block the way, noble gates narrow the traffic lane.

These gates are not intended to serve as gates. Most of them are never closed. They lead nowhere. They have no utilitarian reason for being there. Historical reasons and æsthetic reasons, yes. Someone just thought a great gate or arch would look splendid at that point, so there it stands.

Taxi-ing through London is a dizzy experience. The streets are narrow and all elbows, and anyone used to the broad-beamed American car is sure that the taxi cannot get through, but it seems to draw in its breath and squeeze through cracks that appear only wide enough for a thin pedestrian. So many corners are turned that there is no possibility of keeping one's sense of direction. You have to throw yourself on the mercy of the driver—a good place to throw it; London drivers have seldom been accused of taking innocents the long way round to run up the tariff.

The sensitive visitor to London has an almost terrifying feeling that he is walking on the thin upper crust of many layers of history and mystery. Nothing can be taken at face value. Behind everything there is something else, and, behind that, something else again, and so on back and back for two millennia.

Sixteen feet below the pavement on which you walk is the city founded by the Emperor Claudius. It was only some ten years after the Crucifixion when Claudius arrived on the south bank of the Thames with his Praetorian Guard and his phalanx of war elephants. There he found a ford about half an elephant deep and through it the invaders waded across to a small settlement called Lyn-din.

There he ordered his legionaries to lay out a city which should be called Londinium. Some of these same legionaries may have done duty on Calvary on the occasion of the execution of two thieves and a religious zealot called Jesus. As the walls of Londinium rose, St. Paul was starting his missionary journeys. St. Peter was alive and probably Pilate, and in Rome Seneca had just gone into exile.

Londinium was a Roman city for four hundred years. It was a city of mosaic pavements and fine buildings. The houses were probably warmer than they are today. Beneath the floors were hot-air chambers heated by wood furnaces. A temple to Diana was erected, possibly on the site now occupied by St. Paul's. There were temples to other gods and goddesses, one to the Egyptian Isis. The city was surrounded by a great wall with gates, bastions and crenellated battlements. The wall was so well built that, with occasional repairs, it stood for many centuries and was not pulled down until the reign of George III. Its remains may still be seen, particularly where exposed by the bombs of the Second World War.

Numberless reminders of Roman times have come to light and are still being uncovered by the men who dig the foundations for new buildings or dredge the Thames—cauldrons, shields, sickles, razors, water clocks, coins, tools, brooches, rings, pottery, forceps for the self-emasculation of novitiates entering the priesthood, statuettes of Mercury, Apollo and Jupiter. Even a Roman ship was discovered beneath the black silt of the Thames at the Surrey end of Westminster Bridge.

After the Romans departed the city fell on evil days. Whether the Roman gods had anything to do with the excellence that was Londinium may be questioned, and it was doubtless only a coincidence that as Christianity came in civilisation went out. The Dark Ages were nowhere darker than in the decaying city on the Thames.

Finally the Renaissance with its resurrection of Greek and Roman culture brought new life to Europe and to London. Since that time the story has been one of continuous progress, slowed at times but never halted by England's wars.

London, once notorious for its filth, is now famous for its cleanliness. Visitors from Paris or New York or Chicago are quick to notice a difference in London. Even Philadelphia notices it. Richardson Dilworth, Mayor of Philadelphia, visiting London, wrote a story for his home paper, the Philadelphia *Inquirer*, about the cleanliness of London's streets, walks and parks. He concluded by saying:

"The City of London performs less cleaning service per square mile and per citizen than does Philadelphia, which goes to show that all the street cleaning service in the world is not of much help if the people continue to mess up the streets."

It is true that London still smells, but it no longer stinks. Its pungency is one of its great charms. You have one perfume among the roses of Regent's Park, another in the second-hand bookshops of Charing Cross Road, and quite another in the British Museum. The steak houses of the Strand send out one odour and the printing houses of Fleet Street another. St. Paul's and Westminster Cathedral make quite different appeals to the nostrils. The smell of Bond Street is not the smell of Piccadilly. If you were blindfold in Bloomsbury you would know you were not in Mayfair. Close your eyes in Waterloo Station and you cannot imagine yourself in the Houses of Parliament. Even the House of Lords is different from the House of Commons. The interior of Covent Garden has the romantic smell of a thousand operas and the street outside offers the fresh appetising scent of the fruit market. In Borough High Street you smell hops, in Tooley Street butter and eggs, in Pickle Herring Street dried salted hides. There is the pigeon smell of Trafalgar Square.

There are pepper-smelling streets, wool-smelling streets, streets of spice and tea and coffee. And there's the smell of a healthy young English girl who doesn't need perfume.

London is a healthy city. The English climate may not always be pleasant, but it is invigorating. England stands high in health among the world's nations. Some say that this high level of health is due to socialised medicine; others say England is healthy in spite of socialised medicine.

Just what is socialised medicine? We had an exceptionally good opportunity to find out. Possibly one of the best authorities on the subject is Dr. Angus Macrae, Secretary of the British Medical Association. We bore an introduction from a mutual friend in America and Dr. Macrae and his wife received us in their home for Sunday dinner and tea.

They proved to be strong supporters of the National Health scheme—a term they prefer to 'socialised medicine'. I asked Dr. Macrae if his view represented the general opinion of the British Medical Association.

"I think it does. We were opposed to the plan at first. But the Ministry of Health made so many concessions to our views that we saw no point in holding out against the scheme."

"Do you think it is here to stay, regardless of whatever party might be in power?"

"Oh yes. No Government could do away with it. The people would not permit it. Ninety-five per cent of the people are under the National Health."

"They can choose whether to be included or not?"

"Yes. If they wish to join they register with a doctor. He is paid by the Government according to the number of his registrations. Those registered receive his services free of charge."

"Why doesn't everyone register?"

"A few prefer to remain private patients. As such they have a slight advantage. They are likely to be served more promptly, and the doctor is more easily available for home calls. The

State patient may have to sit a long time in the doctor's waiting-room, and a home call is only made in urgent cases. The paying patient may have a private ward in the hospital whereas the free patient is placed in a public ward, unless his case actually demands seclusion and quiet. If an operation is urgently needed it may be had at once, no matter whether the patient is private or State—but if it is not urgent the private patient may still have it at once, while the State patient may have to wait."

"For example," added the secretary's wife, Dr. Marjorie, "if a child's tonsils should come out, but there is no particular hurry about it, under National Health the operation may be delayed several months. That may be a blessing, for by that time the parents may have found that the tonsils should stay in."

Dr. Marjorie went on to tell how the scheme works in the school clinic she supervises.

"Previously we had mothers bringing children with very serious diseases which we couldn't take care of and they couldn't afford to have treated by specialists. And the mothers themselves would drag on for years with serious chronic ailments. Now we don't get such cases: they go at once to the specialists. Doctors are saying that now for the first time they are able to practise preventive medicine—and that's really the best kind, isn't it?"

"But I suppose some people run to the doctor for very trivial ailments?"

Dr. Angus nodded.

"Of course. There will always be people who will take undue advantage of anything that is free. They cut their finger or get a pimple—off they go to the doctor. It can be a nuisance. But such problems have a way of solving themselves. For example, after a patient has sat in the doctor's waiting-room for an hour he is apt to take stock of his trouble and wonder whether it is worth all the time he is spending on it. The next time he has a cold sore or a case of sunburn he will be inclined to take care of it himself. So it isn't as great a difficulty as you might imagine. At first people ran to the doctors because they were paying taxes for this service and felt bound to get something for their money. There's not so much of that now. Perhaps they've more or less forgotten that they're paying for it—it has become routine."

"The insurance premiums that everybody pays to the Government—do they cover National Health?"

"They have nothing to do with National Health—though many English people are under the impression that they do. They cover retirement pensions and all that. National Health is paid for out of the income tax."

"You were in the United States recently. Did you find the American Medical Association opposed to National Health?"

"Very much so. So much so that they do not hesitate to misrepresent the system as it is working here."

"But the British Medical Association and the rank and file of English physicians are for it?"

"The Association, yes. The doctors, most of them, but a few prefer to keep their private status. They are men who already had a large following of well-to-do patients and they see no advantage in changing. But the young doctor is better off under National Health. The doctors are quite free to choose. They may have either State patients or private patients, or both. We can never expect to see one hundred per cent approval of any State plan—but on the whole both the public and the doctors are pretty well satisfied with National Health."

On the way back to the hotel we asked the cab-driver what he thought of National Health.

"It's like this," he said. "Thousands of people are getting treatment today who couldn't afford it before. You sometimes have to wait, but not too long. Little things are taken care of in the doctor's office. If it's anything important, he sends you to the hospital. My wife is to have an operation for varicose veins. She will get it free. A friend of hers who goes to a private practitioner is going to have the same operation and she will have to pay about seventy pounds. Her husband thinks it beneath his dignity to take anything free. I don't look at it that way. We pay for this in our income tax, so why not take it?"

Visitors do not pay British income tax, except indirectly in the purchases they make, but they are accorded the same privileges as citizens under National Health. However, before making an appointment, the visitor should ask whether the doctor operates under the National Health plan or takes private patients only. Usually the traveller is in a hurry; if so, he will do better to pay for prompt attention.

"You won't find anything doing in London now. Everything closes up for the summer."

So we were told upon arrival in London. We bought a newspaper and turned to the entertainment page. We counted the notices of plays, operas, ballets, symphony concerts, band concerts, music-hall offerings, motion pictures and miscellaneous performances. There were seventy-five all told. And this was the off season!

In a library we consulted a New York newspaper for the same day. The number of attractions announced was forty.

The third of the world's greatest cities is Tokyo. There was no Tokyo paper available, but having lived many years in Japan we knew that summer offerings in Tokyo were only a fraction of those in New York.

London is the entertainment capital of the world. Perhaps it may be said to be the cultural capital as well. A high proportion of the seventy-five attractions announced in the newspaper were for people who wanted to learn something. The lecture, the opera, and Shakespeare are year-round attractions, not confined to brief seasons.

London prints many of England's books, some nineteen thousand titles a year. We think we do well in America to publish twelve thousand, though our population is three times that of Britain. British television does not compare in appeal with the American brand and has not as yet made serious inroads upon book reading. Great art galleries are scattered throughout the city. There are schools and colleges of every sort and London University has a larger enrolment than Oxford and Cambridge combined.

And yet with all this there is no hurly-burly unless you want it. London is a city of noisy spots punctuating great areas of quiet. In our hotel in Bloomsbury Square, and in another in Stanhope Gardens, there was not a street sound to be heard from nine in the evening to nine the next morning.

You can always escape from a busy street into a park, for there is a lot of country in London. The open spaces and parks occupy thirty thousand acres, or ten per cent of the metropolitan area.

The residential districts are pervaded by an ineffable calm. In villages neighbours are for ever chattering at each other over their fences. In London they keep to themselves. You can die in a London flat and be undisturbed for weeks. I do not say whether this is a good thing, but if it's solitude you want in London you can get it.

"Those who prefer the country life," writes the English author, Thomas Burke, "always seem to assume that the man who likes London life must be of gregarious nature, and that the country life makes no appeal to him because of its solitude. But it is just because I like solitude that I like London."

Whichever one desires, constant excitement or profound peace, London will provide it. It has something for everyone, and for everyone's changing moods. You cannot get weary of its face since it does not have one face, but a thousand.

"When a man is tired of London," said Dr. Johnson, "he is tired of life."

Index

[of British names only]

281

Conway, 225, 226
Cornwall, Duchy of, 190, 199
Cotswolds, the, 11, 14, 26–8, 48
Cricklade, 25–6, 29
Cromwell, Oliver, 22, 48, 154, 205, 224
Crummock Water, 235
Cuillins, the, 245
Culzean Castle, 237
Cumnor, 54–7

DARTMOUTH, 189
Day's Lock, 81, 82
Dickens, Charles, 126, 133–4
Drake, Sir Francis, 118
Duich, Loch, 245
Dunster, 204–6

EDINBURGH, 238, 249
Edward I, King, 225, 226
Edward III, King, 103
Eilean Donan Castle, 245
Elgol, 245
Elizabeth I, Queen, 55, 57, 118, 165
Ellen's Isle, 237
Ely, 254
Eton College, 87, 92, 179
Exmoor, 204

FARRINGFORD, 184–5
Fletcher, John, 151
Forster, Sir Anthony, 55–6
Fort Augustus, 248
Freshwater, 185

GAELIC LANGUAGE, 182, 243, 246
Gairloch, 244
Glamis Castle, 239
Glastonbury, 190, 197, 206–8
Glencoe, 248
Glen Shiel, 246

Godstow, 59–61
Goring-on-Thames, 84
Grampian Mts., 239–40
Grasmere, 234
Gravesend, 119–20
Gray, Thomas, 92
Greenwich, 117–18
Guernsey, 185, 187–8

HAMPTON COURT, 98–102, 105, 117
Hannington Bridge, 30
Harlech Castle, 225
Harvard, John, 255
Henley-on-Thames, 88, 90
Henry II, King, 59–60, 137–8, 142, 203
Henry III, King, 91
Henry VIII, King, 75, 98–9, 117–18, 142, 165, 208
Hereford, 215–16
Herstmonceux Castle, 117, 155–6
Holehaven, 122–4
Howard, Catherine, 99, 100
Hythe, 147–8

ILFRACOMBE, 204
Inchnadamph, 242, 244
Isle of Wight, 184–5

JAMES, HENRY, 150–1
Jersey, 187
John, King, 93–5
John o' Groats, 240

KATRINE, LOCH, 237
Kelmscott Manor, 45
Kemble, 13, 15–16
Kempsford, 30
Kenilworth Castle, 214
Keswick, 234
Kew, 110, 111, 112

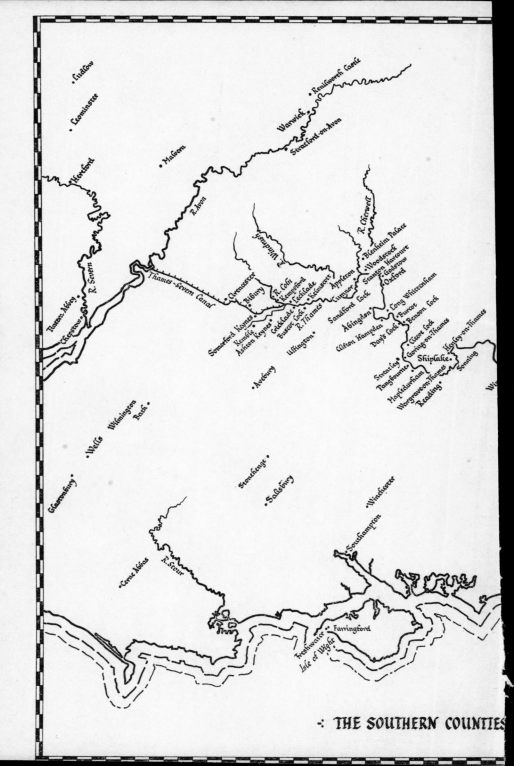

Ludlow

Leominster

Hereford

Malvern

Warwick • Kenilworth Castle

Stratford-on-Avon

R. Avon

R. Windrush

R. Cherwell

Blenheim Palace

Woodstock

Stanton Harcourt

Godstow

Oxford

Thames-Severn Canal

Cirencester

Bibury

R. Coln

Kempsford

Lechlade

Kelmscott

Appleton

Sunner

Tintern Abbey

Chepstow

R. Severn

Somerford Keynes

Kemble

Ashton Keynes

Cricklade

Buscot Lock

R. Thames

Sandford Lock

Abingdon

Clifton Hampden

Day's Lock

Long Wittenham

Burcot

Benson Lock

Clere Lock

Goring-on-Thames

Shiplake

Henley-on-Thames

Sonning

Ulfington

Streatley

Pangbourne

Mapledurham

Wargrave-on-Thames

Reading

Wi

Avebury

Whittington Bath

Wells

Glastonbury

Stonehenge

Salisbury

Winchester

Cerne Abbas

R. Stour

Southampton

Freshwater • Farringford

Isle of Wight

: THE SOUTHERN COUNTIES